Black Dance
in London,
1730–1850

Black Dance in London, 1730–1850

Innovation, Tradition and Resistance

Rodreguez King-Dorset

McFarland & Company, Inc., Publishers
Jefferson, North Carolina, and London

Frontispiece: William Louther performing the revised version of Alvin Ailey's *Hermit Songs*. He is demonstrating a technique and a style that was (and still is) rooted in the black American dance tradition (V&A Images/Victoria and Albert Museum, London; photograph by Anthony Crickmay).

LIBRARY OF CONGRESS CATALOGUING-IN-PUBLICATION DATA

King-Dorset, Rodreguez.
    Black dance in London, 1730–1850 : innovation, tradition and resistance / Rodreguez King-Dorset.
       p.   cm.
    Includes bibliographical references and index.

    ISBN 978-0-7864-3850-1
    softcover : 50# alkaline paper ∞

    1. Dance — England — London — History — 18th century.
    2. Dance — England — London — History — 19th century.
    3. Dance — England — London — African influences.
    4. Blacks — England — London — History — 18th century.
    5. Blacks — England — London — History — 19th century.
    6. London (England) — Social life and customs — 18th century.
    7. London (England) — Social life and customs — 19th century.
    I. Title.
    GV1646.E6K56   2008
    793.3'19421— dc22   2008031662

British Library cataloguing data are available

©2008 Rodreguez King-Dorset. All rights reserved

No part of this book may be reproduced or transmitted in any form or by any means, electronic or mechanical, including photocopying or recording, or by any information storage and retrieval system, without permission in writing from the publisher.

On the cover: *Tregears Black Jokes: Being a Series of Laughable Caricatures on the March of Manners amongst Blacks.* "The Route." Engraving by Hunt after Summers. Published by G.S Tregear, London, c1834 (©National Maritime Museum, London)

Manufactured in the United States of America

McFarland & Company, Inc., Publishers
Box 611, Jefferson, North Carolina 28640
www.mcfarlandpub.com

To my "father" William Louther and to Nicholas Dromgoole.
Without them my work would have been almost impossible,
so a heartfelt thank you to both of them.

Table of Contents

Preface 1

1. Body, Kinesthetics and Dance Theory 3
2. The Origins of African Dance and European Dance 35
   and the Dance Traditions They Established
3. "Savages with No Knowledge of Their Ancestry": 82
   Examples of African Dance Survivals During and
   After the Atlantic Crossing
4. The Importance of Dance for the Black Community 103
   in London and Its Growth and Development in the
   Seventeenth, Eighteenth and Nineteenth Centuries
5. Interpreting the Visual Representation of Black Dance 126
   in London During the Nineteenth Century

Conclusion 157
Chapter Notes 161
Bibliography 179
Index 191

Preface

Most people are surprised to learn there was a sizable black minority population in London between 1730 and 1850. They might be even more surprised to realize there is much more to be learned from examining the ways in which that minority used dance in its struggle to maintain a sense of group identity. The very idea that this black community was highly organized, holding its own festive dance occasions, "black balls" from which whites were excluded, adds a fresh dimension to any study of this period. It also adds a frash element to comparable studies of what was happening to the black minority in the United States of America, and the larger black communities of the Caribbean.

To provide an understanding of how black dance developed in London during this time, this book examines the importance of dance in African culture and analyzes the ways in which dance survived the Atlantic crossing and the traumatic experience of the slave trade, persisting in the new communities established among slaves in the plantations of the Caribbean. The relevance of this dance survival has only recently been realized by historians, and can be used as evidence in the academic controversies over what was culturally lost and what survived from African culture during the horrifying experience of slavery.

After analyzing in detail the dance culture of Africa, the book looks at the European dance culture that produced the quadrille. Having done so, and accepting the subsequent creolization of Caribbean culture (an inevitable mixture of African and European strands in the Caribbean's slave communities) as a result of slavery, the book considers the ways in which Caribbean slaves learned, used and adapted European dance forms, particularly the quadrille. Examples will be analyzed to illustrate the new mindset of Caribbean creole culture which blacks brought with them to London.

Having examined the development of black communities in London in the eighteenth and nineteenth centuries and looked carefully at their Caribbean origins, the book sets out to analyze the various ways in which the London black community used dance, specifically the quadrille, to establish a sense of their own identity, as a means of criticizing the white society in which they found themselves, and as a way of reinforcing their group desire to resist the oppressive ways in which they were treated by the majority.

Diaries, journals, plantation documents, parliamentary papers and newspapers have all been used to provide evidence, as have oral traditions. Since dance is a visual medium, it has been necessary to examine what paintings and drawings have survived to illustrate the evidence. The book concludes that the importance of dance in African society continued to be reflected in both Caribbean society and in London black communities in the eighteenth and nineteenth centuries. Illuminating the ways in which the black community in London used dance adds both fresh evidence for the survival of African culture and interesting new insight into the ways in which the black community in London operated as a group.

The survival of African cultural traditions in the New World, particularly those of dance, music and song, has been a subject of academic controversy since the pioneering work of Melville Herskovits in 1937.[1] Yet even in this controversy the dance culture of blacks in London in the eighteenth and nineteenth centuries has been neglected. What has been overlooked is that when blacks arrived in London from the Caribbean, they brought with them aspects of their African dance culture which had survived their transportation to the Caribbean. Understanding this dance culture can provide important evidence in this controversy. Examining some of the elements of African dance traditions that permeated African culture and persisted well into the nineteenth century will show that a combination of factors contributed to the survival of the African dance tradition in the Caribbean and were carried in the mid–eighteenth century to London. Perhaps the most important factor was the toughness and tenacity of the African dance culture that helped blacks to use dances such as the quadrille in London as part of their struggle for self-identity.[2] This book will help to redress the balance and give black dance in London during the eighteenth and nineteenth century the importance it deserves.

In spite of the upheaval caused by slavery, African dance culture survived so vigorously that black dance continuity played a special role in meeting black people's problems of identity in London up until the moment of emancipation.

1

Body, Kinesthetics and Dance Theory

The Problem

Dance, music and song in the seventeenth and eighteenth centuries played a greater part in African society than they did in European society. And dance, music and song from the cultural traditions of Africa survived better than other elements of African culture after the traumatic experience of transportation to the Caribbean. This book will be concerned only with dance, but dance, music and song are inextricably intertwined in much African culture, and it is difficult to talk of one without implicitly considering the other two.

It is not just a question of dance, music and song playing an important part in African culture. The real difficulty is to make clear just how big a difference there is between African dance and European dance, between African music and European music, between African song and European song.

In a sense these differences lie at the heart of what is referred to here as creolization. The creole culture that emerged in the Caribbean was a strangely assorted mixture of African and European influences and traditions. If the slaves arriving in the Caribbean had brought no culture with them, there would have been no creolization. Caribbean society would simply have been a provincial imitation of European society. That was indeed the case in many of the plantation owners' families. The very fact that black creole culture in the Caribbean, however, was variegated in the different islands and proved to be so different from that of the plantation owners, is the best and most striking evidence that far from bringing a tabula rasa with them on their arrival, the newly arrived slaves brought with them elements of a surprisingly vigorous and sophisticated culture from which they had been untimely ripped.

My own experience and background have helped me to analyze these differences. Although I was born in Britain, both my parents were born and grew up in the Caribbean, and I too grew up in a British ethnic minority that was as much Caribbean as it was English. In other words I was immersed in a culture where dance, music and song still played a more important part than it did in the majority culture. My own great-grandmother was a slave in Barbuda. She fitted into the early process of creolization and retained many dance and musical links with the Africa from which my forebears came. My mother learned directly from her a version of the British quadrille known as the "Kachriil," and indeed learned two versions, one of them deliberately satirizing the way white people danced the steps. She in her turn taught me these and other dances as part of my family upbringing. Yet I was also trained as a professional dancer in the European classical ballet technique and in modern American dance techniques. This helped to sharpen my understanding of the differences between African and European traditions. In the eighteenth and nineteenth centuries, Africans would have had difficulty accommodating their set of dance and music expectations to those of Europe. In the eighteenth century the reverse was also true. Europeans, faced with African dance and music for the first time, found it largely incomprehensible. It requires some imaginative effort to put oneself in the mind of an eighteenth-century African arriving as a slave on a Caribbean plantation. The dance, music and song going on in the plantation owner's house would have been quite outside such a slave's experience. Ira Berlin has helpfully pointed out that a tiny minority of Africans at both ends of the Atlantic crossing familiarized themselves with European ways and already embodied the meeting of the two different cultures.[1] The process of creolization is not generally considered to have taken place until the first generation of native Caribbean-born slaves emerged.[2] In this first generation of native-born Caribbean slaves, the process discussed later in this book of creolization had already started taking place. The new generation would take a great deal from their parents' attitudes, assumptions and knowledge, all rooted in African culture. At the same time they would have been acquiring some of the European culture that now surrounded them. It is in this context that the process of creolization must be considered as it applied to dance, music and song. Former slaves arriving in London from the Caribbean in the eighteenth and early nineteenth centuries emerged from a culture that was neither European nor African. It was a creole culture, but one in which dance, music and song continued to play a greater part than they did in the rest of European society at that time. It is fair therefore to talk of a specifically black aesthetic set of concepts toward dance that was different from an eighteenth-century European aesthetic. Creole culture certainly adopted the minuet and later, in the beginning of the nineteenth century, adopted the quadrille. But the mind-set that creole dancers brought to the quadrille was not the same as that of Europeans. Creoles were embedded in a culture where dance, music and song were much more important as a means of expression than in Europe. So black dancers attending black social dances—or black balls, as they were then called—in London in 1825 may have looked to any European gazing through the window as though they were dancing the quadrille and dancing it in a rather exaggerated fashion. In fact they were doing much more than this. They were dancing what had become their own kind of dance in their own way, and this had become one of the means through which they expressed their sense of their predicament.

There is another difficulty. Academic studies looking at creolization as it occurred in the Caribbean, and in the colonies and then the United States, can trace some kind of continuity from the past to the present. Oral traditions have passed on memories of the not-so-recent past and helped to build up a picture of how things were in the seventeenth and eighteenth centuries. Some dance and music traditions have persisted to the present day. Unfortunately the case is very different in any examination of the eighteenth- and early-nineteenth-century black community in London. By the beginning of the twentieth century this community had largely disappeared.[3] Doubtless it played its part in the gene pool of the majority, but for the most part its very existence had disappeared from living memory. For the present-day historian, there is no living continuity to tap into as there is in the Caribbean and elsewhere in America. The modern historian studying this eighteenth- and early-nineteenth-century community in London must therefore rely on a narrower set of evidence — diaries, journals, shipping documents, parliamentary papers and newspapers, as well as what paintings and drawings have survived. There is also the difficult question of interpretation. The modern historian looks at what evidence in the seventeenth, eighteenth and nineteenth centuries has survived with a mind-set that belongs firmly to the twenty-first century and is sadly subject to the tyranny of what sources are still available. It is always difficult to step back in time and try to empathize with the distant shadows of another period. Although I am myself black, in trying to decode much of the evidence that still exists, I am inevitably looking at a black community in London largely through the eyes of white commentators. Sometimes this has involved a kind of mental double somersault on my part.

Even for European onlookers in the eighteenth and nineteenth century, black creole dancers looked strange. Shane and Graham White make this clear:

> Describing Jamaican dancers in 1790, J. B. Moreton thought it "very amazing to think with what agility they twist and move their joints: I sometimes imagined they were on springs or hinges, from the hips downwards." Mainland slaves performing the Juba dance, William Smith wrote in 1838, displayed "the most ludicrous twists, wry jerks, and flexible contortions of the body and limbs, that human imagination can divine."
>
> The suppleness of blacks' bodies was associated with free movement of the pelvis, the fluidity of black dancers' bodies contrasting with what Lawrence Levine refers to as the "stiffly erect" bodily position commonly assumed in European dance forms, but more was involved than this. A sense of cultural difference pervades whites' description of African American dance. Even if the steps black dancers were using were familiar to whites, those steps were being performed at different speeds, combined in different ways, and executed with different movements of the torso and limbs. Even if slaves were performing European dances such as the quadrille, the cotillion, and the schottische, differences in style — the rhythmic complexity, the persistent improvisation, and unusual body movements — suggested that different cultural values underlay the performance.[4]

My Own Experience

My interest in African dance was sparked by my experience of working with William Louther, the great Alvin Ailey and Martha Graham principal. He was trained by Katherine Dunham, among others, who as well as being a dancer interested in African and Caribbean dance, was trained as an anthropologist by Herskovits himself.[5] My own training mixed the European classical ballet tradition with both West African and Caribbean dance. The tensions between the two, and my interest in dance history, were the original basis for this book.

My personal experience was part of London and England's absorption of a sizeable black community in the twentieth century. I have been fascinated with the parallels between my experience and that of a black ethnic minority in London in the seventeenth, eighteenth and nineteenth centuries.

Frazier/Herskovits Debate in the 1940s

African cultural survival and African dance survival have long concerned historians in the Americas. Academic controversy over what African culture did or did not survive crystallized in the 1940s into two opposing schools of thought. One said that retention of African culture in the United States was more or less nonexistent because the African was almost totally stripped of culture by the process of enslavement. The other school of thought proposed that slavery did not destroy slaves' African culture and that African culture continued to have a defining impact on Afro-American culture in the United States. The two theorists who laid out these initial positions in detail were Edward Franklin Frazier and Melville J. Herskovits, respectively. Although their theories have been superseded, the questions they asked are still the questions that cause debate. Therefore, it is useful to recapitulate some of the basic tenets of their arguments before proceeding to examine modern debates over creolization.

The Herskovits thesis is set out in his book *The Myth of the Negro Past*.[6] The myth that Herskovits set out to destroy was the belief that American Negroes had no past except a history of primitive savagery in Africa from which they had been delivered by contact with European civilization in America. Admittedly, in the early 1940s, studies of African history were still in their infancy, but to deny that blacks in the United States had an important culture and history that was rich in the complexity and tradition in Africa, and to suggest that African culture was not advanced enough to withstand contact with "superior" European culture was to imply that Negroes were an inferior people, which Herskovits could not accept. Herskovits thought it was important to recognize the historical relevance of African continuity in order to assess cultural differences between white and black Americans in sociological and cultural rather than racist terms. He believed that any differences between white and black values and behavior were due not to any black inferiority, but to a different cultural tradition whose roots lay in Africa.[7] At the time, this was an original insight that has proved remarkably influential in later studies of both African and slave history.

Herskovits was an anthropologist who "studied the physical as well as the cultural traits of the Negro, and his investigations included work not only in the United States but also in Africa, South America and the West Indies."[8] He brought to the debate on the survival of African culture a wealth of firsthand knowledge and practical experience built around his broad fieldwork in Dahomey, Dutch Guiana, Haiti, Trinidad and Brazil. He studied the "New World Negro" as part of his research in the slaving area of Africa where a large proportion of Afro-Americans originated.[9] In discussing the culture of black people in the United States he insisted that the situation of the Negroes of North America be placed on a "cultural baseline" with other Afro-American societies, arguing, "It is quite possible on the basis of our present knowledge to make a kind of chart indicating the extent to which the descendants of Africans brought to the New World have retained Africanisms in their cultural behaviour."[10] He wrote, "The scale of the survival of African culture stretches from Dutch Guiana (Surinam) with the strongest and most primary examples of African culture at one end, to the vast mass of Negroes of all degrees of racial mixture living in the South of the United States. Finally, we should come to a group where, to all intents and purposes, there is nothing of the African tradition left, and which consists of people of varying degrees of Negroid physical type, who only differ from white neighbors in the fact that they have more pigmentation in their skins."[11]

Herskovits believed it was necessary to compare the United States with other areas of the New World where Africanisms were present, in order to discover clues to more subtly disguised African patterns of culture in the United States.[12] He believed that apart from Haiti, Trinidad and Brazil, where it had been possible to trace tribal antecedents back to particular West African tribes and localities, slaves in the United States and the Caribbean were of too mixed an origin to make interesting anthropological studies. They could not be ascribed with any certainty to definite areas of Africa, such as Nigeria or Dahomey (although we now have good figures on the places of origin of slaves going to the Caribbean in the seventeenth and eighteenth centuries).[13] Herskovits made up for this difficulty by defining African culture as a single-culture area with an overall similarity and unity despite local differences. He pointed to a "base line" of African culture to serve as a measure for determining Africanisms in the United States. He maintained that within the general culture of Africa there was a center, and that this center was an African religion in which music and dance play a major part. Throughout New World Negro cultures, the strongest Africanisms were to be found in religion, music and dance.[14]

Herskovits emphasized that dance was "also a fundamental element in aesthetic expression everywhere in Africa." He wrote, "Dancing takes multitudinous forms, and all who have had firsthand contact with the area of our special interest speak of the many varieties of dances found there.

These may be ritual or recreational, religious or secular, fixed or improvised, and the dance itself has in characteristic form carried over into the New World to a greater degree than almost any other trait of African culture. To attempt verbal descriptions of dance types requires a technique as yet scarcely developed; since analysis must also await the utilization of motion pictures as an aid to the study of these special aspects of motor behavior, we can here but record the fact of its prominence in the culture, and its pervasiveness in the life of the people."[15] We now have, besides motion pictures, both Benesh and Laban notations that are often used as an analytical aid in dance studies. These support Herskovits's arguments. Indeed, the extent to which his arguments have stood up over time remains remarkable.

Herskovits asserted that Negroes did have a past, a cultural history which made them "as distinctive as the Italians or Germans or Old Americans or Jews or Irish or Mexicans or Swedes (in America).... The tendency to deny the Negro any such past as all other minority groups of this country own ... is thus unfortunate, especially since the truth concerning the nature of Negro aboriginal endowment, and its tenaciousness in contact with other cultures, is not such as to make it suffer under comparison. The recognition by the majority of the population of certain values in Negro song and Negro dance has already heightened Negro self-pride and has affected white attitudes toward the Negro."[16] Herskovits concluded: "The civilization of Africa, like those of Europe, has contributed to American culture as we know it today."[17]

It is important in analyzing Herskovits's thesis and the evidence he presented to remember that he was attacking a myth. The black sociologist Edward Franklin Frazier, the foremost opponent of Herskovits in the 1940s, while conceding the existence of African cultural survival in Latin America and the Caribbean, denied that African culture was able to survive the conditions of slavery to any significant extent in the United States. He admitted that a few individual slaves remembered something of their background in Africa. However, exceptions proved the rule for him. He still maintained that African traditions and practices did not take root and survive in the United States. He said in his book *The Negro Family in the United States*, "These isolated instances only tend to show how difficult it was for slaves, who had retained a memory of their African background, to find a congenial milieu in which to perpetuate the old way of life ... the slaves, it seems, had only a vague knowledge of the African background of their parents."[18] Frazier's work was supported and added to for several decades by Stanley Elkins, Kenneth Stampp and Daniel Patrick

Moynihan, although Elkins and Stampp disagreed over the psychology of the black response to a situation in which they found themselves stripped of their own culture. Moynihan's analysis of the way slavery destroyed the family unit is firmly based on Frazier's theories.[19]

Frazier's theory was that the process of enslavement and the death of earlier generations born in Africa destroyed the culture of the slaves. The gap this created was filled by Christianity, which became the new bond of social unity. The new world view which gave meaning to life was Christianity, expressed in the images and stories of the Bible, as accepted by the slaves and celebrated in their spirituals.[20]

Sterling Stuckey has shown that Frazier's view was simplistic.[21] Stuckey makes it clear that unknown to white plantation society, black slaves "engaged in religious ceremonies in their quarters and in woods unobserved by whites."[22] According to him, "From the time of the earliest importation of slaves ... millions of slaves did the ring shout, unobserved, with no concern for white approval."[23] The ring shout was a ring dance ultimately ending in a "state of possession" by some of the participants. Stuckey makes it clear that far more of a shared music and dance heritage from Africa survived than whites realized at the time and that cultural historians did not know anything about it until recently. This is extremely important when considering the use of dance by the London community in the late eighteenth and nineteenth century. Blacks coming from the Caribbean to London brought this shared music and dance heritage with them from Africa. Stuckey also provides evidence that when black congregations established themselves in Christian churches, they subtly altered the services to fit in with their African heritage. As he noted, "For the African, dance was primarily devotional, like a prayer.... That whites considered dance sinful resulted in cultural polarization of the sharpest kind since dance was to the African a means of establishing contact with the ancestors and with the gods."[24] As Joe Nash has pointed out, the ring shout (also known as the flower dance, the rope dance and the rocking daniel) was a blending of Africanisms and Christianity. To shout was to move in a circle counterclockwise, dancing to the accompaniment of hand clapping and chanting — a form of body prayer. When this moved into Christian churches, crossing of the feet as in dancing was not allowed, but otherwise the African religious form was preserved largely intact.[25] Nothing could better underpin what this book will maintain as a major difference between the mind-set of London's black eighteenth- and early-nineteenth-century community and that of the majority around them, than this direct evidence of the shout. In burial customs too, across the

Caribbean and elsewhere in the Americas, African customs prevailed and continued.[26]

Shane White and Graham White observed that the shout was alive and well later in the nineteenth century, in a description by one M. R. S. who visited a school in Beaufort, South Carolina, in 1866: "After school the teachers gave their children permission to have a shout. This is a favorite religious exercise of these people, old and young. In the infant schoolroom, the benches were first put aside, and the children ranged along the wall. Then began a wild droning chant in a minor key, marked with clapping of hands and stamping of feet. A dozen or twenty rose, formed a ring in the center of the room, and began an odd shuffling dance. Keeping time to the weird chant they circled round, one following the other, changing their step to quicker and wilder motions, with louder clappings of the hands as the fervour of the singers reached a climax."[27]

White and White write, "Though whites generally associated the shout with Christian religious observances, there was some scepticism on this point, as M. R. S's reference to the 'wild droning chant' suggests. Laura Towne saw in the shout 'the remains of some old idol worship' and declared that she had never seen 'anything so savage.'"[28] The Whites add: "As performed by slaves in the antebellum period, the shout seems like a typical African American adaptation, which retained the ring formation, foot-stamping, polyrhythmic clapping, and shuffling of African dance forms and blended them with elements from a religion to which many had by then been converted or encouraged to adhere."[29] The importance of this evidence is that the shout was an African tradition capable of survival and adaptation long after Africans had removed to the Americas and the Caribbean.

The academic debate of the 1940s has been refined and developed since then. Throughout the 1970s those scholars who based their arguments on Frazier faced difficulties. In 1972, John Blassingame brought new research to show that slave communities managed to live and work autonomously in spite of slavery.[30] Herbert Gutman, carrying out research very similar to Blassingame's, set about refuting Moynihan's theories about the collapse of black families.[31] It became clear that a theory midway between Herskovits and Frazier would be needed since, even if Blassingame and Gutman successfully refuted the idea that no African culture survived, it was clear that what African culture did survive, managed to do so in conditions very different from those experienced by arrivals in the New World from Europe. In 1976 the anthropologists Richard Price and Sidney W. Mintz suggested a synthesis of Herskovits's and Frazier's positions. They drew an analogy between creolized culture that focused on "deep structures," comparing "underlying values and beliefs" with "unconscious grammatical principles." They suggested that values and beliefs that existed at a deeper level, undoubtedly did survive the trauma of the slave crossing.[32]

Mintz and Price argued, "[N]o group, no matter how well-equipped or how free to choose, can transfer its way of life and the accompanying beliefs and values intact, from one locale to another. We assert further that the conditions of transfer, as well as the characteristics of the host setting, both human and material, will set some limits on the variety and strength of effective transfers. It goes without saying that Europeans and Africans participated in highly differentiated ways in the process of New World settlement."[33] Since they wrote this, there has been a new impetus in subsequent research emphasizing the social politics of body and dance, with a further emphasis on contemporary feminist and cultural studies coming from Jane Desmond and Helen Thomas. In addition, Lawrence W. Levine has careful analyzed black culture and black consciousness based on the orally transmitted expressive culture of Afro Americans in the United States from slavery onward, asking, "What were the contours of slave folk thought on the eve of emancipation and what were the effects of freedom upon that thought."[34]

Thomas, in particular, asks just how authentic the performance of any dance can be. The question of authenticity will be of particular relevance when looking at the pictures of dance performances in chapter 5. Thomas draws interesting parallels with the approach to authenticity in music performance, particularly with early music.[35] As with music, she asks how we can relate dance "as it was" to dance "as it is."[36] She looks in passing at the term "intentional fallacy," first used in the early 1940s and 1950s in literary criticism in an article by W. K. Wimsatt and Monroe C. Beardsley, attacking the idea of limiting the search for meaning in a literary work to an attempt to discover the author's intentions, rather than looking at the potential for meaning in the work itself.[37] Taruskin in 1995 uses the same argument to decry the idea of looking at the intentions of a composer of music, calling this "consulting the oracle."[38] Taruskin says that judging a performance on that basis "bespeaks a failure of nerve, not to say infantile dependency."[39] He thinks the idea of historical authentic performance is a modernist invention and not a historical restoration.[40] Taruskin maintains that real authenticity is to be found in the actual performer's "imaginative conviction."[41]

Gary Tomlinson, a music historian, has held that Taruskin's theory was itself too limiting and has wanted to transform the term "authenticity" to "authentic meanings." "Authentic meaning" refers to "the meaning that we, in the course of interpretative historical acts of various sorts, come to believe its creators and audience invested in it."[42] Thus, for Tomlinson, meaning not only was to be found in the work as a structuralist might believe, but also arose from the relationship of the work to "things outside it" in a much wider historical and social context.[43] In 1995, Peter Kivy expanded on these assumptions, suggesting there was no single authenticity but a number of "authenticities."[44] He argued, "[T]he gap between 'text' and 'performance' is not only a necessary evil but at the same time a desired, intended and logically required ontological fact. It is in that gap that the work of art is produced that we call the 'performance,' and that I have likened to an 'arrangement' of the work. It was in that gap that personal authenticity can either be or not be."[45]

This academic debate suggested four components for authenticity. Firstly, there was the replication of the creator's intentions. Secondly, according to Taruskin, there was a dependency on the performer's imaginative act. Thirdly, according to Tomlinson, meaning depended on the historical and social context in which the work was created. Fourthly, according to Kivy, authenticities depended on a variety of different kinds of approach. Tomlinson suggested that any consideration of a historical dance performance had to bear in mind the relevance of these assumptions about authenticity.[46] Looking at current revivals of early American dance classics, she said that if the dancers consciously tried to fit into the mind-set of the original creators, "there is a process of not simply dance 'as it is,' but also an attempt to realize dance 'as it was.' So there is still a sense of recovering the past work, even as there is a vivid presentness in performance."[47] It is just this "vivid presentness" that we can see, for example, in so many folk dance solos from Antigua today, as I have observed them. (Interestingly, I have observed many of the same solo movements danced in Ghana today.) These should be looked at with the debate over authenticity very much in mind. Even assuming that the actual movements of the Antiguan dance are historically correct, and even assuming that the performer conveys the right sense of conviction in interpreting them, the process of creolization analyzed by Mintz and Price has completely altered the social context in which the dance is performed and the attitudes and assumptions of the spectators who watch it when this is performed in the Caribbean. Those watching it in Antigua do so with a mind-set which is embedded in Caribbean culture, which is very much a creole culture. Those watching a very similar dance in West Africa see it from the perspective of West African culture. The same dance acquires different meanings and interpretations according to its cultural context.

As Jane Desmond has pointed out, "Dance, as a discourse of the body, may in fact be especially vulnerable to interpretations in terms of essential identities associated with biological difference."[48] Such identities incorporate not only race and gender but also the sexualized assumptions made along with them, as well as associations of national and ethnic identities, which can often be wrapped up with notions of race. As Desmond observes, in the United States dance can often be seen in terms of a racialized difference between black and white. As she notes, "Obviously there is a much more complex matrix of racial and cultural identities occurring between the relationships of the various dance groups, changing in response to events, demographics, economics, and other factors, yet while the black and white divide is ludicrously simplistic it nevertheless holds the field in public attitudes and media as well as within communities and across communities, acting as a very positive marker of cultural identity."[49]

Desmond has noted that modern white Americans tend to associate black people with sexuality, sensuality and an inborn propensity for physical dance ability and expression tending to excess. It followed long-standing cultural assumptions from Thomas Jefferson and even well before him.[50] This allows middle- and upper-class whites to adopt so-called Africanisms in their dance and to move in what is for them a relatively outrageous manner, thus in a sense temporarily adopting "blackness" without having to pay the social penalty for being black. As she says, "An analogue might be 'slumming'—a temporary exertion across lines dividing social classes in the search for pleasure."[51] It should be possible to refer back from this to the process of creolization taking place in the Caribbean in the seventeenth and eighteenth centuries. A similar blurring of the black-white divide was taking place in a fragmentary fashion.

Division according to social class is here almost as important as division according to race and this adoption of the otherness, of different groups, obviously plays a part not only in social dance in America, the Caribbean, and the UK, but also in any consideration of public attitudes and responses to Africanisms in dance performance as well as in social dance itself.

Any discussion of authenticity has to bear in mind the attitude and assumptions of the audience. In discussing the modern black choreographer Alvin Ailey, Ramsay Burt has said, "Where Ailey can be seen to be trying to express black experience and create representations of masculinity that are meaningful to black audiences, white definitions of dance aesthetic, of gender and of 'Otherness' intervene. These stereotypes condemn the black male dancer to be seen as a body and as the objectification of black male sexuality and virility—the source of thrills and fears."[52] In order fully to understand dance forms in Africa, the Caribbean and London, it should be useful to consider these stereotypes associated with the black body as they interacted with dance forms elsewhere. Two examples are dance as it developed in Brazil and dance as it developed in Argentina. Barbara Browning has written perceptively about dance in Brazil, particularly samba, candomblé and capoeira. She points out that attitudes to race differ in Brazil from those in the United States, writing, "As the historian Carl Degler has bluntly put it, 'In Brazil the mulatto is not a Negro, whereas in the United States he is.' That is, in part, why miscegenation has been perceived as a process of 'whitening' in Brazil, and not in the United States. This is the fundamental difference in the two countries' understanding of race. Brazil has, as Degler again succinctly terms it, the 'mulatto escape hatch.'"[53] As Degler says, "When a society develops a place for the mulatto as occurred in Brazil, then certain other responses to the presence of black men in a white-dominated society, such as those that were worked out in the United States, for example, are foreclosed."[54] Brazilian society has a softer version of the inevitable tensions, particularly sexual tensions between white masters and black slaves. Gilberto Freyre (1900–1987), having looked at interracial sexual contact and its consequences, which not only included mixed-blood offspring but also epidemic sexually transmitted diseases and widespread promiscuity, stated, "It is generally said that the Negro corrupted the sexual life of Brazilian society by precociously initiating the sons of the family into physical love. But it was not the Negro woman who was responsible for this: it was the woman slave."[55] Browning comments on this strange reversal that makes a black woman slave responsible for corrupting society. Obviously this reverses the role of sexual power. As a slave the black women has to be sexually submissive. But her slave state became eroticized so that she became the sexual "initiator" corrupting white boys with "physical love." Where the U.S. version of this exchange is a plain and simple rape of a black slave by a white master, Brazil has managed to sidestep this issue and regards the offspring of such miscegenation as being whitened rather than blackened. Hence the widespread acceptance in Brazil of the mulatto. Browning does point out, however, that since the 1970s the resurgence of black confidence in the United States has had its counterpart in Brazil where some mixed-race Brazilians have begun to identify themselves as black, in imitation of the harsher American attitudes. She points out that in Brazil the mixed race body was "eroticized, feminized, and thus effectively depoliticized as the mulata sambista."[56] Sadly, what happened in Brazil does not seemed to have happened in the Caribbean. The offspring of white and black parents were seen as blackened rather than whitened, and so despised in the same ways as the blacks themselves.[57]

Interestingly, Browning also sees the Brazilian candomblé, commonly known as the "possessional" dance, as being close to Yoruba traditions in West Africa and a striking survival of a West African form. In looking at capoeira she echoes Robert Farris Thompson, Kenneth Dossar and Gerhard Kubik, who all describe capoeira's origins in Angola.[58] Browning also considers that the indigenous Brazilians made a significant contribution to its development. She sees the dance as embodying an idea of "breaking out of boundaries, of getting out of control, which is not only figured in the broken circle, the shattered roda where dance explodes into class unrest and violence. Ostensibly, racial borders as well were being broken. The so-called mulatto capoeirista is a figure moving between categories. He exists at the anxious point of contact between blacks and whites. And while that point of contact was sexualized in the body of the mulata sambista, it is made violent in that of the capoeirista."[59] Browning notes that slavery, which was not abolished in Brazil until 1888, was to some extent mitigated in the social tensions both before and after abolition by being transmuted into capoeira.[60]

Martha E. Savigliano has looked at the gendered, racial and political echoes and assumptions that surround the body of the dancer in the tango, a dance form that developed in Buenos Aires, Argentina. She writes:

> Whose embrace was the tango embrace? Tango's choreography emerged out of mutual admiration and scornful disdain among the different races, classes, and ethnicities lumped into one city. The lighter-colored ones imitated the skilful movements of the blacks and, self-conscious of their shortcomings, ended up caricaturing them. The darker ones, in trying to rub on some fashionable white elegance but knowing that this would bring them no more respect, mocked the loose embrace of the quadrilles, mazurkas, habaneras, and waltzes, tingeing it with bodily proximity and sweat. The tango dance emerged from these racial and class conflicts and competed for a place of its own among the dances that were already being danced, pending, as always, benediction in the cultural empires of the world. Male and female bodies displayed tensions of the "correct" and the "incorrect," of the "civilized" and the "primitive," of the "authentic" and the "parody," and all tensions were sexualised so as to render the conflicts natural, universal, and unavoidable.[61]

1. Body, Kinesthetics and Dance Theory 17

The idea of mockery and derision implicit in so many African retentions will be examined later, and it is interesting to note it in the development of the tango, particularly in relation to the quadrille. Savigliano also has much to say about the tango from a feminist viewpoint, asserting, "As a typical example of a macho society, the tango—created, administered and dominated by males—has had at its center a marginal zone, inhabited by women who sang it and danced it."[62] And Savigliano says that "in tango, the marginals are at the core."[63] She cannot accept the tango as another example of patriarchal power: "Tango, both in its lyrics and choreographies, has recorded women's abilities to subvert and negotiate."[64] Savigliano does not suggest that women win in the struggle, but admires the fact that they are struggling, quotes her mother: "No esta muerta quien pelea" (She who fights is not dead).[65]

Savigliano is even more trenchant in discussing what she calls 'the colonizing gaze.' She points out that there are at least three people involved in dancing the tango, "a male to master the dance and confess his sorrows, a female to seduce, resist seduction, and be seduced, and a gaze to watch these occurrences."[66] She maintains that when tango performers and spectators no longer shared a common race, class or culture, tango became exotic. When upper- and middle-class dancers perform, they depend for their looks, hopes and desires on a view of the tango as being exotic and something outside of their own experience. Savigliano considers that the power to exoticize is the colonial gaze. Exoticism emerges from a colonial encounter.[67] She suggests that in the colonial situation an emerging middle class respond to promises of development which she sees as a bourgeois, modern, imperialist drug, "but without exoticism, the hooking up would not be complete. Exoticism creates the need for identity and assures that it cannot be attained. It is the imperialist hook that cannot be unhooked. Exoticism creates the abstract, unfulfillable desire for completeness in the colonized while extracting his or her bodily passion. Exoticism is a colonial erotic game played between unequal partners. In tango the couple dances for the bourgeois colonizing gaze ... following his lead."[68] This is strikingly similar to the way in which would-be colonizers and slave owners looked at African dance. Theirs is Savigliano's colonizing gaze, but whereas the tango, largely because of its European input, was accessible and exotic to those viewing it from outside Buenos Aires working-class culture, African dance was less accessible to European eyes. Sadly, only its sexually and erotic content, the semi-naked bodies, the range of sexually suggestive movement, came to be how it was largely interpreted by Europeans and Caribbean and American planters.[69]

Richard A. Long has greatly clarified the history of Afro-American and Afro-Caribbean dance. He noted that it was not until the 1920s, with the art movement known as the Harlem Renaissance, that a growing pride in black achievement and individuality resulted in increasing attention being given to the three arts fundamental to any sense of black consciousness of a separate collective identity. These were music, singing and dancing.[70] Two developments in continental European scholarship also affected much of the emphasis of British and American anthropological and historical studies. These were the "folk life studies movement" developed by European students of "*Volkskunde*" or regional ethnology, and the Annales school of French social historians. These two movements turned the emphasis away from surviving documents, particularly legal documents, to the actual lives, customs and material culture of the folk.[71] The Annales historians took their name from the journal founded by Marc Bloch and Lucien Febvre in 1929[72] and, largely ignoring politics, wars and treaties, looked at the social life and cultural life of human beings in a given period. They looked at hitherto-ignored evidence in census reports, legal records, deed registries and parish records, and they asked different questions, trying to establish the mental outlook of ordinary people involved in social, cultural, and economic life.[73] These two scholarly traditions helped to extend the range of inquiry into slave and post-slave communities in the Caribbean and elsewhere in America. I hope that they have helped to underpin some of the research methodology adopted in this book.

The groundbreaking work of Lawrence W. Levine also redressed the lack of attention given by history to the actual lives led by the great majority of black men and women during and after slavery. "Upon the hard rock of racial, social, and economic exploitation and injustice, black Americans forged and nurtured a culture," Levine writes, "they formed and maintained kinship networks, made love, raised and socialized children, built a religion, and created a rich expressive culture in which they articulated their feelings and hopes and dreams."[74] He reminds us that "human beings are more resilient, less malleable and less able to live without some sense of cultural cohesion, individual autonomy, and self worth than a number of recent scholars have maintained."[75] Levine tries to "explore and reconstruct the mind of the black folk"[76] and what he has to say about black laughter will be of particular value when looking at black culture's propensity to mockery and derision. Just as Stuckey has made clear how much religious practice continued after the Atlantic crossing, in secret, without white society being aware of it, Levine makes clear the secretive nature of black folk culture in the face of oppression:

> Got one mind for white folks to see,
> 'nother for what I know is me;
> he don't know, He don't know my mind.[77]

This reinforces W. E. B. DuBois's contention that the African American forever "feels his two-ness—an American, a Negro ... two warring ideals in one dark body."[78]

Dena J. Epstein has added to the understanding of black folk culture also, with her careful analysis of black folk music before the civil war in America. She quotes from John Bernard, an English actor touring in the United States around 1800 on his way to Charleston who noticed the passion of slaves for dancing:

> The negroes have ... been ... known to walk five or six miles after a hard day's work to enjoy the pleasures of flinging about their hands, heads, and legs to the music of a banjo, in a manner that threatened each limb with dislocation. (Thomas Jefferson in the eighteenth century wrote of blacks, "the instrument proper to them is the banjar which they brought hither from Africa.") Bernard observed a dance at which the Negroes 'laughed, jumped, danced, and sang all their favourite ditties—"The Praise of Bumbo," "Virginny Nigger Berry Good," "I Lost My Shoe in an Old Canoe," etc., etc.[79]

None of the songs mentioned have survived, which reinforces Levine's account of how so much of the ordinary black culture was lost. Epstein makes it clear that in both the Caribbean and in the southern states of America, music and dancing were widespread among slaves. In existing sources and written evidence that has survived from this period, however, music and dance are seldom mentioned. This was partly because white commentators regarded dancing as sinful and something that should be stopped, so tended not to mention it often, and also because observers did not feel such "ordinary" pursuits worth commenting on. It was also partly because those in favor of abolition wanted to show the slaves in abject misery, a state with which exuberant dancing and singing did not fit, so they too tended to ignore it. Epstein writes, "Today we can understand that dancing and singing could coexist with a forced labor and bitter suffering, providing the slaves with a psychological escape that helped them to survive. It no longer seems necessary to depict slavery as unrelieved misery in order to condemn it. What the singing and dancing represented to the slaves themselves is not fully understood, but there can be no doubt that secular music and dancing were widespread despite the religious opposition to them. Church members frequently refused to participate in them, but not all blacks were church members."[80] It should be clear that music and dancing played an extremely important part in the lives of black communities in the Caribbean and in America, but also that their attitudes and assumptions would have been shared by black minorities in London. It was not just a question of singing and dancing coexisting with suffering, but rather that singing and dancing were a necessary outlet for the emotions such suffering involved.

Peter H. Wood has looked carefully at the self-same African characteristics of music and dancing in the worlds of slavery and post-slavery days. Even more importantly for the arguments put forward here, he has helped to analyze what made African slave and post-slavery dance different from European. He quotes one slave song that endured in the Gullah dialect, asking dancers to "gimme de knee bone bent." He points out that many Africans considered that straightened knees, hips and elbows implied death and rigidity, while flexed joints indicated energy and life. Slaves would refer to the "knee bone bent" as a praiseworthy ability to "get down."[81] Bernard, looking at the black dancers, refers to their "flinging about their hands, heads, and legs." In fact, the dancers would have been embodying the African characteristics—with ankles, knees, hips and elbows all bent—that Wood wrote about. They can all be observed in a rare watercolor titled *The Old Plantation*, painted in South Carolina toward the end of the eighteenth century and produced as visual evidence by Peter Wood.[82] Wood points to an illustration, *A Bivouac Fire on the Potomac*, by Winslow Homer, from *Harper's Weekly*, December 21, 1861. (*See overleaf*).[83] Here a black, freed slave is dancing to the music of a fiddle played by an elderly black and is watched with varying degrees of incomprehension by Union soldiers sitting around the fireside. Homer was white, of course, and his depiction of the dance done by the Negro, certainly looks closer to the European jig (discussed in chapter 2) than anything a black person was likely to have been dancing, but this must remain speculation. What can certainly be noticed is that the upright stance of the jig has been replaced by a semi-crouch, the "knee bone bent," thus giving it an exotic difference even for a painter like Homer, who, judging by his other productions, was little concerned with the true characteristics of African retentions in black dance.[84]

Peter H. Wood would have been less likely to write so perceptively about African dance, had he not benefited from earlier studies initiated by Katherine Dunham.[85] She was an earlier pioneer attempting to analyze the African background of New World dance as a result of her research in Africa, the United States and the Caribbean. She separated out three processes as being important factors in what African culture brought to the creolization of Caribbean and American black communities, and in their effect on the European culture which New World settlers brought with them. These were the way African religious dance was absorbed into Christian worship the complete secularization of dances which in Africa had been religious, and the way these now secular dances interacted with each other.[86] Dunham's work became the starting point for a serious study and analysis of what had been until then largely ignored as of little interest, and had been generally ascribed to the oddness of black behavior. In putting together a dance company and in performing, Dunham tried to convey the redemptive, exalting and spirit-enhancing role of dance in the African diaspora. She tried to convey it to people who had never known it, to those who had largely lost it and to those who only knew it in a fragmented and distorted form.[87] In a sense she was peeling back some of the layers which creolization had built for twentieth-century Caribbean and American black communities. She was, of course, also doing much more than this. She was highlighting a whole area of culture that had been largely ignored and was opening it up to new academic disciplines studying culture and the arts.

Even so, for students of culture and dance during nearly two decades there were only two book-length studies of Afro-American dance practice, Marshall and Jean Stearns's *Jazz Dance: The Story of American Vernacular Dance* (published in 1964) and Lynne Fauley Emery's *Black Dance in the United States from 1619–1970* (published in 1972).[88] The limitations in the first are already present in its title. A detailed account of professional artists nevertheless limits jazz dance to being merely "vernacular," even suggesting that "art dance and vernacular dance will combine more and more effectively as time passes."[89] The idea that dances based on the African diaspora might be considered as good an art form as any other kind of dance is never entertained. Emery's *Black Dance*, with its many illustrations, is a kind of whirlwind tour of Afro-American presence from the Atlantic crossing to the Caribbean and to the plantations of the United States and onward. In covering so much, from slave festivals, to nineteenth-century popular entertainment and twentieth-century dance forms, the book is admirably encyclopedic but inevitably leaves too much out, including any real attempt at dance analysis, with a tendency to see "primitive" dance burgeoning after the civil rights movement into something more sophisticated and secondary anyway to white American dance history. This reflects an unfortunate racial prejudice.

In the Stearnses' work, their beginning section on the characteristics of African dance was particularly useful. They based this on research by

A Bivouac Fire on the Potomac, by Winslow Homer, from *Harper's Weekly*, December 21, 1861. (© British Library Board. All Rights Reserved. G.13318, 11770.:2, Harper's Weekly 1861, No. 808/9)

Robert Farris Thompson, who eventually published a groundbreaking analysis of African dance and music performance in 1966.[90] Thompson's analysis highlights "the dominance of a percussive concept of performance; multiple meter; apart playing and dancing; call-and-response; and, finally the songs and dances of derision."[91] Derision was an important element in many African dances. In the Caribbean and later in London, derision added a political dimension to black dance that was an important outlet through which an oppressed minority could express its frustration. Dealt with in greater detail in chapter 4, this element of dance clearly referred to experiences in the world outside of dance. In the 1960s a growing consideration of black dance underpinned the new renaissance of the so-called "black aesthetic" referred to earlier.[92] By the 1990s the performance characteristics analyzed by Thompson were being reconceived as "Africanist retentions" or "Africanisms." Thomas DeFrantz listed them:

> Africanisms discernible in concert dance, for example, are qualities of design and execution based on insistent rhythmicity, angularity, percussive rupture of underlying flow, individualism within a group dynamic,

and access to a dynamic "flash of the spirit" that simultaneously confirms temporal presence and ubiquitous spirituality. These qualities are not particular movements so much as composition strategies that may inform any given moment in a dance. As such, they are recurrent aesthetic imperatives that may be employed both by African diaspora artists and, significantly, by others following this tradition. While some scholars have resisted this theoretical approach because of its implication of a narrow and singular "African dance" idiom, the identification of these conceptual traditions has created the most consistent approach to documenting Africanist performance across generations and geographies of Afro-American dancers and choreographers, as well as in work by others, including white Americans, Europeans, and Asians.[93]

These traditions are as applicable to any analysis of eighteenth-century African dance as they are to the nineteenth and twentieth centuries. DeFrantz objected to the term "black dance" since it tended to be defined as something opposed to its racial opposite, "white dance." As DeFrantz says, "the black body in motion does not render itself as an alternative to anything; as Fanon writes, 'it is.'"[94]

The British writer Christy Adair reinforces the view that the term "black dance" is too limiting. Looking at the history of a contemporary British troupe, the Phoenix Dance Company, admitting that the company is exclusively male and exclusively black, and that the company's dance is largely concerned with firsthand experience as an ethnic minority, she objects to the responses of dance critics in the media tending to see blackness as one-dimensional, based on "colonial imperialist paradigms."[95] Phoenix Dance Company achieved early success and within four years was established with an Arts Council grant, but the company changed its directors and personnel until it saw itself as part of the general contemporary dance movement in which black dancers played an important part, but were not limited to notions of a specifically black culture and experience.[96] Adair regretted that some critics were unable to expand their horizons sufficiently to accept this. In effect she was restating, in a British arena, criticism already made by DeFrantz, and even more trenchantly by Brenda Dixon-Gottschild. Dixon-Gottschild wanted to go further. She wanted dance critics to be knowledgeable about what made African dance different from European dance so that they would be able to write knowledgeably about African dance. At the same time she did not want critics to limit Afro-American dancers to their black heritage, but to see them as part and parcel of American dance to which African retentions had made such an important contribution anyway.[97] A typical example of what Adair and Dixon-Gottschild were objecting to was cited by Shane White and Graham White, who noted the response of Benjamin Latrobe in 1819 when faced with hundreds of Afro-Americans, both slave and free, watching dancers performing to drums, banjos, violins and other instruments in the then-famous Congo Square dances in New Orleans. Latrobe experienced only strong feelings of cultural alienation. "I have never," said Latrobe, "seen anything more brutally savage and at the same time dull and stupid."[98] The Whites write, "Others, more observant of the dancers themselves, have left accounts which suggest a strong West Indian influence, a predictable enough development given the cultural links between New Orleans and the Caribbean and the fact that the Haitian Revolution of the 1790s and early 1800s had prompted many Haitian planters to migrate to the city, bringing their slaves with them."[99] *Plus ça change, plus c'est la même chose.* Just how real and important are the differences between Latrobe and the attitudes of the modern critics that Christy Adair and Brenda Dixon-Gottschild complained about so bitterly?

Shane White and Graham White make interesting parallels between the slaves' color sense and their music, both related to an underlying sense of rhythm, different from and alien to Euro-American cultural forms.[100] Thompson thought the clash of colors and patterns gave Mande textiles their sense of vibrancy and "aliveness."[101] For John Miller Chernoff, the "clash and conflict of rhythms" had much the same effect in African music. As he adds,

> The relationship of dance to both African and African American music is so intimate that these forms of cultural expression should probably be considered as one. Like African American music and textile design, black dance is characterized by rhythmic complexity. It too, privileges improvisation over predetermined form. As with black music, whether from the slave period or after it, and as is also true of black quilts and clothing, African American dance conveys an impression of "aliveness" and "vibrancy," the "unpredictable rhythms and tensions" of the performer evoking a sense of "constant surprise." Just as the clashing colors and irregular patterning of slave textiles and the multiple rhythms and unreproducible sounds of slave music jangled white sensibilities, so the movements of the black body in dance often seemed alien and unaccountably strange.[102]

The sense of strangeness, of course, was only felt by most white people. For blacks it was a source of pride. As the black ex-slave Solomon Northup wrote to his supposedly white readers: "Oh, ye pleasure-seeking sons and daughters of idleness, who move with measured step, listless and snail-like, through the slow winding cotillion, if ye wish to look upon the celerity, if not the 'poetry of motion'—upon genuine happiness, rampant and unrestrained—go down Louisiana and see the slaves dancing in the starlight of a Christmas night."[103] Solomon Northup was obviously glorying in the difference between Afro-American dance and the more restrained dance of the European tradition discussed above.

Paul Gilroy emphasizes something that is easy to underrate. He uses the term "racial terror," because in his view no aspects of the black diaspora can be grasped without an understanding that the full horror of the experience of slavery is somehow bound up with them and is always present in the background, either as direct experience or as racial memories rooted in folk culture.[104] This terror is, in his words, "unsayable"; words are somehow inadequate. Language and writing are usually considered among the most important expressions of human consciousness. Gilroy suggests that the power and significance of music and dance have a special place within the black diaspora in Europe, the Caribbean, and elsewhere in America. This is precisely what this book is attempting to emphasize. As Michael Dash has pointed out, "The slaves' access to literacy was often denied on pain of death and only a few cultural opportunities were offered as a surrogate for the other forms of individual autonomy denied by life on the plantations.... Music becomes vital at the point at which linguistic and semantic indeterminacy/polyphony arise amidst the protracted battle between masters, mistresses, and slaves. The oral character of the cultural settings in which diaspora musics have developed presupposes a distinctive relationship to the body."[105] This idea was expressed with exactly the right amount of impatience by Glissant: "It is nothing new to declare that for us music, gesture, dance are forms of communication, just as important as the gift of speech. This is how we first managed to emerge from the plantation; aesthetic form in our cultures must be shaped from these oral structures."[106]

Cultural Erasures, Retentions, and Creolization

Antonio Benitez-Rojo has carefully analyzed the complex syncretism of Caribbean cultural expressions, which he calls "supersyncretism," which emerged from the coming together of European, African and Asian elements within the plantation systems of the Caribbean.[107] He is only too aware of the difficulties inherent in any analysis: "As soon as we succeed in establishing and identifying as separate any of the signifiers that make up the supersyncretic manifestation that we're studying, there comes a moment of erratic displacement of its signifiers toward other spatio-temporal points, be they in Europe, Africa, Asia, or America, or in all these continents at once. When these points of departure are nonetheless reached, a new chaotic flight of signifiers will occur, and so on ad infinitum."[108] He takes as a vivid example the cult of the Virgin de la Caridad del Cobre in Cuba. He suggests that this cult has three sources of meaning: first, its aboriginal origin (the Taino deity Atabey); second, the European Virgin Madonna; third, a deity from West Africa (the Yoruba Orisha Oshun).[109] He points out that these "origins" could give rise to a warmly patriotic pride in their history for Cubans. Yet also by immersing themselves in the cult of the Virgin they could transcend their sense of nationality altogether. He then looks at the different origins of each of these elements in turn, and points out that each has a different set of associations and assumptions so that each signifier leads on to other signifiers, ad infinitum.[110] This brilliant analysis highlights the problems when discussing Caribbean culture. Each layer of acculturation as it is peeled away reveals only further layers beneath it. This is depressingly apposite in any attempt to analyze the development of creole dance in Caribbean society. When is the "shout" not the "shout"? When is the minuet not quite what Europeans interpret as the minuet?

Benitez-Rojo also spends time revealing yet another important aspect of the process. Different Caribbean islands were colonized in different ways at different times, making it remarkably difficult to generalize about Caribbean culture at all. He points out that the presence in the Caribbean of Spain's European rivals happened almost from their first years, at the same time as quite an astonishing demand for sugar and other tropical products, as a result of the growing prosperity and hunger of Europe's capitalist economies. What started off as a society of small landholders and artisans served by workers of the same race and creed changed with surprising speed into a quite different plantation economy with continuous slave imports. As an example, the English landed in Barbados in 1625. The early labor force was made up of colonists, Carib Indians, deported criminals, deported political prisoners and indentured servants. In 1645 there were 18,300 whites (11,200 of them land owners) and 5,680 Negro slaves. This was three whites for every Negro, in an economy largely based on a small-holding cultivation of tobacco. In 1667, there were 745 owners and 82,023 slaves. The sugar plantations had arrived, sweeping away the tobacco smallholdings and taking up nearly all the land on the island. In 1698, just thirty years later, there was a ratio of nearly eighteen slaves for each white man.[111]

The dizzying speed of these developments bypassed Spain's colonies.

Spain itself was in a state of economic, political and social decay under its Hapsburg rulers and was involved in a succession of wars in Europe. It did not participate in the commercial expansion and capital accumulation that France, Holland and Britain found so profitable. Its Caribbean colonies were under frequent attack from privateers and pirates from 1523 until piracy ended around 1720.[112] Its Caribbean colonies concentrated on the construction of forts and defensive measures to protect not just the port cities but also the galleons circling the Caribbean collecting gold and silver in Cartagena, Portobello and San Juan de Ulua, en route for Spain.[113] These Spanish possessions stayed outside the plantation economy and did not experience the massive importation of slaves, so that the percentage of slaves compared to the rest of the population was much lower in the Spanish colonies than elsewhere.[114] At the beginning of the eighteenth century, the island of Cuba was more a colony of settlement than of exploitation, with a limited economic activity. As a result, Havana grew as a city in a way very similar to Spanish cities in Spain, with civic institutions like the church and schools, the book industry and the press, patriotic societies and the university, consulate and department of public works, botanical garden, opera house and theaters. Consequently Havana was "a city of plazas, esplanades, towers, walls, and palaces and theatres" well before the plantation system finally arrived in Cuba.[115] Kingston, Jamaica, on the other hand, grew with the plantations. In the eighteenth century it was little more than "an urban precinct with sugar warehouses, commercial offices, the governor's house, the fort, the docks and the slave shacks."[116] As a result, throughout the British colonies when compared with the Spanish, there was less economic diversification, smaller numbers of smallholders and artisans, a restricted internal market, a less adequate system of transport, a smaller middle class, a less effective institutional life, an inadequate system of education, a greater conflict with the language of the mother country and a slower emergence of arts and letters.[117]

These differences make any attempt to generalize about Caribbean culture much less valuable. As Paul Gilroy says, "The cultural and political histories of Guyana, Jamaica, Barbados, Grenada, Trinidad, and St. Lucia ... are widely dissimilar."[118] Each island's residents tended to think of themselves as different from those on other islands, and this has to be born in mind in any consideration of creole culture. It is Benitez-Rojo's opinion that "the negro slave who arrived at a Caribbean colony before the plantation was organized, contributed much more toward Africanizing the creole culture than did the one who came within the great shipments typical of the plantation in its heyday." Benitez-Rojo continues: "In spite of the natural differences of opinions held by different investigators of the Caribbean, the judgment that the slave on the sugar plantation was the most intensely exploited and repressed seems to be 100 percent unanimous. In my opinion, consequently, this slave would have been the least active African agent in the process of communicating his culture to the creole social milieu."[119]

The process of syncretic creolization suggested by Mintz and Price provided Afro-Caribbeans with a new and different sense of their own identity and culture. What did the Afro-Caribbean bring to this process? Frazier, of course, would have said that he had very little to bring because of the destructive, dehumanizing Atlantic crossing and the experience of slavery itself. Followers of Herskovits would suggest a variety of African retentions that provided some sort of cultural continuity with the African past. For example, Peter Wood and later Judith Carney have shown in convincing detail how the cultivation of rice, a staple food in West Africa, arrived in the Carolinas. The black slaves brought with them the knowledge of how to produce the crop and their West African skills helped to transform Carolina's economy and cultural practice.[120] Similarly, Margaret Washington Creel's analysis of the ways in which African religious practices combined with and in some ways transformed European Christianity among the Sea Island Gullahs in the coastal region of South Carolina during enslavement helps to provide striking evidence of African retentions.[121] Equally impressive evidence of African dance retentions has been provided by Charles Joyner's examination of South Carolina folk culture during slavery.[122] Ira Berlin has also pointed out that a minority of free Africans at either end of the Atlantic crossing had already immersed themselves in European culture in order to deal commercially with the European slave traders. They too would have provided, at the Caribbean end, some contribution to the process of creolization.[123] Richard Cullen Rath would propose a link between language and culture as a theoretical base for cultural creolization.[124] This, and the work of Henry Louis Gates Jr. and Edouard Glissant, are a useful base from which to examine how Afro-Caribbeans used their own and European dance forms as part of their struggle for a self-directed rather than an other-directed identity in the eighteenth and nineteenth centuries.

Mintz and Price's process of syncretic creolization describes the building of a native identity in a situation where it has not arrived naturally. The process occurs among the descendants of a forcibly displaced immigrant population drawn from various sources. The immigrants themselves go through a process known in linguistics as "pidginization," a simpler way of dealing with language and cultural practices within a number of different native identities. The children of these immigrants arrive in a society that still has a fragmented sense of identity. The children take this fragmented inheritance and build a more creole identity from it. Once large numbers of fresh immigrants disappear, this process of creolization gradually transforms the whole society from a fragmented one into a creole culture. Obviously creole language and culture generally tend to be the product of slavery, which provides the horrifying conditions from which creolization emerges.[125] These conditions make creolization special as a way of forming cultural identity. "Pidginization" is obviously different from creolization and is only its first stage, but the different geographical sources, enforced work, geographical transfer, subsequent procreation, racial prejudice and inequality all make creolization different from other processes involved in the establishment of a culture such as syncretism, the mating of different traditions, geographical moves, acquisitions, continuations or translations. Creolization is only useful as a concept if its special conditions are kept in mind.

It is not enough to liken cultural creolization to the process of linguistic creolization. The two cannot be separated. As Rath maintains, language is bound up with culture and culture is bound up with language. Both help those within a creole world to make sense of their society and their relations with others. Each is integral to the other.[126]

From the 1930s to the 1950s, structuralist linguists put forward the idea of rules that they termed "transformations" that linked culturally specific underlying grammatical structures with the way that a particular language expresses itself. In 1957 Noam Chomsky suggested that such structures were universal, and that the human brain was already wired to acquire language.[127]

By the mid 1970s it was generally agreed that these innate abilities for language were to be found in the underlying structures rather than in the transformation of those structures into actual expressions. Different languages are produced by differences in the transformations that result in expressions.[128] While accepting that the underlying structures of human language are an innate capacity wired into individual minds, the transformations that a speaker of a different language uses are clearly culturally conditioned. Otherwise everybody would speak the same language. Transformations, the ways that meaning filters through underlying structures to emerge as particular expressions, are culturally specific.[129]

These transformations represent a useful way of looking at and defining culture. They are the means by which the individual makes sense of the world. The process will certainly have an effect on, if not being wholly responsible for, transforming underlying structures into a whole range of different culturally specific expressions. The underlying structure is not culture. The body of expressions does not make up culture either. Culture is the way they act on each other. This is a definition of culture that is firmly located within individual consciousness, but perhaps the most useful way of defining culture is to see it as the way in which individuals can place themselves and understand their function in the world in which they find themselves. Defining culture in this way makes clear the relationship between culture and language. And because culture does not exist outside those making it, variety and conflict become all too explicable. It is a useful definition when approaching creolization.

There have been different ways of approaching creole identity. "Creole" has been used widely as a term to cover anyone in the Caribbean or the Americas born with forebears from elsewhere, including Europe. Jack P. Greene and Benedict Anderson have used the term to describe the arrival of American identities in the eighteenth century.[130] Anderson has used it with reference only to Europeans. Others have thought of it as a set of attitudes and assumptions produced in those whose forbears experienced the traumas of slavery, and have looked at these attitudes and assumptions as essentially African in origin. Caribbean authors like Edward Brathwaite and Edouard Glissant have examined their regional histories in the light of these assumptions.[131] Even more importantly, anthropologists and historians have examined creolization using linguistic models to analyze Afro-Caribbean and Afro-American culture. By looking at how dance and culture work together, it should be possible to integrate these approaches, taking advantage of Mintz and Price's comparison of "underlying values and beliefs" with "unconscious grammatical principles" as an entrée into Afro-Caribbean culture.

There are yet other ways of looking at creolization. There is something sadly similar between Edouard Glissant's novel *Malemort* and Orlando Patterson's concept of social death.[132] Glissant paints a depressing picture of the French Caribbean island of Martinique. Martinique is a French department administered from Paris and, as with most French possessions, it is administered efficiently and with humanitarian understanding.[133] Yet there is a positive policy of assimilation concerned with the dissemination of the French language.

Glissant makes it clear that this has caused the process of creolization to stop almost dead in its tracks and that Martinique runs the risk of being overwhelmed by French language and culture and of never evolving its own "langage."[134] As Glissant says, "*Pour qu'un multilinguisme ne soit pas dévastateur il faut qu'il soit consenti et vécu librement, par delà son institutionnalite, par la conscience libre de la communauté*" (for a multilingual encounter not to be devastating, it must be agreed to and lived freely, beyond its official status, within the free consciousness of the community).[135] Since this is not happening in Martinique, Glissant is discussing a sad confrontation, a tormented interfacing of "*langue*" and "*langage.*" What Glissant would go on later to describe as "*Poétique de la relation,*" would be forced into being as a result of "this opposition between a language one uses and an idiom one needs."[136] Setting the conservative values of "*langue*" against the creolizing force of "*langage,*" Glissant sets out one of his heartfelt themes, the importance of the non-systematic and chaotic in Caribbean attitudes. Glissant uses this concept of "*langage*" to evoke a whole area of responses within a given society to its experience of the world. "*Langage*" becomes a structured and conscious series of attitudes, and refers to that zone in which the peculiarities of a community's worldview or sensibility are formed.[137] In that sense, dance is also a "*langage,*" and it is worth remembering that across the Caribbean so many African dance forms have been subsumed into European dance forms, while retaining sufficient African characteristics to make them creole rather than European. Glissant considers that the French language has progressively impoverished creole and that "dispossession, lack of technological responsibility, absence of control over the everyday and the circuits of the economy deprive the Martiniquan community of its opportunity to evolve, of its own consciousness and personality."[138] As a result, the citizens of Martinique tend to use language itself in a remarkably flowery and overdecorated way, almost as a psychological and near-hysterical outlet for their frustration at not being able to achieve a collective sense of their own identity. Elsewhere in the Caribbean both language and dance have been able to develop according to regional needs and so have helped the creole culture to achieve a sense of its own identity.

Glissant's analysis of the process in Martinique correlates well with Orlando Patterson's view that so traumatic were the experiences meted out to slaves in the plantations that they suffered what he calls "social death" and lost much sense of their own individual identity.[139] Patterson gives, as one of many examples, the case of a slave who with his parents and other siblings witnessed the brutal flogging of an elder sister by the slave master for the minor offense of breaking a clock. The family witnessing this brutality did nothing about it because such were the conditions of their slavery; there was nothing they could do about it. Patterson asks, "[H]ow ... could persons be made to accept such natural injustice?"[140] His answer: "[D]enying the slave's humanity, his independent social existence, begins to explain this acceptance."[141] Perhaps it is cynical to suggest that we do not know the value of the clock, as it might have been of more monetary value than the slave. Since this was an incident remembered sixty years later, it hardly looks as though the family did accept it. The memory of the horror appears to have rankled over a period of sixty years. This is hardly acceptance. And while no doubt there is some truth in what Glissant and Patterson have to say, the lively evidence of creolization which is to be found in every Caribbean island, however different from each other, and in the slave states of America, would seem to make it clear that both Glissant and Patterson have a tendency to overstate their case.

With Glissant, it is not so much that creolization may or may not be used as a form of resistance; he is regretting that in Martinique the process of creolization has been arrested. Yet elsewhere, he considers that even when creolization has taken place, it is still more a way of coming to terms with the loss of freedom and the loss of their parents' homeland than anything else. Glissant was writing in a particular historical moment, the incorporation of Martinique into France, which influenced what he had to say. As we have seen, however, there was generally a hidden agenda in the relationships between blacks and whites. Many black activities and much black knowledge were concealed from the whites. The sporadic outbreaks of revolt imply both organization and shared views of which the whites knew little or nothing. One of the areas that whites seldom understood and often tried to ban was dance and the music, drumming and singing with which it was inextricably linked. These could be used as a way of expressing desperation over loss and as a way of lamenting the slaves' predicament, but it could also be used as a way of expressing active resistance. It was always imbued rather more with exuberant life than with Patterson's "social death." As will be made clear in chapter 3, dance and music could play a decisive part not only in establishing a sense of common identity, but also as a means of forwarding active resistance leading to open revolt.

Terminology

Since it is widely acknowledged by historians such as Folarin Shyllon and Simon Schama that the vast majority of the slaves that came to

London in 1730–1850 were from Africa via the Caribbean, for the purpose of this work, "black dance" means culturally black, as well as biologically black, a dance culture and identity that is rooted in Africa; unless otherwise stated, the term "black" must be recognized in this context.[142]

Talking of "blacks" as a group may also be too much of a generalization. Historically they have been made up of many groups. Nevertheless, there are general points that apply across the board to a wide variety of different groups. There are refutable exceptions, but these are refutations to a general pattern that has persisted across cultural Africa for most of recorded history, although the term "Africa" covers a large, diverse and far-from-homogenous area.

There are obvious difficulties in attempting to write about dance just as there are about music. Dance is a form of movement by humans, that expresses their response in movement, generally to music, but sometimes without music, to emotion. It needs to be seen, and either experienced in practice, or kinesthetically appreciated by the visual observer, who is supposedly imaginatively experiencing the dance as a physical exertion, even though not actually moving. For academic study, dance is difficult to describe in words, and just as music has developed its own notation, so, fortunately, dance has developed workable notations, but only in the twentieth century. (Rudimentary notations have existed from at least the fourteenth century onward, but are in general too rudimentary to be of much use, at least until ballet's Stepanov nineteenth-century notation). Neither music notation nor dance notation are used in the following pages. Drawings and paintings are used to illustrate the following chapters, but these represent a moment frozen in time, whereas dance is essentially movement, or, to use Susanne K. Langer's intriguing philosophical theory, dance is "virtual power" whereas music is "virtual time."[143] There are, of course, recordings of dance on film, but it is not possible to use this medium within the confines of a book. Anyway, the camera frame itself presents another problem. This imposes a square or rectangular border to what is viewed. Unfortunately, a dancer in making the moves required by the dance, tends to move out of the frame and the visual effect of the dance depends on being able to view the whole body of the dancer. If the camera operator appreciates this, and moves the camera further away from the dancer, so that the whole body can be seen whatever movement it makes, then, unfortunately, the dancer has a tendency to look too small within the frame, more like a performing flea than a human being. This is generally the reason why tribal dances and dance designed for the theater stage seldom seem to work properly when viewed on film. Only when a choreographer like Fred Astaire, who really understood the problems of the film medium, designs dances to fit and be seen within the camera frame, can the dance really take off in this new medium.[144]

The Next Chapters

The next chapter will look in detail at the origins of both African and European dance and indicate some of their interactions in the Caribbean. Examples will be demonstrated and analyzed in chapter 3 of the cultural mindset which black Caribbeans took with them to London in the eighteenth and nineteenth centuries. There will, however, be one further area to explore before looking at the actual evidence of the ways black Londoners used dance. How did the black minority *get* to London, and what sort of a minority society did they manage to build when they got there? This will be covered in chapter 4, before we can profitably analyze the various roles dance played in the life of that minority in chapter 5.

2

The Origins of African Dance and European Dance and the Dance Traditions They Established

This chapter will look at aspects of African traditional dance culture, and then look at the very different dance culture that had developed in Europe by the eighteenth and nineteenth centuries. Only after both of these very different dance cultures have been examined and analyzed will it be possible to observe what effect they had on each other in the process of creolization. Without a reasonable understanding of the important role dance played on the African mainland, an importance which would already have conditioned the minds of African slaves arriving in the Caribbean from Africa, it would be impossible to understand the cultural interchange between African and European influences involved in the creolization. This process produced the mind-set that blacks from the Caribbean brought with them when they arrived in London. The black community they would have found already existing in London when they got there would have shared this mind-set. It is this minority community's dependence on dance, and the particular ways in which they used dance, which will be examined in chapters 4 and 5. In Africa, some of the cultural dance traditions of which we have evidence from the eighteenth century have persisted to this day. This area of study is one in which it is possible to include written evidence by European explorers and also to include the scanty writings of Africans living in London in the eighteenth century. Enough was written to give a fair picture of our chosen period.

Europeans first reached what was to become known as the Gold Coast in the Kingdom of Guinea in 1426.[1] They often briefly mentioned and sometimes inexpertly described local West African dances in the accounts of their journeys and in the letters they sent to Europe. Blacks transported to London from West Africa via the Caribbean, such as Olaudah Equiano, wrote with more clarity and authority when describing the importance and meaning of their dance.[2] Since dance is our subject matter, both in the Caribbean and in London, and with the African influence as well as the European influence upon that dance, it is clearly important, if not crucial, to be able to establish from where in Africa most of the Caribbean slaves originated. David Eltis has helpfully collated much of the evidence available, although without any particular reference to dance. As he says, "The new data will probably modify currently accepted estimates of the size of the trade less than it will change knowledge of most other aspects of the trade. Nevertheless, the data do support a revised aggregate estimate, and, more importantly, they provide the basis for more accurate assessments of who carried the slaves, from which part of the African coast they embarked, and where in the Americas they were taken."[3]

The cultural dance of the Gold Coast will be examined as an example, at least partly because the Akan people's asafo dance figures prominently in one of the planned slave revolts to be examined. It is important to realize, as Philip Curtin has made clear, that only 18 percent of slaves exported by the English from 1690 to 1807 came from the Akan people in the Coast. About 30 percent came from the Bight of Biafra. In Jamaica, the percentage of Africans coming from the Gold Coast in the eighteenth century was no more than 25 percent.[4] David Eltis would raise these estimates to 27.7 percent for the period 1651–1808, but as Trevor Burnard and Kenneth Morgan make clear, "Heterogeneity of ethnic origin was a conspicuous feature of Jamaica's slave trade."[5] After 1710 the Bight of Biafra and later Angola became the primary markets for slaves sent to the British Caribbean. As a result, by 1813 in Trinidad only 8 percent of slaves came from the Gold Coast.[6] This diversification of origin and the process of creolization, aided by intermarriage, meant that by the late eighteenth century a sense of identity shared by blacks in the Caribbean was based more on skin color than on national differences.[7] It is important to realize that any reference therefore to the Akan people and their asafo dance must be seen as only one example among many possible from a wide variety of different African origins.

Even while emphasizing that regional differences in Africa existed and were significant in shaping cultural patterns, it is equally important to recognize the common features which African culture shared. Examples of this, particularly relevant here, would be both African attitudes to dance and the dance techniques that are widely shared across many of the regions of Africa. Common aspects of African dance technique were set out in chapter 1. African attitudes to dance will be analyzed later in this chapter. It is important to realize that slaves arriving from different areas in Africa shared some common culture.

The area of Africa first discovered by Europeans, which they called the Gold Coast, is now incorporated in modern Ghana in West Africa, bordered by Burkina Faso on the north, Togo on the east, the Atlantic Ocean on the south and the Ivory Coast on the west.[8] A coastal plain parallels the 350-mile shoreline. In the west a forested belt extends north from the plain, verging in the east into the hilly Asante region where 14.8 percent of modern Ghana's estimated 19 million people live. The Akan are the largest ethnic group, making up 49.1 percent. Farther north is a high, rolling savannah. It covers 92,000 square miles and contains no less than seventy-five languages and dialects.[9] While no reliable data exists for the population in these regions in the eighteenth century, it is reasonable to assume that the Akan then represented much the same percentage of the total population as they do now.

According to Herbert M. Cole and Doran H. Ross, "Stone-age man probably first inhabited Ghana roughly half a million years ago, while a knowledge of agriculture and pottery appears in the archaeological record about 2000–1500BC. The descendants of these early peoples form the population base of present-day Ghana, despite numerous migrations into and within the area. Iron tools developed somewhere between 500 and 1000 A.D., with more advanced technologies such as brass casting and weaving following several hundred years later."[10]

Written history really begins with the European arrival on the Gold Coast in the fifteenth century. It is generally believed that the Portuguese were the earliest Europeans to visit the gold-producing districts between the rivers Ankobra and Volta in 1426.[11] So much gold was obtained in this area that it was named Mino by the Portuguese and Côte d'Or by the French, a name which was later adopted by the English — "Gold Coast."

In their commercial activities, the Portuguese at first concentrated on the natural products of the west coast of Africa, such as gold, pepper, salt and ivory, as well as slaves. With the "discovery" and colonization of the Americas in the fifteenth and sixteenth centuries, and especially with the establishment of sugar and tobacco plantations there and a need for a regular supply of slave labor, trade in humans became more profitable. From its beginning in 1441, the trade with West Africa became increasingly dominated by the need for human slaves to supply European developments in the Caribbean and the Americas.[12]

In 1441, ten Africans from the northern Guinea coast were shipped to Portugal as a gift to Prince Henry the Navigator.[13] A subsequent expedition brought back 235 Africans who were landed at the Portuguese port of Lagos. The choicest of these Africans were presented as an offering to the chief church of Lagos, and one little boy was sent to Cape St. Vincent to be educated. He grew up as a Franciscan friar.[14] The trade continued to expand and until 1660 the Europeans concentrated their activities entirely along the coast of Ghana. In 1482 the Portuguese built the castle of Fort São Jorge da Mina. The castle helped the Portuguese to maintain their exclusive monopoly over the coast, as well as to obtain an impressive trading center in gold and slavery. Envious of the profit margins the Portuguese were making from slaves and gold, other European traders started to invade Portuguese territory from 1598 onward. After the Dutch, who captured Elmina castle from the Portuguese, came the English, French, Belgians, Danes, Swedes and Germans.[15]

In the eighteenth century, early European adventurers such as the Dutch trader William Bosman, became interested in Ghana. He visited the Ashanti in 1700. Bosman called them "Asiante." Twenty-two letters he sent to his uncle in Holland were translated into English by James Knapton and Daniel Midwinter in 1705 and published as *A New and Accurate Description of the Coast of Guinea, Divided into the Gold, the Slave, and the Ivory Coast*.[16] It remains of sufficient academic interest for a new edition to have been published in 1967.[17] In one letter Bosman stated, "The Inland Potentates, such as Akim, Asiante, &c. are ... able to over-run a Country by their numerous Armies."[18] He could understand the idea of armies but much of the rest of West African culture seemed beyond his understanding. In fact, eighteenth-century Europeans visiting Africa were faced with an alien culture, surprisingly different from their own. As Graham Connah states, "Outside Africa itself there persists, amongst people in general, a deeply ingrained conviction that precolonial tropical Africa consisted only of scattered villages of mud or grass huts, their inhabitants subsisting on shifting cultivation or semi-nomadic pastoralism. What is more surprising, and more disturbing, is that this sort of stereotype seems also to have had some effect on scholars considering the emergence of cities and states as global phenomena."[19] It is only in recent years that the academic world has started to pay more attention and give more respect to the cultures and empires established and flourishing in black Africa long before the arrival of any Europeans. The role played by dance in these cultures and empires was much more important than most Europeans realized.

Every culture has an impulse to dance as an expression of movement in response to music. There is no society known to history or anthropology that does not dance as an important part of its artistic activity.[20] We all dance. Yet different cultures develop different conventions, different styles, and different ways of expressing this common impulse. Oriental, Hindu, African, Arab and European dance are recognizably different, each embedded in its own culture, with its own sets of associations, ideas and responses. Indian dance, for example, has a set of hand movements, called mudras. Anyone outside Indian culture who is told that a particular mudra represents the god Shiva would find such information not very helpful. Most of those inside the culture can respond to all the ideas and associations that the concept of the god Shiva conjures up. For them the mudra is very important and meaningful indeed. For anyone who has difficulty understanding why this information in dance is culture specific, it should be enough, if they are European, to show them an Indian mudra, a hand movement, chosen at random. When asked what it means, they will not know. Most Indians will know. The information is culture specific.

On this subject, Belinda Quirey says, "We never in the West make the symbolic arm and hand gestures that are characteristic of so much Eastern, particularly Indian dancing."[21] Akram Khan, an Indian dancer and choreographer who now lives and works in England, gave performances at the South Bank Center in London from April 12 to April 16, 2005, called *Third Catalogue*, which included a Kathak solo exploring Hindu gods. He had also performed the same work in India. When performing it in England he found it necessary to have a spoken commentary from the stage explaining what was meant by the movements the dancers were making. He has himself reported that when performing the same work in India, he would not have dreamed of doing any such thing, as an Indian audience knew exactly what the mudras meant, whereas an English audience would have had no idea. He says, "My set-up is a bit like a lecture, I talk on the microphone. I wouldn't do that in India, where they know the story behind every movement, because they would probably feel insulted."[22] This is similar to the report St. Augustine gives in his *Confessions*, written A.D. 397, about a group of mime performers from Rome, appearing where St. Augustine lived in North Africa. The Roman audience understood the mime gestures without needing an explanation, but St. Augustine noted that the North African audience needed a verbal explanation during the performance, just as the South Bank Center audience did in 2005.[23]

African dance sets up the same kind of responses for Africans. In African society almost every emotion, every social ritual, every area of social interaction can readily be expressed and translated into dance.[24] Emotions such as joy, pity, fear, anger, love and reverence can and are specifically expressed in the conventions of African dance. The social rituals of worship, sowing crops and reaping harvests, marriage and death, are clear examples which have a wide range of dance attached to them, much more so than in European culture. Moreover, as an example of social interaction, the relationships between the hierarchies of tribal life are all precisely delineated in African dance. It is generally agreed by analysts of African culture that dance plays a greater part in African social life than it does in other cultures such as the European or the Eskimo. Dance is a long-standing feature of African life.[25] As Opoku wrote, "Much has been written about African dance but few realize that ... for the African ... the fullest expression of the African life is the dance."[26] Thus Opoku can say of African dance that "a study of the African dance is a study of its peoples."[27] Alphonse Tierou comes from the Ivory Coast and has been a specialist in African dance for the last thirty years. He founded the Bloa Nam dance school in Nimes, which was the only school in the world at that time that researched African dance. Tierou says, "Whether or not he is a musician, the African perceives the music of the interior. He lives with it, experiences it, plays it with an energy of which westerners are scarcely capable. The content of traditional African music is poetic because it is more animated. This is the way it must be approached and understood and not through that nauseating formula 'they have rhythm in their blood.'"[28] As W. Ofotsu Adinku explains in his discussion on traditional Ghanaian dance forms within a cultural context, "Discussion centers on three different areas: ritual, social and recreational. The ritual area links dance to the expression of cosmic principles and helps the mediums (traditional healers) in attunement, the social area dwells on the place of dance movements in expressing role differentiations as well as traditional norms, while the recreational type is restricted to the entertainment needs of the users."[29]

For most Africans during the period examined here, dance was a central part of their lives. Robert Hinton writes, "Dance was central to African society in the days before the European intrusion, permeating every aspect of African culture, both sacred and secular."[30] R. M. Stone maintains, giving an anthropological and ethnographical explanation of African dance,

2. African and European Dance and Their Traditions 41

This would seem to call for a concept of movement signature, defined as an element of movement that consistently marks dances from a given culture, and distinguishes them from dances of other cultures. Ewe communities, and those of their Ghanaian neighbours, recognize the emphasis they place on sharp upper-torso movements, specifically rotation of the shoulders, upward-downward movements of the shoulders, and contraction-release of muscles over the shoulder blades. The neighbouring Ga emphasise shuffling foot-movements, derived partially from the flow of the energy of hip movements. The Ashanti emphasize arm-and-hand gestures that succeed soft shoulder movements; the Dagbani emphasise rippled lower-torso movements, using stomach muscles. The Kasena-Nankani emphasise the raised knee. Masai men punctuate their prancing with jumps, and Zulu dancers make leaps. The Nuer make high jumps in lines, their kinetic signature. Similar signatures are the Kikuyu's runs and leaps, and the Dogan's brief, repeated, motive figures of little amplitude.[31]

All these variations in dance were nevertheless part of a shared collective dance culture. This culture and the tribal social organization in which it played such an important part is still sufficiently in place for the dances themselves to have survived, often largely unchanged.[32]

Increasingly, African dance has been studied, recorded and analyzed on film, video and even in dance notation. The anthropologist and professor John Blacking from Belfast University employed Benesh dance notators from the Institute of Choreology in London to record the rich dance culture of the Venda of Northern Transvaal in valuable work over many years. In 1974 he met Rudolf Benesh, the inventor of Benesh notation, and discussed with him the use of movement notation for African dance. Choreologists (or notators) then recorded African dance. The system has been mostly used by choreologists for recording dance movements that could be reproduced later, in the same functional way as sheet music.[33] A notator must be familiar with the dance vocabulary being recorded and also the movement styles. The basic styles in common use are ballet and modern dance styles (based on American modern dance)[34]; however, the notation has been used for recording ethnic dance, such as Bharata Natyam[35] and Aboriginal dances.[36] An interesting aspect of the Benesh system occurred when notators were asked to record a dance movement in an anthropologist's film. The notators realized, as with every culture they studied, that each culture developed its own language of movement. Notators needed to learn the language before they could record the movement. (The nearest analogy would be with a written language using a different alphabet. It is not enough to know the letters of the Greek alphabet. The Greek language has to be learned in order to write down the spoken words. Choreologists found it was the same with dance. They needed to know the whole dance language in order to write down "sentences" within it). As they got to know the society under the instruction of the anthropologist, they still found themselves unsure of how to record the movements that were not part of their western dance movement repertoire. The problem was resolved when it was realized that the hip and not the thigh was the essential source of the movement.[37] The recording proved difficult without some knowledge of the cultural context. The study highlighted the fact that "definitions" of dance are meaningless if they do not take into account the cultural background. It also provided a reminder for the anthropologists in the field to take more note of movement and cultural physical expression. The Benesh notation system is a cross-cultural shorthand for what might otherwise take pages of writing, as well as being a tool for movement analysis. It generates questions, useful distinctions and criteria for distinctions and so provokes further analysis.

The important point to note is that skilled dance notators from Europe at first found African dance so alien, and so culturally specific, that they had difficulty coming to terms with it at all. Nothing could better show how African dance is integrated with African culture than the notators' need to analyze the culture in order to understand the dance. In order to understand the dance sufficiently well to be able to notate it, choreologists found they needed to learn a new language of movement. They were dealing with a language embedded in a different culture, setting up all kinds of associations, meanings and echoes in the minds of an African audience, that were unknown to Europeans. From a historical point of view, this gives some idea of the difficulties that seventeenth- and eighteenth-century Europeans experienced on their first encounters with Gold Coast culture. Just as Akram Khan needed to explain Indian dance to a South Bank audience, just as Roman mimes had to explain their movements to a Carthaginian audience in North Africa in the days of St. Augustine, so African dance had to be explained and understood in terms of all its cultural associations, even in the twentieth century, before European notators could begin to analyze it. Earlier Europeans obviously faced even greater difficulties.

A good example of these points can be found in the life of Olaudah Equiano, a black abolitionist and leader of the black community in London, who claimed he was born in 1745 in West Africa. He was wrenched from a culture where dance was integral. At the age of ten he was kidnapped by slave hunters, together with his sister, from whom he was separated while still in West Africa, and transported to America. After passing from one owner to another, enslaved in America, in the Caribbean, and in England, he purchased his freedom with his own savings in 1766, at the age of twenty-one. In 1789 his autobiography, *The Interesting Narrative of the life of Olaudah Equiano, or Gustavus Vassa, the African*, was published in London.[38] *The Narrative* begins with an account of Equiano's family and the customs of his native village. He describes the importance of dance to his people as follows:

> We are almost a nation of dancers, musicians and poets. Thus every great event, such as a triumphant return from battle, or other cause of public rejoicing is celebrated in public dances which are accompanied with songs and music suited to the occasion. The assembly is separated into four divisions, which dance either apart or in succession, and each with a character peculiar to itself. The first division contains the married men, who in their dances frequently exhibit feats of arms, and the representation of a battle. To these succeed the married women, who dance in the second division. The young men occupy the third, and maidens the fourth. Each represents some interesting scene of real life, such as a great achievement, domestic employment, a pathetic story, or some rural sport; and as the subject is generally founded on some recent event, it is therefore ever new. This gives our dances a spirit and a variety which I have scarcely seen elsewhere.[39]

Equiano was an Ibo, not an Akan, but it should be clear that the importance of dance was common across the collective culture of Africa in spite of regional dance differences.

Some early commentators have suggested that Equiano was incapable of writing the *Narrative* and mentioned the "very unequal style" of his writing. *The Monthly Review* had one observer who wrote, "It is not improbable that some English writer assisted him in the complement, or at least the correction of his book, for it is sufficiently well written."[40] Vincent Carretta has even suggested that Equiano lied about his origins and was born not in West Africa but in South Carolina.[41] Critical opinion is still divided about this. Nobody seems to have noticed that the remarks quoted above by Equiano about dance and music in West Africa are not only remarkably perceptive, but would seem very strong evidence that he was born in West Africa, not South Carolina. As far as his writing ability is concerned, Paul Edwards concedes, "We must remember Equiano received schooling even when a slave, had mixed constantly with Englishmen, and from the age of twenty-one had been a free man working as a valet, regularly in the company of educated people. There is no reason why he should not, at the age of forty-four, be perfectly fluent in English."[42]

Dance and its accompanying music were and are part of a wide-ranging culture. It is not surprising that elements of it survived in spite of the early and horrific conditions of the slave trade in the Caribbean and the Americas. Chapter 1 looked at the creole culture that emerged as a mixture of African elements, combined with the horrific experiences of slavery and the new European culture of the plantation owners.[43] Unfortunately neither Burton nor Price and Mintz have examined the dance that permeated so many aspects of African culture (Burton's description about jonkonnu being an exception).[44] As noted in chapter 1, Richard Cullen Rath presented a forthright and challenging analysis of what survived from Africa in both Caribbean and American slave worlds. He saw any attempt at distinguishing between language and culture as artificial. For him, both were integral, depending on each other, as, in his words, "making sense of the world," which he saw as one of the primary functions of both language and culture generally.[45] His emphasis was more on music than dance, but as we have seen, in Africa it is impossible to separate one entirely from the other.

In Africa, christenings, initiations, weddings, and funerals were social occasions where dance and music played a pivotal role. In 1796, Captain J. G. Stedman published a book entitled *Narrative of a Five Years' Expedition against the Revolted Negroes of Surinam, in Guiana, on the Wild Coast of South America, from the year 1772 to 1777: Elucidating the History of that Country, and Describing its Productions, viz. Quadrupeds, Birds, Fishes, Reptiles, Trees, Shrubs, Fruits, & Roots, with an Account of the Indians of Guiana, & Negroes of Guinea*.[46] In this book Stedman includes a list of elegant self-made drawings of the wide-ranging musical instruments used by the blacks in Guinea. These instruments described by Stedman are still in use in Ghana and are still used by the musicians for Ghanaian dance groups. It is clear that the instruments he describes in Surinam are essentially African. He also notes the interdependence of music and song, observing, "Such are the musical instruments of our African brethren, to which they dance with more spirit than we do to the best band in Europe."[47] He also talked of the spirituality associated with the dance performances. He showed a real sympathy for what dance meant to Africans that made him exceptional for his time if we judge by all the other accounts from which we have quoted, given by Europeans when confronted with West African dance.

Hans Sloane was another rare exception of a European attuned to African sensibilities, as evidenced in his account of the slave songs transcribed for him by a French musician named Baptiste. His recording of slave dances also showed a similar appreciation of African music and dance. He noted the key importance of rhythm in both African music and dance: "Their dances consist in great activity and strength of body, and keeping time if it can be."[48] Stedman noted in his account, "It is indeed upon the whole astonishing to see with what good-natured and even good manners their dancing societies are kept up, of which I repeat they are so fond, that I have known a newly-imported Negro, for want of a partner, figure and foot it nearly the space of two hours, to his shadow against the wall."[49] The varied and complex musical instruments he described may have led him to believe that there were similar complex structures in the dances that Africans danced, since "they dance with uncommon pleasure and at times foot it away with great art and dexterity."[50] He was far more perceptive than others, such as Mungo Park, who saw African dance as consisting "more in wanton gestures, than muscular exertion or graceful attitudes."[51] T. Edward Bowdich referred to African dance as "the gesture and distortion of maniacs."[52] Both men traveled to the same continent and observed the same people doing the same type of dancing. Unlike them, Stedman wrote of the blacks as his "brethren" and seemed almost able to view the role of dance in black society with African eyes.

So what is it about the African dance culture that makes it so different from the European dance? All stages and events of life from birth to death — worship, sickness, ritual, planting, harvesting — are celebrated by dance in Africa. This is less true of European dance as it has a different aesthetic, as will be seen later in this chapter. It is normal to attend a European funeral without having to dance at all. This includes both the service in the church, the carrying of the coffin to the grave, the service at the grave itself and the consumption of food and drink at the social occasion that follows. At all of these events most Africans would expect to dance, and have culture specific dances for each of them. In *Dancing*, Lilly Grove, despite her racist language and cultural arrogance, makes the difference between African and European dancing clear, when she writes, "Some African tribes might be instanced, who could not live a single week without their dances.... It is not with him a mantle to be assumed on high days and holy days ... in his daily life the dance takes a large share."[53] Although she wrote this in 1893, the essential differences between European and African dance were still as applicable then as they had been in the eighteenth century.

In Africa there are customs that include national celebrations where dance plays a leading part. K. A. Opoku writes that "dances marking phases in life take many forms. Some (African) societies emphasize birth, puberty, and funerals."[54] Cole and Ross write, "Birth celebrations include the 'outdooring' ceremonies."⁵⁵ The end of adolescence in Africa involves learning the music and dance of a rite of initiation into manhood. There is also an element of this dance tradition which allows for spontaneity in the ritual where the impulse to express the joy of moving to music is allowed to take place. Opoku sheds light on this when he says, "Dances are agbadza, adowa, adenkum and nagla. They serve to bring the young of both sexes together in a clean atmosphere which results in marriages. They encourage the youth in providing opportunities for creating new rhythms, dances, songs and presentation."⁵⁶

An African funeral is an occasion for one of the more formally staged dances. The dances for this occasion are not downbeat. There is a time for grieving, normally confined to the hours immediately after death. The funeral dances are in homage to the dead. The dancers use the dance vocabulary to describe the life of the departed. Improvised movements and gestures are used to describe the dead person's achievements. A relative sings and dances this as part of the African dance funeral process. Dance scholar and practitioner J. H. Nketia says that the accompaniment drumming for this is called "ayi-mnyam," which literally means "sympathy."⁵⁷

Another of the important functions of dance in African society entailed warfare. Dance helped to rouse men to battle or to describe events on the battlefield. Nketia writes, "The atran piece is designed for war and grave emergencies. In the days of warfare, it was played at the battle front to urge the troops to go forward."⁵⁸ Emmanuel Kingsley Braffi adds another interesting dimension to the importance of the war dance history, explaining that "every male in Asante was born with an allocated place in the war formation which could be conveniently compared with ants on the march."⁵⁹ He notes also, "The Asante child born in the humblest hamlet believes he is Kotoko, the Porcupine, the animal that can fight with 'arrows' stuck in his body, and for Kotoko he is to live and die. The porcupine is the emblem of the Asante Nation."⁶⁰

This suggests that when performing war dances, the warriors had the same place in the dance formation as the place that they actually took up in the fighting of a war. Cole and Ross note, "Emphasis is on full participation and group performances rather than individuality, although some solo dances are found. Dancing tends to be abrupt and angular. Although there are some subdued women's dances, men's events involve powerful strides, leaping, exaggerated arm movements."⁶¹ These war dances, while no longer performed for the same purpose as they were in the eighteenth and nineteenth centuries, are still performed today for entertainment by the Ashanti people in Ghana.

In a similar way, the original functional use of hunter dances have changed. Oral tradition specifically states that a hunter dance would tell the story of the hunt. The dancing would show the hunter stalking prey, the animal's reaction, the hunter being in danger, his courage in conquering his own fears, how the animal escaped, and how the warrior finally hunted it down, captured it and returned victoriously to the village. Opoku says, "Hunting dances, at least in Africa, are not performed to bring success to the hunter but to retell the adventures encountered in a successful hunt. The abofoo of the Akan and their frafra version bear testimony to this."[62] In this way the young also learn the part they will have to play in the hunt when their time comes. This process of dance imitation had the same purpose in the warrior dances. The use of dance to instruct young men was typical of early traditional African dance.

Opoku also has much to say about the importance dance plays in the role of a West African chief. "The chief or paramount leader," he notes,

> is the visual focus of court panoply. As such he commands varied modes of dress for different occasions; indeed, one of the characteristics of high Akan office is that many outfits, not just one, are available for any particular event. After a new leader is enthroned he must add to the state wardrobe or treasury one or more items with which he is to be particularly identified.... He may also receive gifts from his own people. Ordinarily the political senior leader present at any event is also the most sumptuously attired, and accounts indicate that it used to be improper (and punishable) for a lesser chief to attempt to surpass a higher one.[63]

Just as authority figures had to dress well, they also had to be capable dancers. Leaders reinforced the trust and respect of their people partly by the way they dressed, and partly by the way they danced. Traditional African etiquette meant that they took dance instruction before taking up an appointment. As youngsters learn to dance by imitation from the moment they are able to walk, there would have been an element of continuity here. The chief would have absorbed the dance tradition almost from birth. The youngsters attending dance rituals would dance along on the outside edges of the crowd surrounding them. In *The Dance in Traditional African Society*, A. M. Opoku states, "A chief's dance movements must at all times reflect his position to win the acclamation of his people, who while exhorting him to make graceful, studied and regal gestures, use stronger dynamic forms of the same movement patterns to express pride in him as the embodiment of the highest within his society and their willingness to die for him in peace or war."[64]

From this standpoint, the need for a chief to be a good dancer helps to show the importance of dance in African society. Dance was not only used to differentiate one social class from another. At the same time it was a common language of movement which everybody understood. This use of dance as a common language, like the use of musical drumming as a common language, provided much of the basis for subsequent creolization in the Caribbean.

Opoku continues: "In the African dance expression we are made to *see* the music, as it were, and to *hear* the dance ... the dance in Africa then must express fully and clearly through movements, the inner feelings, which are acceptable to a region, and is disciplined by the rhythm suggested by the music in the mode or form of that social group."[65] Traditionally, these dances were and still are performed within a ring made by onlookers. The musicians could form a part of the circle, or they could be in the center with the dancers moving around them, or they could move freely within the ring. As already mentioned, in formal events each participant knew his place in the staging, when and how to dance. Those surrounding the dance action were expected to respond at certain points in the same way that a religious gathering may have call-and-response moments where chanting and gesticulation takes place.

Even today in Africa, the musician's art is usually handed down from father to son. The kora for example, is a classical West African instrument dating back to the 14th century. The world's foremost kora player, Toumani Diabaté, can trace his griot lineage back to the 14th century, the instrument handed down from father to son in an uninterrupted line. It is still made the same way—calabash, cowskin, leather rings for tuning, and fishing wire for the twenty-one strings circling the wooden bridge.[66] A person with a talent for music who does not come from a musical background will be apprenticed to an established musician. (During the eighteenth century most musicians were connected to the court of a chief.) Notably, mothers dandle their infants in time to music and later teach them songs accompanied by clapping. All this has been carefully observed and documented by the anthropologists and photographers Angela Fisher and Carol Beckwith, who went on even more importantly to observe that many childhood and initiation ceremonies take place within a framework of clapping, singing and dancing.[67]

This musical gift is developed very early in West African babies as they are very often wrapped on the back of a dancing female. The wrapping cloth is important, as Cole and Ross observe, "We do not know precisely when large cloths became universal formal wear among the Akan, but they probably became widespread during the eighteenth or at least nineteenth century when the wealth of the south had dispersed through the population. A notable feature of these voluminous wrappers is the more or less constant 'dance' of adjustment which involves several expansive, fluid, unwrapping and wrapping gestures."[68] Women wear long wrap-around skirts consisting of a two-yard length of material, the width being the waist-to-ground measurement. This is wrapped while standing with legs apart to ensure room for comfortable walking. With this a blouse is worn. Over this a top cloth is wrapped from waist to the middle of the thigh; the upper edges at the left side of the waist are rolled under to keep the cloth in place. But it gradually loosens, and one of the habits of women is the frequent readjustment of the top cloth; this continues while they are dancing and may even be used to enhance the feeling of the performance. Although there were many different dances in the various tribal organizations of Africa, Africans had more customs in common than they had differences distinguishing them from one another. Music, particularly, with its emphasis on rhythm, crossed these boundaries and was shared by all, and so did the major characteristics by which we can distinguish African dance as a whole from dances of other continents. A baby wrapped on the back of a dancing female is probably more likely to appreciate the importance of musical rhythm than a European baby in a pram. In the analysis of African dance, it is these common characteristics that are outlined and analyzed.

The man's version of the female wrap-around cloth among the Akan is called a kente. It has about ten yards of material, one-third of which goes across the left shoulder from behind; the other end, coming from behind and under the right shoulder, is flung back over the left. The yards of cloth tend to slip down the left arm and are lifted back to rest on the shoulder. In dance, the cloth may be flung with a flowing, swooping undulation of the arm, perhaps triggering spin, at the same time as the body moves rhythmically. The raising of the cloth back to the shoulder may lead to stooping.[69] One of the signs of a competent dancer is the craft with which the dancer uses the technique of manipulating the cloth. Bystanders wave at the dancer while dancing toward him. Other forms of admiration include waving a handkerchief at the dancer and wiping the sweat off the dancer's brow. Pressing money to the dancer's sweaty forehead is also common. The dancers then pick up the money and often share it with the musicians as both are equally involved in the dance.[70]

The importance of the musicians, particularly their drumming, cannot be overemphasized. In most African languages, every syllable has a certain tone. Changing the tone may change the meaning or dissolve the meaning of the word altogether. This is also true of Akan drumming. As J. H. Nketia, an expert on Ghanaian drumming, notes, "Drum orchestras are not only vehicles of music for dancing. They have also functions akin to those of signal drums and talking drums. Accordingly, drum orchestras would always perform whether there were dancers in the ring or not in the hope that the chief, their master, would be listening and that he would be appreciative of their efforts to set him high above all others."[71] In other words, the treble and bass drum have a language made up of tones and rhythms that can be beaten and translated. These are "talking drums." During a dance the master drummer may greet the dancers as they move into the ring, often using an asafotwene drum.[72] He may have a "dialogue" with the dancers. Often this will involve the drummer "praising" the movement quality of the dancer, or visa versa. Some drummers will be dancing and drumming at one and the same time. (The name for this is "*ntan*.")[73]

This integration of dance, music and rhythm is an important part of African dance and music culture. The techniques involved in performing African dance are very different from those of dance that has its origins in Europe. As we have seen, Benesh notators had to learn a new dance language in order to notate African dance. As dance historian Belinda Quirey writes when discussing European dance from its roots to the Renaissance, "Western dancing is quite different from Oriental dancing; different too from such primitive dance styles as we can still find in undeveloped countries today." Even if her patronizing approach to African dance sounds too prejudiced for modern tastes (she was writing in 1976), she still perceptively sees the major element in African dance compared to that of European dance. She argues, "Not percussion, therefore, but the melodic phrase is the rhythmic basis of our dancing. The nearest we get to a percussive rhythm is the transferring of our weight from foot to foot on the pulse of the music." She goes on: "What seems as a rule to have been avoided was an unnecessary expenditure of muscular energy by stamping, or beating, or banging our feet on the ground."[74] Attitudes to movement reflect the cultural climate at any particular period. For example, "being pulled-up," "centered," and "lifted" are concepts that belong to Western ideas about dance. They suggest an emphasis on balance that is essentially vertical. In European social dances the technique centers on a desire to overcome the downward pull of gravity. This can be seen clearly in all the European dances mentioned later in this chapter.[75]

In African dance, the opposite is true. There seems to be much less need to fight against the downward pull of gravity, nor is the upper body constrained as it is in European dance. The pull of gravity is recognized. There is a downward sense of gravitation toward the earth. The knees do not fully straighten. There is a greater sense of "feeling" and of "the spirit of the dance taking over the dancer." There is an attitude of humility toward those who are older. (In Europe the older dancer is thought to be handicapped by age.) African movement quality has a greater sense of free flow. Several body parts tend to move simultaneously. In European dance, on the contrary, the body is usually controlled so that movements in one part do not unintentionally create movements elsewhere.

Sometimes European eyes see a tendency toward sameness in African dance. The dance may seem repetitive to those outside African music and dance culture because much of the excitement for an African comes from the subtle interplay between the rhythms of the dance and the rhythms of the music. (This should become clearer in the following paragraphs). To generalize about the differences between African and European music, most musicologists, including John Miller Chernoff, would agree that the major emphasis in African music is on rhythm, while the major emphasis in European music tends to be on melody. As Chernoff writes: "The African dancer may pick up and respond to the rhythms of one or more drums, depending on his skill, but in the best dancing the dancer, like the drummer, adds another rhythm, one that is not there. He tunes his ear to hidden rhythms, and he dances to the gaps in the music."[76] Paulla A. Ebron has reservations about what Chernoff has to say about African music. While recognizing much of the force and popularity of what he has to say, she feels that Chernoff already has a concept of Africa which colors his approach to African music and particularly drumming, and makes what he has to say less valuable. All the same, Chernoff is perceptive about dance.[77]

In the same context, Marshall Stevens makes clear the differences between the harmonic complexities of European music from the rhythmic complexity of the African. He argues that African music is polyrhythmic, with as many as five or six different rhythms played simultaneously. The African dancer can use different parts of the body to respond to different rhythms. The feet may be moving in 4/4, while the hips sway in 4/3, and the head in 6/8.[78] Music professor Leonard Goines attests to this, saying that "in much of African dance the polyrhythms of the accompanying music are reflected in the dancer's body; the arms might move in one rhythm, the head in another, and so on for the shoulders, trunk and feet."[79] Chernoff writes, "In African music, excellence arises when the combination of rhythms is translated into meaningful action; people participate best when they can 'hear' the rhythms, whether through understanding or dance."[80] Chernoff describes this ability among African musicians to keep so many rhythms in place all at once. With "the formal components of a complex rhythmic system built around cross rhythms and responsive rhythms, and in the notions of apart-playing and off-beat accentuation," he writes, "rhythms work together, cutting and conversing with each other, [and] we begin to sense the distinctiveness of the African approach to music. (And dance)."[81] Given the dance and musical expertise of both of these scholars, it should be easier to accept that rhythm and the ability to respond to a number of different rhythms at the same time are an important part of the average African musician's approach.

As Marshall Stevens makes clear, European musicians are seldom expected to keep more than four rhythms going in their mind at one time. Africans, well versed in a musical tradition that constantly emphasizes rhythm, can keep up to a dozen different rhythms interchanging in the mind simultaneously. This gives richness and complexity to African dance and its rhythmic music, which is sometimes difficult for those brought up in the European musical tradition to comprehend. This richness is substantiated by Chernoff, who argues,

> Western music possesses a remarkable sensitivity that enables observers to say, after hearing only a few notes, whether it is Rubinstein or Horowitz playing the piano. Such discrimination rarely can be applied beyond a select group of virtuoso players. I found this sensitivity regarding their own musicians extremely widespread among my African friends, who were quick to point out that they admired how a certain musician had his own "way" with his instrument. In Tamale one day, Alhassan easily identified all members of a distant party of drummers from "the way they talked." When an African responds to you because of "how you say something," he may mean it literally and not in reference to the particular words you chose: style of speech is more important to him than to us. Readers familiar with African and Western European idioms will recognize that even in American music, distinctions of musical touch are perhaps more readily apparent among Afro-American musicians, particularly jazz players, than among Western European musicians."[82]

These differences are certainly not innate; they are culture specific and culturally acquired. It is a matter of a difference of emphasis between one culture and another. The African dancer may also break away from the accompanying music and add his own inner rhythms.[83]

Dance can be defined as the joy of expressing a response to music through movement. Yet black dance is born out of a culture and tradition that is not European but African, where both music and movement set up images, echoes and associations that are very different from European culture. The African dances practiced in the Caribbean stem from the diverse dance styles that existed in Africa at the time of the Atlantic slave trade. The funeral dances, for example, where a good send-off from an Akan point of view commenced with the customary last drop of water to the dying, also included drumming and dancing as part of the funeral rites.[84] What is particularly interesting is how well the funeral dances of the Akan culture in West Africa survived in the Caribbean.

The aim in examining African dance in this chapter has been to establish clearly the dance background from which Caribbean slaves were brought and to emphasize the "tenaciousness"[85] of the music and dance culture from which they came. The black Londoners attempting the quadrille in their social dance at the beginning of the nineteenth century carried with them what survived in the Caribbean. The striking continuity between African dance culture and what those black Londoners were attempting will become clearer as this analysis proceeds.

The European Dance Tradition

It may seem abrupt to move from a careful analysis of African dance culture and to skip both geographically and chronologically in order to look at European dance in the eighteenth and nineteenth centuries. Yet if we are to consider the full background of those African slaves who finally ended up in London via the Caribbean in the eighteenth and nineteenth centuries in a more or less free condition, it is just as important to consider the dance culture in which they found themselves.

The discussion will focus on some European dances, and show how they were very different from African dance traditions discussed above. It will also examine the social climate and the changes in the way Europeans related to their dances in the eighteenth and nineteenth centuries. These factors had some impact on black dance in the Caribbean and in London.

European social dance in the seventeenth, eighteenth and nineteenth centuries is well documented.[86] In a world of aristocrats and peasants, dance was an important way for a male aristocrat to display his virility, status, glamour and importance. In the late seventeenth century, John Locke wrote in *Some Thoughts on Education* of "dancing being that which gives graceful motions all the life, and above all things, manliness."[87] Even in the eighteenth century, Lord Chesterfield could write to his son: "You must dance well.... Take particular care that the motions of your hands and arms be easy and graceful; for the genteelness of a man consists more in them than in anything else, especially in his dancing."[88] Nowadays we are quite out of tune with such attitudes. In the modern theater a male dancer now carries a faint stigma of effeminacy. This was very different from the court of Louis XIV, where in a court ballet performance the king would take the leading role, supported by Britain's Charles II in exile, by Louis' brother, the Duc d'Orleans and by Charles's brother, the Duke of York, all of them displaying regal manliness in the way they danced. All this was to change.

Aristocrats did remarkably little actual work of any kind, and so had time to concentrate on their leisure pursuits. As the industrial revolution progressed in the eighteenth and nineteenth centuries, the middle class steadily increased in numbers, status and importance. Inevitably their views played an ever-greater part in the ideology of the period. The middle classes were working hard at actual jobs, helping the industrial revolution on its way. They had little time for leisure, and they tended to judge status and importance in terms of economic achievement and the possession of goods.[89] Social dancing began to become a more marginal activity as the middle class increasingly dominated the media of communication which set the standards for social behavior and social priorities generally. Dance lost its central role as a way of displaying status. As Mr. Darcy remarks in *Pride and Prejudice*: "Every savage can dance."[90] In terms of the "civilizing process" proposed by Norbert Elias, an urban, industrial regime was replacing an earlier one based on agriculture, dominated by aristocrats and peasants.[91] Nicholas Dromgoole, in his book *The Playwright as Rebel*, gives an informative account of the industrial revolution and its influence on social culture. The use of gesture in performance is also perceptively covered in his fascinating book *Performance Style and Gesture in Western Theatre*. Dromgoole links it with the social conventions of the period.[92]

In the earlier aristocratic world of that agricultural regime, still dominant in the early eighteenth century, where social dance was used to show off male vigor, virility, glamour and importance, the dances of the period were the sarabande, the minuet, the *passepied*, the jig, the cotillion, the chaconne and passa caglia, musettes, the gavotte, the rigaudon, the hornpipe, and the bourreé.

The sarabande was originally a Spanish dance in triple meter that was popular from the sixteenth century to the second half of the eighteenth century. In its early days it was considered a licentious dance bordering on the obscene, and condemned and banned by the authorities. The sarabande exemplifies a process that was taking place all through medieval and renaissance dance, certainly up until the period covered by this book.[93] Far from dance being an aristocratic pursuit and then slowly drifting down, as it were, from the court and the aristocracy, the reverse was almost invariably the case. Dance forms started off as peasant forms and then were adopted upwards in society by aristocrats and the court. Far from being an elitist activity that gradually became more popular, dance moved upward from being "base, common and popular" until it was adopted by the social elite.[94] (It can be noted in passing that almost every form in classical music began and was linked with a popular dance form, so the process applies almost as much to music as it does to dance.) This process is evidence of just how widespread dance activity was and how it permeated all levels of society, although not, in the all-embracing way in which dance dominated almost every area of social activity in Africa. In the upper levels of European society, whose leaders were usually the arbiters of fashion and taste, there has always tended to be a passion for novelty. Thus anything happening lower down the social scale was often soon adopted and refined. By the seventeenth and eighteenth centuries, dancing masters and theatrical performances in the court and in the city proved an effective means by which the adoption of new dances up the social scale were effected.[95] It has often been remarked that every step of classical ballet, as codified by the French Royal Academy of Dance established by Louis XIV, had its origin in a peasant form. Even the entrechat, where the dancer leaps up in the air and crosses his feet in little beats before landing again, can still be found in Basque folk dance.[96]

Thus folk dances that may originally have been despised as being beneath aristocratic notice could be taken up and become newly fashionable. There is also a subtext. Aristocrats may have had doubts and even guilt about the social divide between the rich aristocratic few and the impoverished majority. By adopting peasant dances they could emphasize their links with the majority at little actual cost to themselves or their position. (It is probably this same unspoken subtext that led Marie Antoinette, even as the French Revolution of 1789 loomed ever closer, to dress up and enjoy behaving as a milkmaid in a supposedly rural atmosphere.)[97]

There might seem to be a paradox, in that the aristocratic world developed a taste for innovation and change, but the actual change seems to have almost invariably depended on dances being done at the peasant level of society. If there was to be innovation, why did the aristocrats not invent it for themselves? Probably the answer partly lies in the general illiteracy in the lower ranks of society. The widespread use of dance throughout society has already been noted, but dance as a means of expressing emotion probably became more powerful among the illiterate than among the educated few. This has already been noted in a different context in chapter 1, with relation to Gilroy's "racial terror."[98] Dance innovators are few, in any case, and in terms of numbers, the popular base for folk dance was much more numerous than the much smaller aristocratic elite. It therefore follows that there was far more likelihood of change and innovation in folk dance than elsewhere. Once aristocratic circles had taken up a folk dance, it was certainly then refined, added to, and became more sophisticated. Yet the original impetus invariably came from below.

By the end of the sixteenth century the sarabande had become a more respectable dance and it was performed in enclosed spaces, city squares, dance halls, and ballrooms as a circle dance by women alone or by men and women together. It existed in both fast and slow versions. The sarabande (*zarabanda*) traveled to England via France and is mentioned as early as 1616 in Ben Jonson's play *The Devil Is an Ass*. Nearly all Baroque composers wrote a sarabande as part of a suite for various instruments, including keyboard and instrumental ensembles. Sarabandes can be found in the works of Johann Sebastian Bach. The dance was often included in French operas and ballets and became one of the most popular ballroom dances at the court of Louis XIV. Even later, in 1771, there is a sarabande in *Zemire et Azore*, a comedy ballet in four acts by Gretry (1741–1813) dedicated to Madame du Barry.[99]

The minuet had its origins not in noble surroundings, but from rougher stock, the *branle de Poitou* (the English called it "the brawl"), which was akin to the galliard. It began to be received into the French courts in the seventeenth century.[100] The term "minuet" usually stands for a French court and theatre dance in moderate or slow meter, but it also refers to a musical composition or a symphonic movement. The clearest description of the dance, including its steps and rhythms, occurs in Kellom Tomlinson's *The Art of Dancing Explained by Reading and Figures*.[101] The minuet consists of an introduction and four figures: an S-shape as the main dancing figure; the presentation of right hands; the presentation of left hands; the S-figure and the presentation of both hands. The dance is preceded and concluded by "honors" (a deep bow) to the "presence" (the person or persons of highest social rank) and by partners to each other. While other *dances à deux* are choreographed to specific music, the minuet can be danced to any music with a moderate or slow meter. Its unique characteristic among the Baroque dances is flexibility. The S-figure may be repeated as frequently as the male partner chooses. When dancing the minuet, the man, according to Tomlinson, must lead with consideration so that the speed at which he performs the honors will dictate where the couple begins the dance, within the music. It is also the man's responsibility to see that he and his partner begin on the first beat of 3/4 measures, whether during a musical strain or at its beginning. He must signal in advance his intention to change from the S-figure to the presentation of hands; otherwise the female would dance past him. While holding both hands, circling, and looking at the lady, he must keep sight of the top of the room for fear of opening out in the wrong direction, and thus bowing with his back to the "presence."[102]

The minuet is a refined expression of ritualistic courtship. The dancers face each other almost continuously; they approach, pass, and retreat. Their only physical contact is holding hands at arm's length while circling.[103] It was danced in a patriarchal and male-dominated society and obviously reflected social presumptions about gender.

It is quite clear that the minuet was a couple dance, with couple after couple gradually joining the dance, but dancing with each other and not as part of a group. The dancers' skill in performance was a test of their wit in dancing and mastery of social graces. Feldtenstein wrote, "The minuet, the queen of dances ... the test of every dancer who seeks perfection and honor ... the positions and movements of which illuminate the essence of the art of the dance ... offers the best opportunity to demonstrate as much beauty and charm in Nature as the body is capable of assuming."[104]

The eighteenth-century dancing masters never failed to mention this importance of bearing, dignity, and what Giovanni-Andrea Gallini in 1772 called "easy-genteelness" in the performance of social dances.[105] It is important to remember how different from the lives of ordinary people the lives of aristocrats were. Everything they did — entering a room, greeting each other, even just walking — was done differently from how the majority behaved. Dancing masters taught them not only to dance but how to stand, how to walk, how to sit, how to eat, and so on. Every action seems to have been carefully choreographed, no doubt largely to impress the lower orders with the impossibility of their ever attaining the excellence of their betters. Once again, in terms of the sociological analysis of Norbert Elias, this would have been an example within an agricultural regime, of aristocrats looking down on and disdaining the world of the peasants and making efforts to differentiate themselves from it.[106]

The minuet was a leading social dance in the early eighteenth century. As the descriptions at the end of this chapter will show, whole sections of the manuals of dancing masters such as Feldtenstein, Rameau and Tomlinson were devoted to this dance alone. Feldtenstein preferred certain figures of the dance performed at "a social gathering where many are dancing."[107]

The minuet was also popular in the Caribbean. M. L. E. Moreau de Saint-Mery's book *Danse,* published in 1796 and translated in 1946 with comments by Lillian Moore, described the balls given by French colonial plantation owners. Their balls would have been similar to those given by English plantation owners. Both French and English plantation owners frequently traveled back and forth between their mother country and the Caribbean. Saint-Mery's whole passage is interesting because it reveals how closely whites in the Caribbean followed European practice:

> Formerly, the pleasure of the dance was lessened by a sort of pride, which had established a particular ceremonial for the balls. Elaborate systems and even research were necessary in order to decide who should open the ball, and in what order each guest should dance his first minuet.... Finally it was realised that relaxation is not a course in etiquette, and for some time now, after the grandparents have made a show of starting the minuet, contredanses are informally arranged. The host and hostess watch to see that everyone has a good time.... At intervals the contredanses are interrupted by minuets, danced by the older people or by dancers whose talents are capable of winning applause, in spite of the severity with which it has been customary to judge minuets in recent years. When the gentlemen begin to tire, and the ladies speak of leaving, that is the signal for all the other dances: the allemandes, the anglaise, and the minuet congo.[108]

It is clear from the quotation that planter society in the French Caribbean was faithfully reflecting the differences in assumptions and attitudes that were transforming revolutionary France and industrialized England, although actual planter/slave society in the Caribbean was very differently organized from the society emerging in England and France. The English agricultural and industrial revolutions had changed society, changed the way people lived. The old formality and elaborate etiquette of eighteenth-century dance, allowing the male to show off his virility, had made dance a central activity in cultural life. With the increasing importance of the emerging middle class, social dances became a more marginal activity, since the man of this class simply did not have the time or inclination to devote to it that the eighteenth-century aristocrat had. Until industrialization took hold, French and English aristocratic society had many similarities, although the country dances, which the French called *contredanses,* had always been more popular in England. In its way, industrialization changed English society almost as radically as the French Revolution altered French society. There are dangers, of course, in using a French author writing about French planter society to make a point about what was happening in English planter society, but the situation in the English Caribbean islands would in all probability have been very similar.

Gallini's emphasis on the importance of the minuet proved irrelevant in the nineteenth century. The social climate had changed. The minuet represented old customs of the past, too stiff and regulated for popularity in any but the most old-fashioned social circumstances. About the minuet congo, Lillian Moore wondered, "What on earth could it have been?" This will be discussed later in this chapter, as part of a discussion on possible African influences in European dance.

The *passepied* was a French dance dating from the sixteenth century or earlier. It was mentioned in 1548 by Noel de Frail, who describes it as a court dance of Brittany. The Baroque *passepied* was set to music in triple meter, usually with a 3/8 time signature and an eighth-note upbeat. The dance had the same step vocabulary as the minuet, one step-unit requiring two bars of music, but with a faster tempo. Raoul-Auger Feuillet has at least twenty-one extant *passepied* dances in his notation, simply showing the positions of the feet. The *passepied* occurred as part of a dance suite, a set of two or more contrasting dance types performed consecutively without a pause. Because it had a jolly character, the dance was more often found at the end of such suites. Characteristics of the dance include a floor pattern in which the partners moved parallel to each other rather than in the more usual symmetrical shapes, a limited step vocabulary and a shift in rhythmic stress in the music. The parallel floor patterns are either circular, with the couple holding inside hands, or rectilinear. A folk dance called *passepied* is still performed in parts of France today, but any connection with the earlier version can only be speculative.[109]

The jig (or French *gigue*) has a long history. It developed as a stage form, generally as an "after piece," in Elizabethan drama. But its origins go further back to medieval drama and medieval festival performances. In Elizabethan times it was a song with a mimed accompaniment that was generally farcical, which acted out the story of the song. Elizabethan drama companies touring Europe took it with them where it proved so popular that the Germans adopted it as their own *singspiele*. In social dance the term was used to cover any dance accompanied by song and music. The sailor's hornpipe was thought of as a jig in this sense.[110]

The jig's dance element came to embody a variety of up-and-down movements.[111] Where did they come from? This will be examined later in this chapter, as part of a discussion on possible African influences on European dance. The French *gigue* was in fashion in European court dances of the late seventeenth and early eighteenth centuries. The *gigue a deux*, a dance for which no clear indication is given for its intended performance in either the ballroom or the theater, can be found in Feuillet's *Recueil de dances*, published in 1700. The liveliness and gaiety of the *gigue* were expressed in springing steps, such as the jeté. The ballroom *gigue* demanded stamina, agility and a sure technique. The *gigue* served to demonstrate skill and lightness of step. As in all Baroque court dances, however, the required agility had to be accompanied by a calm and elegant bearing.[112]

The cotillion was a social dance of eighteenth-century French origin. According to Andrew Lamb, the cotillion takes its name from the words of one of the earliest tunes to which it was danced: "*Ma commère, quand je danse mon cotillion va-t-il bien?*"[113] It was danced in square formations, like country dances, with a large number of steps. The music was often no more than a series of waltz tunes or incorporated polkas, mazurkas and galops in 2/4 or 6/8.[114]

In the 1780s, William Creech described in *Fugitive Pieces* the dances enjoyed at the various balls: "The minuet with its beautiful movement, the cheerful country dance, the joyous jigg, the ... courtly cotillion."[115] Fifty years later, he would have had to delete the minuet, the jig and the cotillion and add the courtly quadrille, the waltz and the polka. These dances will be discussed below as dances that were in great favor in the early days of Queen Victoria.

The chaconne and passacaglia were two eighteenth-century dances in triple meter.[116] Of the two, the chaconne had a longer history as a dance, spanning two hundred years from the late sixteenth century to the late eighteenth century, whereas the passacaglia developed later and declined in popularity sooner. According to Cuthbert Girdlestone, the chaconne

> was licentious in character and associated with the sarabande in the condemnation of moralists, being included in the dances whose performance was forbidden on stage. The period of its greatest vogue in Spain was from 1600 to 1625. ...it was known in France by 1625. ...the earliest description of the dance, by Feuillet, dates from 1701 when it had long been established as a theatre dance.... It seems that, as with the passacaglia, Spain provided the dance and Italy developed the instrumental form. The fusion of the two took place perhaps in France where it (they) came to be used for prolonged displays of dancing on a large scale, especially at the close of an entertainment.[117]

Both of these dances were primarily theatrical dances and among the most difficult of their period because of the virtuoso technique required of the dancers and the stamina needed to last the distance of the dance. Though little is known about the choreography of the chaconne beyond the opening "sexual" character of the dance, Kellom Tomlinson gives a description of the actual steps in his book, *The Art of Dancing*: "The chaconne is composed of three movements, viz. first a bound, secondly a hop, and lastly a bound, or ballon, and it is most usually taken from the third position. The left foot disengaged and at liberty behind the right, in the position aforelaid, begins the first movement by making a bound, in the manner already shown in treating of that step, which, as I have there said, is accomplished by a sink or bending of the knee."[118]

Only three dances of musettes are known to survive. The first two were made for the theater. The third is a ballroom dance for a couple, published in Paris in 1724. It consisted of three figures, and the dance was fairly typical of ballroom dances found in the annual collections around the 1720s and '30s.[119]

The gavotte was a French folkdance that is still performed in Brittany. The dance developed in the sixteenth century into a popular court dance and continued to be performed as both a social and a theatrical dance through the nineteenth century. The dance seems to have originated with the peasants of Gavotte, in the Alpine region near Gap in southeastern France. Others state that the dance took its name from a word in the central French dialect, "*gavaud*," meaning "bent-leg," which is a feature of one of the gavotte steps. It was danced in duple time with four- and eight-bar phrases, but the addition of hops to the double steps gave it a lively character. The theatrical dance version, which was usually danced by one or two men, included difficult steps and was sometimes in a much slower tempo. The social *danse à deux* was performed at court or at other formal balls. Although these dances used a number of different steps, they could usually be distinguished from other Baroque dance types by their frequent use of the assemblé to create short, well-defined dance phrases. The assemblé was often preceded by a *contretemps de gavotte*, a step combination of smaller and smaller steps. The gavotte continued to be danced in the theater even after it was no longer popular as a social dance. Jean-Philippe Rameau used it more than any other dance type in his stage works (1733–1764), and danced gavottes were also included in works by Mozart. In late eighteenth-century England a minuet and gavotte were often danced in the theater as entr'acte entertainment, and both dance types were still being performed at the Paris Opera as late as 1817.[120]

Dance on stage in the theaters reflected the assumptions of the period and helped to extend such changes occurring in other areas. Theater itself became more important for the newly leisured women of the emerging middle class, as a way of passing time, and also as a way of embodying and passing on new ideas and the spirit of the time. The wide varieties of dances described above belong to the aristocratic world of the eighteenth century. As that world changed, this rich array of dances slowly fell out of use, to be replaced by simpler dance forms. In the same way, dances in the theater altered too. Costumes in the closing years of the eighteenth and the early years of the nineteenth century took on a series of changes for both the male and female dancers. The panniers that were associated with the minuet began to disappear after 1780. The world of fashion in England changed as well; long, clinging skirts and a very high waistline known as the Empire style came into vogue from 1800. Skirts were becoming fuller and of ankle length.[121] This allowed the dancers to move more freely. By 1790 puffing up and powdering of the hair had ended for women and the natural hair was arranged at the top of the head with soft curls.[122] Aristocratic elaboration was being replaced by middle-class practicality. Men too discarded their wigs and powder and wore their natural hair. Knee breeches were discarded and replaced by trousers.[123] The complicated etiquette of eighteenth-century social dance, and the demanding complexity of its music and movements were giving way to a simpler and more practical world that needed these changes in social dress. As has already been made clear, all these changes were faithfully reflected in the planters' balls in the Caribbean, even though their society, based on slavery, was very differently organized from an England that was adapting to industrialization.

The Baroque dance expert Violet Alford says that the lively rigaudon was popular at the French court of Louis XIII — that is, from about the first half of the seventeenth century. From there it spread to London. The musical accompaniment was in duple time and had a quarter-note upbeat, with almost all phrases four or eight measures in length. Throughout the seventeenth and eighteenth centuries, the rigaudon was a well-known musical dance form, used for instance by Rameau, Purcell, Handel, Gluck, Lully and many other composers.[124] The rigaudon was danced both as a social dance and a ballet *entrée*, to both instrumental and vocal music, and echoed the elegant manner of the court. The steps of the rigaudon were the usual ones of French court dancing: pas de bourrée, contretemps, glissade, jeté, and *sissonne*, but most rigaudons also had at least a single *pas de rigaudon*. This step unit had several springing movements together with leg gestures to the side. It was normally seen no more than two times in a dance and signified a climax. The figures of this dance followed the geometric pattern that was very typical of French court dancing, with both dancers of a pair normally doing identical steps, but on opposite feet, thus creating a mirror image.[125]

I have already mentioned some of the dancing masters who were associated with these seventeenth- and eighteenth-century dances. They include Beauchamps and Pecourt, Louis XIV's great dancing masters, and Pierre Rameau (not to be confused with the composer) and Feuillet, who published the notation system called sténochorégraphie.[126] The French Baroque technique is sometimes referred to as the Beauchamps-Pecourt or the Feuillet-Rameau technique.[127] The dances described above are some of the more familiar ones. Some lesser known ones are described below.[128]

The hornpipe is unique to Great Britain. It should be characterized as belonging to the step-dance tradition, which emphasised leg actions and beating (or sounding) rhythms with the feet. In its most traditional form, it was an important source for later tap-dance movements. Historically, according to Margaret Dean-Smith, the name derived from the instrument that is used in playing the music for the dance.[129] The hornpipe dance fell into three types. The first was performed by one person, or by two or more people dancing at the same time, but independently. In England this form of dance had existed since the sixteenth century. It was essentially a peasant dance and in time became associated specifically with sailors, and by then may have been influenced by some African dance practice. It was one of the forms of the jig and is discussed later in this chapter in the context of possible African influences in European dance. The second type was a rustic round dance for both men and women in hornpipe tempo, and the third type of hornpipe was a longways country dance from the late seventeenth century, in 3/2 time, created by dancing masters for assembly rooms or for private patrons. Its figuration was intricate. Movements labeled "hornpipe" using the rhythm of the country dance type, were often found in the dance suites and incidental theater music from the sixteenth to the eighteenth centuries. References to this can be found in the works of Purcell and Handel, who included two hornpipes in his "Water Music" (nos. 9 and 12) and the chorus "Now love, that everlasting boy" in Act 2 of S*emele* which is headed "alla hornpipe."[130]

The bourrée was one of several dance types, like the minuet, sarabande, *passepied,* gavotte and rigaudon, that were refined and changed to suit aristocratic tastes for the court of Louis XIV. Wendy Hilton states that the dance "usually took between two and three minutes to perform, and a step-sequence would occasionally be repeated." She comments, "Within the structure of court life, dancing alone with a partner before a crowd of spectators must have seemed quite unexceptional."[131] The dancers moved with a graceful and strongly centered carriage, and used swiftly flowing steps to form a variety of floor patterns in geometric figures common to French court dancing in the period. There was less ornamentation and subtle footwork than in many of the other popular court dances. The tempo was quick, and the music was in duple meter on all levels and had a quarter-note upbeat, with many phrases four or eight bars in length. The most common step was the pas de bourrée, a step unit performed to one measure of music. It had a demi-coupe, which is a step with a plié and élevé, followed by two *pas marchés,* that is, two plain steps without a change of elevation. The pas de bourrée could begin on either foot and was therefore handy whenever a change of leading foot was required. The third of the three steps was sometimes performed with a tiny leap or demi-jeté, for extra jollity. A form of the pas de bourrée is still used today in ballet, and varieties of it occur in many folk dances. Bourrée entrées occurred frequently in French Baroque ballets and operas from about 1650 until 1750. The bourrée was highly regarded as a social dance at court. It was popular both as a piece for one couple dancing alone, which as already mentioned was a *danse à deux*, and, from about the 1680s, as a *contredanse*, with several couples dancing at once. The *danse à deux* was performed by one couple at formal ceremonial balls while the assembled court watched. A *contredanse* often followed a *danse à deux* and was easier to perform, as a constant repetition of the four-bar step sequence was carried out and the dancing figures were not so difficult.[132]

From the nineteenth century onward, dance tended to lose much of its former central role as a social activity for an aristocratic class in which nobody did much work. As the middle class became more dominant, its male members were working hard to make the industrial revolution ever more effective. Dance for them was a more marginal activity, only possible in their rare leisure time.[133] The role of the famous assembly rooms in Bath, dominated by Beau Nash, reflected the older importance dance had occupied in the aristocratic world of the eighteenth century. This persisted with Beau Brummel during the early years of the Regency period, but by mid nineteenth century, the importance of the Bath assembly rooms was greatly diminished. Social changes in the late eighteenth and early nineteenth century meant that balls and dance generally were beginning to count for much less in polite society, so that by the end of the century the middle class were beginning to represent the dominant ideology.[134] E. H. Gombrich explains:

The late eighteenth century is also the period of the attempted distinction between ("external") "civilization" and ("internal" or "human") "culture." It is moreover the period of the newly general modern meaning of "the arts" and "the artist," as terms indicating more than specific practices and practitioners and now centrally including conceptions of general (and then often alternative or oppositional) values. The independent formations, alternative and oppositional, are directly related to this complex process and set of ideas. Yet the possibility of actually establishing effective independent formations depended, obviously, on general social conditions. This is why, though the ideas were becoming common from the late eighteenth century, effective alternative and oppositional formations became common only in the second half of the nineteenth century and increased markedly towards the end of the century. One factor in this development, within particular societies, was the change in the internal structure of the dominant classes. Within aristocratic and mercantile societies, (there were) conflicts about style and tendency, as well as more general social and economic tensions and conflicts in arts practice....[135]

All the same, social dance echoed other social changes. Previously, social dancers moved side by side, both facing in the same direction and generally as part of a larger group dance. With new dances like the waltz and the polka, it was the couple that become important. The couple faced each other, to the exclusion of the others on the dance floor. They not only danced with each other, but also they held on to each other in a very intimate way. This echoed the new importance of man and wife, the middle-class couple creating a middle-class family in a much smaller household than the aristocratic one. It also indicated a general loosening of social mores, allowing a more public intimacy. Paradoxically, women became more wrapped up in voluminous clothing, primmer, more demure and more modest at the same time as dance became more intimate, more personal and more couple-oriented.

The dances of the polka and waltz both mirrored and attested to this change. In the eighteenth century, for a man to put an arm around his female dancing partner was more or less unthinkable. It was practically forbidden by social etiquette. From the introduction of the waltz and the polka, such bodily contact, so outwardly expressive of the joy of dancing, was the acceptable norm. Choreographically both these dance styles involved the dancers facing each other as opposed to being side by side, as they had been in the past. When dancing in the eighteenth-century "polite society" manner, the acceptable norm meant moving in a style and following a floor pattern that echoed the typically reserved social etiquette of a society dominated by its aristocrats. Social dance now echoed the new dominance of the middle class. Belinda Quirey, writing of the *danse à deux*, refers to it as an example of "inclusive mutuality." In the nineteenth century, she writes, "we get the two dancers, not only in each other's arms, but turned inwards, towards each other, and cut off from, though surrounded by, a throng of similarly closed couples."[136] The quadrille, which developed from English country dances (*contredanses*) and was very much a group dance, survived in spite of these new dance styles and continued to be danced throughout the nineteenth century. It was not a *danse à deux* but remained very much a group dance.

The waltz in the nineteenth century was danced to a simple three-beat rhythm. English folk music and popular music up until the eighteenth century were among the most complex and sophisticated of their kind in Europe. England had a very strong musical culture that reached down through society. The industrial revolution did much to diminish this musical culture. It is only necessary to look at the table below of dance forms, each of which has its appropriate music, to realize the complexity of English dance music available in the eighteenth century compared with the less-rich English dance forms available in the nineteenth century. The working class in the nineteenth century emerged with relatively simple hymn tunes and music-hall songs. Much of the complexity and sophistication of folk music was lost. It is in this context that the success of the relatively simple rhythmic form of the waltz should be understood.

European Dances in the Eighteenth and Nineteenth Centuries

Eighteenth Century
English country dances

sarabande	tambourin
gigue	musette
minuet	gavotte
passepied (later, allemande and cotillion)	rigaudon
chaconne	bourree
passacaglia	hornpipe

Nineteenth Century

quadrille	lancers
waltz	galop
polka	cakewalk[137]

After a period of transition during the political and industrial revolutions, Europeans developed new dance forms and new dance rhythms that embraced the new conditions of life, socially as well as psychologically. In London, as in the rest of Europe, this reflected the sense and sensibility of a powerful middle-class world.[138] One of these new dance forms was the quadrille.

The origin of the word "quadrille" may derive from Italian "*squadra*," meaning a troop of armed horsemen formed into a square for military defense and tournament games.[139] The word was in general use in eighteenth-century France to mean any group of people who had rehearsed together for the purpose of performing in front of an audience, including drama as well as dance. In this book the word is used to mean a dance for four couples arranged in a square pattern. Each dancer in turn, either with his or her own partner or with the dancer opposite, dances in floor patterns with or around the other dancers. Each quadrille lasts between three and five minutes. Sets of quadrilles are normally danced in collections of three to seven separate quadrilles.

The beginnings of the quadrille as a social dance are to be found in the *contredanses* or, as the English called it, country dances, and secondly in the cotillion. Feuillet in his *Recueil de contredanses* in 1706 defined a *contredanse* as "a dance figure repeated continually, first by two, by four, by six, by eight, by ten and finally by as many couples as were present. A figure in respect of *contredanse*, was a certain number of movements capable of filling out an air."[140] In other words, this was an invented set of movements danced to a refrain, and then repeated again and again as fresh couples joined in. In fact, a number of different refrains, just for the pleasure of variety, could make up the dance.

Out of these easy and repetitive dances grew a more complex form of dance known as the cotillion. This dance was equally a group dance, with all the characteristics of the *contredanse*, but was much longer, had far more steps and variety, and was quite difficult to remember and dance correctly. By the early nineteenth century, dancers found it more and more difficult to be correct in the overcomplicated cotillion and so the quadrille emerged as an easier form. As Thomas Wilson pointed out in 1818 when referring to the quadrille, "this fashionable species of dancing is entirely of French origin, and only differs from the cotillion by leaving out the changes, being much shorter, and frequently composed of figures that require but four persons to their performance ... although eight persons generally stand up for the sake of convenience ... and also to gain room in the formation of the sets, particularly as many cotillion figures are now introduced in quadrille dancing that require eight persons, and as most of the finales contain some figure or figures requiring that number in their performance."[141] Thus, although social dance changed radically in the nineteenth century, balls continued to include charming survivals from an earlier age. The new forms of dance like the polka and the waltz were exhausting. They tired the dancers out. It was helpful to have a slightly easier group dance in between the couple dances to enable dancers to conserve their energy. This partly explains the survival of the quadrille, but there is no doubt also that as interest in history and past traditions increased, dancers felt a sense of continuity with the past when attempting these surviving group forms. Much the same applies today to the vogue for Scottish dancing. These dances are fun to do but they also reinforce a sense of cultural identity and reinforce links with a romanticized past.[142]

During the first decade of the nineteenth century, many combinations and variations of cotillion figures were strung together and called "sets of quadrilles" while dance manuals, books, and pamphlets on the subject proliferated. Thomas Wilson's *Quadrille and Cotillion Panorama* (1822) offers no fewer than fifty-two configurations.[143] The word "cotillion" was still being applied to the new quadrille.

This French quadrille was introduced into exclusive London society, at Almack's, by one of the then leaders of fashion, Lady Jersey, in 1815.[144] Whereas in the past, peasant dances had been refined and made more complex as they were danced in the upper echelons of society, particularly the court, it is typical of the changes occurring in the nineteenth century that the quadrille was introduced at an aristocratic level, and then spread downward. Far from refining and making the dance more complex, the quadrille was a simpler version of the cotillion, and easier to remember. The dominant ideology in both France and England was becoming less aristocratic and more middle-class. The origins for these changes were different. In France a bloody political revolution had initiated far-reaching social changes. In England industrialization had produced a similar social upheaval. By the nineteenth century both France and England were industrializing, with many of the same consequences, but England, where industrialization started, had gained a considerable lead. As a result, by the beginning of the nineteenth century there was less time available for the middle-class male to indulge in leisure pursuits. The middle class needed a simplified version of the cotillion, and that largely explains why a dance introduced at the aristocratic level at Almack's, spread downward and outward so quickly. The quadrille still had some difficult figures, and some of the steps were far from easy, but it was simpler than the cotillion, and it was soon being danced everywhere at any social occasion which included dancing. It could be done by any even number of couples, each couple dancing with its opposite pair. After eight beginning bars of music, dancers launched into the five figures, which were called *Le Pantalon, L'Été, La Poule, La Pastourelle* (or *La Trenise*), and *La Finale* (nowadays sometimes called the Flirtation).

Music for the quadrille, adapted from popular operas, ballets, songs, and anthems, was arranged to fit the dance form precisely. Many famous composers contributed to the repertory. A quadrille band was often made up of a string quartet with added flute, harp, piano, and cornet. The tempo varied with each figure, and a pause of about twenty seconds was observed between figures. The tempo was given as 112 beats per minute, although later in the century the tempo was increased. Johann Strauss the Younger allowed fifteen to twenty minutes for the quadrille on his court dance programs.

The figures were danced to a specified step pattern, in a combination of chassé, jeté, and assemblé. Carlo Blasis in 1828 gave a list of additional steps for women and men.[145] The intention was for the couples to show grace and agility during solo sections. In the 1840s, with the introduction of the waltz, polka, schottische and other couple dances, the quadrille step was reduced to a simple glide walk or *pas marché*. Cellarius in 1847 commented on "the young people of the present day, who are so often accused of walking instead of dancing (the quadrille)."[146] One of the nicest things about the quadrille was the breathing space it gave dancers for polite conversation during the pauses, which was very difficult during the more energetic waltzes and polkas.

By 1850, the five-figure lancers' quadrille rivaled the French quadrille in popularity. The last figure in the lancers' was a tribute to the Royal Lancers' Regiment, which has the dancers marching in single and double lines. The double lancers', the caledonians (to Scottish airs), the saratoga, and the polo quadrille followed soon after, and waltz and polka figures were introduced into the quadrille. As new quadrilles grew, the need for dancing masters to prompt the dancers became unavoidable, and "calling" became necessary.[147]

The quadrille finally fell out of fashion following the First World War, when jazz and a new informality made it appear as old-fashioned as the cotillion. The quadrille should be thought of as being not very different from the cotillion, which itself stemmed from a seventeenth- and eighteenth-century dance form, the *contredanse*, but the quadrille was simpler. It was a group dance, rooted in the social etiquette of the past. In the radical dance changes brought about by the waltz, the polka, and their successors, its sturdy survival made it something of a phenomenon. As they danced it, people felt in touch with a more formal past, and yet it was fun to do, and could be danced to any combination of the latest dance music, like the polka or the waltz, although it was, in the nineteenth century, generally done to a medley of popular airs, more operatic than not, usually ending in the last figure, with a galop.[148]

When we look at the development of the quadrille, it is quite clear that there are recognizable steps and movement patterns which date back to the eighteenth century and the cotillion. This evolution in ballroom dance styles stems from the political and social changes which the dancers found themselves in at the time. Aristocrats no longer dominated social dancing as the middle class became steadily more powerful and influential. Yet the now-dominant middle-class male had less leisure, was working hard to keep the industrial revolution going, regarded dance as a much more marginal activity and needed simplified versions of the earlier complex forms.

Paradoxically, slaves in the Caribbean and in London retained, as I will show in the next chapter, memories of an African culture in which dance played a very important part.[149] They arrived in the Caribbean and in London at a time when dance was beginning to play an even less important part in European culture than it had previously done. In adapting European dance forms, all they had available to them were these simplified dances. They adopted them with ease and added something of their own when they started to dance them.

Social dance in the nineteenth century lost much of its earlier-eighteenth century complexity, but this does not apply to dance in the theater, which became steadily more specialized throughout the nineteenth century. Raymond Williams's remarks about increasing specialization in the arts as a result of the industrial revolution certainly applied to dance as a profession among theater performers, making the gulf between the professional and the amateur even greater.[150] Whereas the middle-class amateur was performing simpler forms of social dance, because dance was no longer seen as an important activity as it had been in the eighteenth century, ballet as a spectacle was increasing in popularity. Dancers attracted attention by developing an increasing virtuosity. The ballerina started to dance on point and acquired a whole range of virtuoso skills as a result, at the very time when middle-class society was simplifying the cotillion into the quadrille. Marie Taglioni introduced point work to the public in the Meyerbeer opera *Robert le Diable* in 1831 at the Paris Opera. The ghosts of nuns rose from their graves and glided about the stage in an apparently effortless manner on the tips of their toes. This created a sensation at the time, and opened the way for an increasing range of technical development in the steps available to the ballerina.[151]

The virtuosity of ballet performances in Europe had little influence on developments in the Caribbean, and there seems to be no evidence that ballet made any impact at all on black society in London in the eighteenth and nineteenth centuries. It is true that in 1781 a sitting of the House of Commons was suspended to allow the members to get to the Opera House to see Gaetano Vestris (1729–1808), the great French dancer who was creating a sensation in London at the time.[152] Alexander Pope referred to Gaetano's son Auguste (1760–1842), "who on one leg could do what erst no mortal could achieve on two."[153] Is it reasonable to assume there were no black members of the audience at the Opera House? If there were, their views have gone unrecorded. It is the changes occurring in English social dance that are of prime importance, changes which were faithfully echoed by the dominant white planter society in the Caribbean. It was the process of creolization, which was the combining of influences from African and European culture that produced the mind-set of the blacks in London in the eighteenth and nineteenth centuries.

Possible African Influence on European Dance Forms

During the second half of the nineteenth century and throughout the twentieth century there was clearly an amazing and recognizable African influence on European dance.[154] This book is concerned with a much earlier period and with a process of creolization during which blacks of African origin were forming a culture for themselves that was both different from, and at the same time a part of, the Caribbean and American societies into which they had been thrust. Yet it would be unwise to ignore the fact that writing at the beginning of the twenty-first century, it is possible to see with hindsight that African dance forms have had a considerable influence on European dance forms. Armed with this knowledge, the dance historian can then venture back even farther, trying to see if at a much earlier stage European dance forms might have started to adjust and adapt to a different dance culture arriving from Africa via the Caribbean and elsewhere in America.

The evidence is scanty but interesting. Earlier in this chapter it was noted that Americans in 1876 considered the jig to be an African dance form.[155] In fact, it had long been a European dance form stretching back into the Middle Ages.

Kemps nine daies vvonder.

Performed in a daunce from London to Norwich.

Containing the pleasure, paines and kinde entertainment of *William Kemp* betweene *London* and that Citty in his late Morrice.

Wherein is somewhat set downe worth note; to reproove the slaunders spred of him: many things merry, nothing hurtfull.

Written by himselfe to satisfie his friends.

"*Kemp's Jig*," London. "Printed by E. A. for Nicholas Ling, and are to be sold at his shop at west door of Saint Paules Church. 1600." (Courtesy British Library)

Yet the jig changed, incorporating new up-and-down movements of the legs and feet, at about the same time as the British slave trade was expanding. Even more importantly, in the form of the hornpipe, the jig came to be a dance specifically associated with sailors. (Chapter 3 will cite evidence that some form of dance by black slaves was a regular occurrence on slave ships.) It should also be remembered that the crews of British, Caribbean and other American ships almost invariably contained black sailors.[156] They, too, would have played a part in any African influence on European dance forms like the hornpipe. Is it just speculation to assume that there was some similarity between the up-and-down movements of the leg and feet of the African dancers and the new steps being incorporated into the sailors' hornpipe? Perhaps it is time to look again at illustration number 1, *A Bivouac Fire on the Potomac*. Here it is not a white dancer but a black dancer dancing to a black musician. The half-crouching position of the dancer is as much African as European. The steps being performed by the feet look very similar to those of the jig, performed in the sixteenth century. This illustration is dated 1861. In another ten years someone would be claiming that the jig was an African dance. By going back over a hundred years to the 1740s, is it not possible that a distinctly European dance form as done by British sailors on a slave ship was beginning to acquire characteristics that would make it easy for a creolized black not only to slip into the dance in 1861, but to think of it as being black and not European at all?

There is even stronger written evidence in Moreau de Saint-Mery's book *Danse,* which gives an account of a French colonial plantation owners' ball. Among a host of European dances mentioned, one name is very significant. It is that of the minuet congo. Dance historian Lillian Moore, in her translation of the book, wondered, "What on earth could it have been?"[157] Is it not reasonable to assume that here we have an example of African influence? Something that is specifically African crept into the European form of the minuet, and because it is African it has been given an African name, the minuet congo. Even more importantly, the fact that it was African was not considered sufficiently out of the ordinary for the movements to be described in any detail. It appears to have been taken for granted, just as the new up-and-down movements in the hornpipe were taken for granted. It is safe to assume here that this is evidence of a process that was to become unstoppable and inescapable in the twentieth century.

The 1762 edition of Giovanni-Andrea Gallini's *Treatise on the Art of Dancing* provides further evidence. He notes,

> The Portuguese themselves, among whom I will not however include [in] the higher ranks of life in that nation, but, at least [a] number of the people who adopted, from the Caffrees, or Negroes of their African possessions, [have] a dance called by them *las chegancas,* (Approaches) [which]

the late King of Portugal was obliged to prohibit ... by a formal edict. The reason of which was, that some of the motions and gestures had so lascivious an air, and were so contrary to modesty, that the celebrated *Frey Gaspar*, a natural son, if I mistake not, of the late King of Portugal, represented so efficaciously to his Portuguese Majesty, the shame and scandal of this dance being any longer suffered, that it was put down by royal authority. Nor was this done without occasioning heavy complaints against *Frey Gaspar*, against whom there were lampoons and ballads publickly sung, upon his having used his influence to procure that prohibition.[158]

Here a European dancing master clearly stated that the Portuguese "adopted" an African dance. Nothing could be clearer. Here are Europeans using an African dance form and using it so well that they scandalized the Portuguese establishment in much the same way as we have seen so many European travelers to West Africa equally scandalized by West African dance. Admittedly the Portuguese experience was special in that large numbers of Africans were being incorporated into Portuguese society, but was this really so very different from what was happening in the Portuguese colony of Brazil, or French and British colonies in the Caribbean? Just as in Portugal they could adopt *las chegancas*, so French Caribbean planters could adopt the minuet congo and British sailors could adapt their hornpipe.[159]

Las chegancas did not disappear, although banned by the Portuguese. It surfaced again as the *chica*, and fortunately for dance historians was described in detail by one of the few perceptive and widely educated commentators to write about dance in the Caribbean in the eighteenth century. He was M. L. E. Moreau de Saint-Mery, a distinguished French émigré who had been forced to flee from Paris during the revolution of 1789. For four years he was part of a distinguished group of French aristocrats in exile, living and meeting regularly in Philadelphia, including the Duc d'Orleans (the future Louis Philippe) and Talleyrand, who was a particular friend of Saint Mery's. It was at this time that Saint Mery wrote a book entitled *Danse*, published in Philadelphia in 1796, dealing with "primitive" dance in general and looking particularly at Negro dance on the island of Haiti (then called Saint-Domingue).[160] (Carlo Blasis in his well-known *Code of Terpsichore*, published in 1830, brazenly plagiarized several pages of Moreau de Saint-Mery's work.)[161] The final twenty pages of *Danse* give an account of the dances brought by slaves from Africa to the Caribbean and provide excellent evidence of just how much dance survived the Middle Passage. Among other dances, he describes the *chica*:

Our Creole customs have adopted another exotic product which, also coming from Africa, has had the most general influence of all the negro dances which I have described. It is a dance known almost everywhere in the American colonies, under the name of the chica, which it bears in the Windward Islands and in Santo Domingo. When one wishes to dance the chica, several instruments play a melody, which is absolutely dedicated to this kind of dance, and in which the rhythm is very plainly marked. For the women, who hold the ends of a handkerchief or the two sides of her apron, the art of this dance consists chiefly in moving the lower part of the loins, while holding the rest of the body almost motionless. To enliven the chica, a man approaches the woman who is dancing, throws himself suddenly forward, falling so that he almost touches her, draws back, and then darts forward again, while seeming to implore her to yield to the desires which she seems to feel.[162]

Saint-Mery even suggests that the origins of the Spanish fandango are to be found in the *chica*, although this is a wild surmise that modern scholarship would not support.[163] Interestingly, just as in Portugal, planter society in the Caribbean found the *chica* too licentious and Saint-Mery tells us: "The chica is now banished from the balls of the white ladies, and is only sometimes performed in a few circles."[164] He praises the negresses in the Dutch island of Curacao for the way they dance the chica and tells his readers that "the chica comes to us from the countries of Africa where every tribe dances it, and particularly the natives of the Congo."[165] "This dance was so universal throughout South America and the West Indies that at the commencement of the present century," Saint-Mery says, "it was always danced in religious ceremonies and processions."[166]

James H. Sweet supports a "revisionist" generation of African diaspora scholars, including Paul Lovejoy, John Kelly Thornton, Colin Palmer and Michael Gomez, who shift the focus of diaspora studies away from any analysis of creolization toward the varieties of African cultures in Africa and the ways differences persisted and can be traced after the Atlantic crossing. This brings greater specificity to African survivals and retentions.[167] Thornton suggests that whatever the ethnic groups in the primary slaving areas of Africa, the pattern of their arrival can be divided into three main sources of origin, Upper Guinea, Lower Guinea and Central Africa. This would group the British Caribbean colonies largely within the Lower Guinea and Central Africa area. Thornton reinforces what has been suggested here, that despite regional differences, people from Lower Guinea and Central Africa had much in common, mutual understandings, and shared beliefs, values and customs, both in Africa and in the colonies of the Caribbean. This would mean that the influences on the minuet congo and the hornpipe should be traced back to the Lower Guinea and Central African regions.

All the same, whatever their geographical sources in Africa, and however homogenous the region from which they came, the process of creolization was, as we have seen, inevitable and widespread. Dance and music played a considerable part in the process, but there was another whole area that must now be considered. The part played by humor in black slave society has been carefully analyzed by writers like Lawrence W. Levine, but it should always be remembered that although verbal humor played an important part in black humor, dance and music were important too.[168] No doubt a black dancer could perform the hornpipe for fellow black slaves in ways that could satirize the white oppressors.

Satire

This book has already referred to the use of satire and humor generally as means by which black slaves and the black minority in London in the eighteenth and nineteenth centuries tried to cope with their experience as an oppressed minority. Humor is a difficult concept to define adequately. As Monro puts it: "Humor is one of the unsolved problems of philosophy."[169] A number of conflicting philosophical theories of humor hold the field, but in the words of Berlyne, "Most of the philosophical theorists erred in singling out one or two as the critical prerequisites for laughter, so that their theories fitted certain instances of humor very well, but accounted for other instances less convincingly."[170] Humor tends in fact to be dragged in almost as an afterthought, as part of a philosopher's general theory. A Freudian gives a Freudian explanation of humor, a Gestaltist gives a Gestalt account, a linguist gives a linguistic analysis, a structuralist presents a speech act or script theory, and so on.

It can be generally agreed, however, that whatever is meant by a sense of humor, it seems to be a uniquely human attribute. There is some debate as to whether other higher primates have a sense of humor, and it would be difficult to establish whether dolphins, with their admittedly considerable intelligence, possess it, but apart from these possibilities, humans would appear to be unique in having a sense of humor, in being able to enjoy laughter. Yet, every human attribute has evolved with some biological purpose. They are there because they fulfill some function. It may well be asked, what is the function of humor? What biological purpose does it serve?

Set against this important question, some of the philosophical theories seem a bit thin. Even more importantly if we are to analyze the ways in which blacks in the Caribbean and in London used humor in their dance, it will be necessary to have some definition of humor in mind.

Monro gives a very acceptable list of the different classifications within which humor can be considered. They are: (1) Any breach of the usual order of events. (2) Importing into one situation what belongs to another. (3) Anything masquerading as something it is not. (4) Word play, puns. (5) Nonsense. (6) Forbidden breach. (7) Novelty, freshness, unexpectedness.[171] This list may be usefully compared with a similar list presented by Cicero. After trying to define a difference between jokes of language and jokes of thought, Cicero in *De Oratore* classified jokes of thought as: (1) Deceiving expectation. (2) Satirizing tempers of others. (3) Playing humorously on one's own tempers. (4) Comparing a thing with something worse. (5) Dissembling. (6) Uttering apparent absurdities. (7) Reproving folly. (8) Surprise. (9) Deceit. (10) Verbal distortion.[172]

It is probably most useful to view these lists, so similar across so many hundreds of years, as lists of the various mechanisms that allow humor to operate. Humans have a propensity to laugh. They need opportunities, mechanisms, for this propensity toward humor to have a chance to operate. But the question still needs to be asked, what is the biological function of humor? What purpose does it serve?

The psychologist Hans Jurgen Eysenck listed four approaches to the study of humor: cognitive theory, conative theory, affective theory and instinct theory.[173] There are inevitably a host of others, including the ambivalence theory of humor as conflicting emotions, the behaviorist theory of humor as a physiological process, the psychological theory of humor as arousal, and the configuration or Gestalt theory.

When looking at black dance, it will probably be most helpful to concentrate on Eysenck's "instinct" theory. The term "instinct" is a vague one. According to Warren A. Shibles it could mean unlearned behavior, unalterable behavior, hereditary behavior, behavior not involving reason, behavior attempting to remove tension, and unconscious behavior.[174] When looking at black dance, it is behavior attempting to remove tension that will best serve the purpose.

This theory links directly with Freud's *Jokes and their Relation to the Unconscious*.[175] Freud's theory of the unconscious has come under increasing attack since his death, but the concept of humor as a way of releasing tension, as a discharge of energy in the mind, remains an attractive one. There are many different theories of humor, each with its own values, and each seemingly well able to analyze at least some elements of humor, so that the idea of humor operating as a release from tension is not all-embracing and does not attempt to cover every aspect of humor. It does help to define the area of humor here. At least it makes the biological function of humor clear. One kind of humor, the humor to be discussed here, operates as a release from tension, a vital safety valve. If anybody needed a safety valve as a release from tension, it must have been those enmeshed in the horrifying conditions of slavery. Even those blacks who had escaped to the comparative safety of London carried with them the knowledge of what was still happening to their relatives and brethren back in the Caribbean, and the knowledge, too, that they were still part of a small and despised minority.

It is worth noting in passing, and this should give it some additional respectability, that this theory of humor as a release from tension, links directly with Aristotle. In his *Poetics*, Aristotle proposed that a Greek audience attending a performance of tragedy, by identifying with characters on stage and imaginatively "acting out" with them the fictional experiences taking place on stage, worked the tensions out of their systems as it were, and did not need to experience them in real life. They had, by a process of "catharsis," purged themselves of their tensions.[176] In *The Tractatus Coislinanus*, Aristotle applied the same theory to humor and comedy: "Comedy is an imitation of action that is ludicrous and imperfect ... directly presented by persons acting and not in the form of narrative; through pleasure and laughter effecting the purgation of the like emotions."[177] Lawrence Levine devotes a whole section of his book on black culture and black consciousness to what he calls "black laughter." If the operation of humor can be seen as providing a release from tension, then clearly the development of many specialized forms of humor in black slave and post-slave society can be all too easily understood. In the hell of plantation life, humor, it may be assumed, acted both as a palliative and as an escape. As Levine points out:

> Assuming that for the erection of a psychic inhibition some expenditure of psychic energy is necessary, Freud reasoned that jokes brought pleasure by disguising aggression sufficiently to get it past both external and internal censors, thus relieving the joke-teller and his audience of the need to expend this inhibiting energy. Humor allowed economy in the expenditure of that energy used for the purposes of inhibition or suppression by liberating feelings which normally had to be contained. This liberation brought with it immense feeling of relief and pleasure, a fact that certainly helps to explain why an active humor has been so notably present among people who seem to outsiders to have so little to laugh about. Freud used the term "tendentious" to characterise those jokes that accomplished this end:

"tendentious jokes are especially favoured in order to make aggressiveness or criticism possible against persons in exalted positions who claim to exercise authority. The joke then represents a rebellion against that authority, a liberation from its pressure."[178]

The folk culture of blacks that developed as a result of creolization often made vicious fun of the whites, but it also made equally vicious fun of the failings of the black community itself. Levine devotes another section of his book to analyzing the popularity of the Uncle Remus tales about Brer Rabbit and Brer Fox and so on, which often pillory the failings of the black community itself.[179] These tales, too, are imbued with a subtle and delightful sense of irony and satire that has so far passed the test of time. They are a tribute to at least one of the ways in which the black community dealt with its predicament.

It is against this context, so carefully described by Levine, of a whole culture of using humor as a way of coping with life's problems, that the use of humor in dance needs to be viewed. As the process of creolization got underway, European dance forms were both adopted and then adapted to the particular context of the Caribbean life style. Given the attitudes already mentioned, it was to be expected that the upright rigidity of the European dance, which for African dancers implied being closer to death than life, should give way to flexed and bended joints seen as more indicative of life and energy in the African tradition. There is nothing necessarily satirical or humorous about this. Black Caribbeans might well incorporate some of their own dance traditions in the way they performed European dances. A European watching them doing so might laugh with the superior sense that blacks were somehow unable to fully appreciate how to perform European dance. Black Caribbeans would be dancing like that because for them their way of dancing would be more indicative of life and energy than the European way of dancing. Europeans might find it funny, but black Caribbeans would not. If humor was to operate for black Caribbeans it would be necessary for them to make fun of Europeans, to exaggerate the ways Europeans danced their own dances. This would mean not dancing them in a black Caribbean manner but on the contrary, dancing them in a way that exaggerated the European upright rigidity, until it became ludicrous in black Caribbean eyes. Creolization would blend African and European elements. Satire would deliberately distort European elements for the purposes of humor.

As Levine maintains, quoting from Bernard, an Englishman living in the United States from 1797 to 1811: "While slaves often learned the dances of the whites—the quadrille, the reel, the cotillion, and even the waltz—their own dance style remained distinctive."[180] Levine then pointed out:

> There is a wealth of evidence in contemporary accounts and slave recollections to buttress Melville Herskovits' assertion that dance "carried over into the New World to a greater degree than almost any other trait of African culture." The basic characteristics of African dance, with its gliding, dragging, shuffling steps, its flexed, fluid bodily position as opposed to the stiffly erect position of European dancers, its imitations of such animals as the buzzard and the eagle, its emphasis upon flexibility and improvisation, its concentration upon movement outward from the pelvic region, which whites found lewd, its tendency to eschew bodily contact, and its propulsive, swinging rhythm, were perpetuated for centuries in the dances of American slaves and ultimately affected all American dance profoundly. Dance no less than song could become an instrument of satire at the expense of the whites. And was useful for slaves hoping to avoid punishment by being "non-verbal." In 1772, the *South Carolina Gazette* printed an account of a clandestine county dance attended by sixty slaves on the outskirts of Charleston. "The entertainment was opened," the anonymous correspondent reported, "by the men copying (or taking off) the manners of their masters, and the women those of their mistresses."[181]

Levine makes clear that dance, as satire for humorous purposes, was widespread in creole society. Mocking, satirizing, "taking-off" the way whites behaved, was particularly appropriate in dance, which obviously lends itself to just this kind of humor. It has already been referred to several times in this book and will be looked at again in the analysis of the visual evidence in chapter 5.

Conclusion

Now that we have looked at both African dance and European dance, it should be possible to understand what survived from each in the mind of the average black creole Caribbean. Some particular African dance forms, particularly the shout, survived the Atlantic crossing. Even more importantly, African attitudes to dance—giving it major importance in most social functions—also survived the crossing. In the particular context of slavery, dance could also be used in humor and satire, partly as a release for powerful emotion and partly as a language for expressing collective feelings of resistance. Yet, increasingly as the process of creolization continued, blacks succumbed to the dominant artistic ideology of the whites, even in dance. They adopted the social dances performed in the world of the planters, even if in many cases they took them over only to use them for their own purposes, which could often be to make humorous and slighting comments on their white masters. It is this strange combination of different factors, stretching back over time into two quite different dance cultures and traditions, which merged in black Caribbean creole culture. It was this mind-set which blacks carried with them when they arrived from the Caribbean in London. Before looking at their use of dance in London, the next chapter will illustrate the themes of this chapter, with three striking examples of black dance under the appalling pressures of slavery.

3

"Savages with No Knowledge of Their Ancestry": Examples of African Dance Survivals During and After the Atlantic Crossing

Before considering the ways black slaves and former slaves based in London in the second half of the eighteenth and early part of the nineteenth centuries approached the quadrille, it will be necessary to examine and attempt to analyze the mind-set they brought with them from the Caribbean. The great majority of blacks in London came from the Caribbean, but as we have already emphasized, the slaves who survived the Atlantic crossing shared much that was common to African culture. They also represented, in their variety, the many striking cultural differences to be found across the regions of Africa.[1] African dance is an obvious example of this, sharing common characteristics while at the same time showing a wide variety of regional differences. This chapter will look in detail at the way dance was used on the slave ships and then at the planned slave revolt in Antigua in 1736, where dance played a particularly important role. The dance that proved to be of prime importance there was the Akan war dance, but it should be seen in the context of what is said above about African culture, as should the South Carolina revolt, which is also analyzed in this chapter.

As we shall see in chapter 4, most of the blacks making up the London community arrived from the Caribbean. We have looked at how African culture and European culture together provided the strange mixture that made up the mind-set of Caribbean slaves, and indeed continued to do so after emancipation. This chapter and the next will attempt to analyze the new ideology that this mixture represented. This mixture is one for which the term "creolization" is a useful label. The aim is to show that the Africans brought to London elements of their dance traditions and practices that flourished during the plantation era.

It should be made clear that on the slave ships themselves there were two kinds of "dance." The slave traders used the word "dance" to describe the way they made the slaves move about in the hope that exercise would keep them healthy. They did this by whipping them so that they moved about, even when they were in irons. In order to analyze and appreciate the importance of a print by Isaac Cruikshank, *The Abolition of the Slave Trade*, it is necessary to examine what dances were possible on the slave ships to which this print refers. In no sense was the traders' enforced exercise "dance" as it was understood in African culture. But even on the slave ships, African traditional dance was often allowed to surface.

The following entry was made in Thomas Phillips's Journal on May 21, 1694: "We often at sea in the evenings would let the slaves come up into the sun to air themselves, and make them jump and dance for an hour or two to our bag-pipes, harp, and fiddle, by which exercise to preserve them in health; but notwithstanding all our endeavour, 'twas my hard fortune to have great sickness and mortality among them."[2] In April 1789 the abolitionist Thomas Clarkson and a committee for the abolition of the slave trade in London produced a three-dimensional diagram of a slave ship. They based the diagram of the loading of the slaves in the hold on the dimensions of the slave-trading ship *Brookes*.[3] The slaves were forced to lie front-to-back like sardines. As such it was physically impossible for the slaves to dance in the hold. The only way dance could possibly have taken place was if slaves had been moved onto the deck of the ship. We have evidence that this was so from the account of a surgeon on board *Brookes*. Commenting on a 1783 voyage, Dr. Thomas Trotter stated that the slaves were forced to take part in a ritual after their morning feed, called "dancing the slaves": "Those who were in irons were ordered to stand up and make what motions they could, leaving a passage for such as were out of irons to dance around the deck."[4]

In 1791, Alexander Falconbridge, who worked as a surgeon on a slave ship, testified before the select committee of the House of Commons,

The Abolition of the Slave Trade. Or the Inhumanity of Dealers in human flesh exemplified in the cruel Treatment of a young Negro girl of 15 for her virgin modesty, **by Isaac Cruikshank (1756–1811). Published by S. W. Fores, No. 3 Piccadilly, April 10, 1792. (© National Maritime Museum, London)**

"After meals they are made to jump in their irons. This is called dancing by the slave dealers."[5] Apart from the practical need to clean out the holds below deck, there were also questions of economic viability. It made economic sense for sea captains to use dance in keeping the slaves healthy. The healthier the slave the more money the captains made when it came to selling them at auction. This is clear from the evidence given by James Arnold, testifying in London before the Parliamentary Committee for the Abolition of Slavery:

> In order to keep them in good health it was usual to make them dance. It was the business of the chief mate to make the men dance and the second mate danced the women; but this was only done by means of a frequent use of the "cat." The men could only jump up and rattle their chains but the women were driven in one among another all the while singing or saying words that had been taught them, "Messe, messe, mackarida," that is: "Good living or messing well among white men," thereby praising us for letting them live so well. But there was another time when the women

were sitting by themselves, below, when I heard them singing other words and then always tears. Their songs then always told the story of their lives and their grief at leaving their friends and country.[6]

In 1807 a youth named Richard Drake kept a journal of the slaving voyages he was making. Drake wrote, "The Captain and I had a chat about this African business. He says he's repugnant to it, and I confess it's not a thing I like. But, as my uncle argues, slaves must be bought and sold: somebody must do the trading: and why not make hay while the sun shines? This voyage (he was a few days out in the Atlantic) proved particularly sickly: We had half the gang on deck today for exercise; they danced and sang under the driver's whip, but are far from sprightly.... Last Tuesday the smallpox began to rage, and we hauled 60 corpses out of the hold ... we stimulated the blacks with rum in order to get their help in removing corpses.... The sights I witness may I never look on such again. This is a dreadful trade ... some of the blacks are raving mad, and screech like wild beasts."[7] This extract suggests that some of the Africans expressed the agonies of the death and disease about them in a terrible dance and music that was incomprehensible to the European sailors. The strong connection between African song and dance is clear when we turn once again to Alexander Falconbridge:

> Exercise being deemed necessary for the preservation of their health, they are sometimes obliged to dance, when the weather will permit their coming on deck. If they go about it reluctantly, or do not move with agility, they are flogged; a person standing by them all the time with a cat-o'-nine-tails in his hand for that purpose. Their music, upon these occasions, consists of a drum, some times with only one head; and when that is worn out, they do not scruple to make use of the bottom of one of the tubs.... The poor wretches are frequently compelled to sing also; but when they do so, their songs are generally as may naturally be expected, melancholy lamentations of their exile from their native land.[8]

It is clear from these quotations that the term "dance" is used with cynical irony. The prime necessity for the traders was keeping slaves healthy during their voyage across the ocean. Therefore they made the slaves move about, even when wearing chains, by beating them until they were exercising. This was not dancing in any African sense. All the same, we can read into these accounts a quite different story. Whenever they were allowed to do so, the slaves sang and danced as a way of expressing their emotions. Inevitably, at this stage, the only dance they would have known would have been their own dance from Africa. They did what they had been accustomed to doing in their own African societies, where dance and song were unself-consciously used to express a wide range of feeling and cover a wide range of activities. Even in the horrifying environment of a slave ship, whenever they could, the slaves reverted to their African dance tradition not only as a defiant means of protest but as a desperate means of cultural survival. Drake, who spent fifty years in the slave trade between 1807 and 1875, made this clear in a report. He began trading the very same year that it became illegal to trade in slaves in England. On a voyage aboard a slave ship Drake reported, "Our blacks were a good-natured set, and jumped to the lash so promptly, that there was not much occasion for scoring their naked flanks. We had tambourines on board, which some of the younger darkies fought for regularly, and every evening we enjoyed the novelty of African war songs and ring dances, fore and aft, with satisfaction of feeling that these pleasant exercises were keeping our stock in fine condition, and of course enhancing our prospect of a profitable voyage."[9]

George Pinckard, a London physician, gives a description of a dance aboard a slave ship in 1816: "We saw them dance, and heard them sing. In dancing they scarcely moved their feet, but threw about their arms, and twisted and writhed their bodies into a multitude of disgusting and indecent attitudes. Their song was a wild yell, devoid of all softness and harmony, and loudly chanted in harsh monotony."[10]

The "disgusting" dance that Pinckard described was also noted by another observer, Sir William Young, who described life aboard ship after a visit to St. Vincent: "In particular I was disgusted with a general jumping or dancing of the negroes on the deck, which some, and perhaps many of them, did voluntarily."[11]

These quotations make it clear that African dance was beyond the comprehension and well outside the dance experience of most European observers who could only see it as "disgusting and indecent."

The dancing aboard ship did not only consist of Africans dancing together at the crack of the lash, but also dancing employed for the questionable physical pleasures of captain and crew. As Young noted: "Once off the coast, the ship became half bedlam and half brothel. Ruiz, our captain, and his two mates, set an example of reckless wickedness, and naught but drinking and rioting could be seen among the men. They stripped themselves, and danced with black wenches, whilst our crazy mulatto cook played the fiddle. No attempt at discipline; but rum and lewdness seemed to rule all."[12]

Sometimes this conduct aboard slave ships involved white men raping black slave girls. In May 1763, Robert King, a Quaker from Philadelphia, who owned many vessels, bought Olaudah Equiano from Equiano's previous owner, one Captain Duran. Equiano worked on board King's slave ships on voyages around the Caribbean until he bought his way to freedom in 1766. In his published autobiography, Equiano gave a vivid and brutal account of a horrific incident while aboard a slave ship to the Caribbean. Unfortunately, as he made clear, this was not just an isolated incident:

> I was often a witness to cruelties of every kind, which were exercised on my unhappy fellow slaves.... It was almost a constant practice with our clerks, and other whites, to commit violent depredations on the chastity of the female slaves; and these I was, though with reluctance, obliged to submit to at all times, being unable to help them. When we had some of these slaves on board my master's vessels to carry them to the other islands or to America, I have known our mates to commit these acts most shamefully, to the disgrace not of Christians only, but of men. I have even known them [to] gratify their brutal passion with females not ten years old; and these abominations some of them practised to such scandalous excess, that one of our captains discharged the mate and others on that account. And yet in Montserrat I have seen a black man staked to the ground, and cut most shockingly, and then his ears cut off bit by bit, because he had been connected with a common prostitute: as if it were no crime in the whites to rob an innocent African girl of her virtue; but most heinous in a Black man only to gratify a passion of nature, where the temptation was offered by one of a different colour, though the most abandoned women of her species.[13]

Resistance at times included the slaves' refusal to dance their African traditional dances aboard the slave ship at the beck and call of the Captain. The print by Isaac Cruikshank called *The Abolition of the Slave Trade* is proof of this.[14] The hand-colored etching by Cruikshank was based on the trial of Captain Kimber who was tried at the Admiralty on June 7, 1792, on a charge of murdering a slave girl by terrible punishments for refusing to join the other slaves in dancing while on board a ship. The prosecution had two eyewitnesses, the ship's surgeon and one of his shipmates, both of whom gave evidence before the Committee for the Abolition of the Slave Trade — and both of whom were committed for perjury after Kimber was acquitted. Subsequently, although unable for legal reasons to make direct accusations, they mentioned the murder to William Wilberforce the day before one of his speeches calling for abolition. Wilberforce believed Kimber substantially guilty and thought the witnesses "scandalously" used, but according to Wilberforce's biographer, "Kimber took a different view. When he was released, Kimber demanded 'a public apology, £5,000 in money and such a place as will make me comfortable.'"[15]

In his book *Blind Memory,* Marcus Wood wrote that the subject in the print *The Abolition of the Slave Trade*

> concerns a notorious case brought before the House of Commons. In parliament, Wilberforce accused Kimber of murdering a teenage slave girl. She had refused to "dance" on the deck of his ship, the common form of exercising slaves, and as a result it was claimed he flogged her to her death. In the subsequent case, very inefficiently handled by the abolitionists, Kimber was in fact cleared, but the caricaturists took up and travestied the story. Isaac Cruikshank introduces sexual elements: the girl is strung upside down virtually naked before the leering captain and apparently punished for refusing Kimber's advances, an element which did not appear in any official evidence. Her agony and degradation are the stimulus merely for bawdy innuendo on the part of her torturers, one of whom, while gazing between her legs, makes an allusion to the availability of white women in the London docks: "Jack our girlies at Wapping are never flogged for protecting their modesty." "By God that's too bad if he had taken her to bed with him it would have been well enough." While the young black woman hangs mute and inverted, grinning, fully clothed, white males flank her. The title *The Abolition of the Slave Trade* bears an ironic relationship to what is shown in the print. The viewer's sympathies are invited to be with the white men; the black girl, whose breasts and buttocks are fully exposed, is not permitted to show her face.[16]

Wood concludes: "As material for the graphic satirist blacks are a strange combination of the familiar and unfamiliar. Part of the semiotic inheritance has represented them as alien beings, mysterious objects, of their essence funny, but the site for terrible anxieties and repressions involving white sexual confusion and guilt about the slave trade. But as well as being represented within this confused iconographic inheritance, blacks were also very much a social reality."[17]

Wood is looking at the print in terms of not only the white caricaturist but also of the white viewers at whom it was aimed. He is probably right in suggesting that whites' feelings about blacks were strangely ambivalent. As the movement for abolition grew in importance, many Londoners who looked at the print must have disliked and felt guilty about the slave trade. They also equated black nakedness with their own guilty feelings about eroticism and sex generally. They also found whatever evidence there was of black culture, such as the dancing, the singing and the rhythmic drumming, altogether beyond their comprehension. Certainly the sailors shown in the print have no appearance of guilt, but are habituated to the trade in human beings.

Wood argues that "the viewer's sympathies are invited to be with the white men." This seems unlikely. Kimber is depicted as a red-necked, bibulous tyrant. His toothless, open mouth adds to this lecherous profile, giving him an unsympathetic air. Our sympathies (viewers of any sex or color) are only with the black women in the print (three of whom sit in the background). It is their traumatic experience that grabs our sympathies.

Wood makes no mention of the three naked women in the background. They are important in this horrific image. The middle figure is clearly in grief, similarly to the figure in Edvard Munch's *The Scream*. This black woman is not screaming but wailing. She is the mirror image of the fifteen-year-old girl. She is reacting to the action in front of her. We sense the agony of the slave girl who is strung up and clutching her forehead. Much of the pain is in the apparent movement of her body. She is off-center; the arched back and bent right leg add a physical sense to her struggle. She is refusing to hang passively, implying that she is a fighter. This is a powerful image of black dance as protest. For the slave girl, in what ways was the significant meaning of her dancing in Africa changed when she was forced to "dance" those Africanized movements for her white oppressors aboard a slave ship? Was she prepared to die rather than submit to the captain and crew? Does the print suggest a degree of black solidarity?

In several respects the central black woman in the Cruikshank etching grabs the sympathy of viewers. It is against this background of grief for the black woman and scorn for lustful white men in the painting that DuBois wrote in his essay "The Damnation of Women":

> I shall forgive the white South much in its final judgement day: I shall forgive its slavery, for slavery is a world-old habit; I shall forgive its fighting for a well-lost cause, and for remembering that struggle with tender tears; I shall forgive the so-called "pride of race," the passion of its hot blood, and even its dear, old, laughable strutting and posing; but, one thing I shall never forgive, neither in this world nor the world to come: its wanton and continued and persistent insulting of the black womanhood which it sought and seeks to prostitute to its lust.[18]

The etching's text representing sailors' words does take some of the focus away from the girl's protest as its theme. In many ways it is an erotic image and meant to appeal to white eyes as such. Yet it is important to remember that for whites the rape of black women was perceived as being different from the rape of white women. According to Angela Y. Davis, rape of African women during the European slave trade was manifested in an "institutionalised pattern": "It should be a mistake to regard the institutionalized pattern of rape during slavery as an expression of white men's sexual urges, otherwise stifled by the specter of white womanhood's chastity. That would be far too simplistic an explanation. Rape was a weapon of domination, a weapon of repression, whose covert goal was to extinguish slave women's will to resist, and in the process, to demoralize their men."[19] As we have seen, it was common for blacks to be forced to dance against their will. By refusing to dance, the African girl was possibly asserting herself as a human being.

The Antiguan Revolt

Kimber's ship might well have been one of the many slave ships intending to unload their cargo at Antigua. Had they done so, the newly arriving slaves might very well have been told of what was by then part of the folklore of Antigua, the slave revolt of 1736. Antigua, a small Caribbean island, is situated forty miles north of Guadeloupe and twenty-five miles northeast of Montserrat. Written history really begins with European arrival in the fifteenth century when Christopher Columbus saw the island in 1493 and named it Santa Maria de Antigua after a church in Seville, Spain. According to his brother Ferdinand, the locals (Caribs) called the island Yaramki (Jamaica) and described it as a "country abounding in springs."[20] Even though it has wonderful harbors and sheltered bays, Antigua remained unsettled by Europeans until 1632, when an Englishman named Edward Warner led an expedition there.[21]

For the next ten years, the settlers focused on producing tobacco. This was deemed unprofitable since the tobacco market was flooded with cheaper and better tobacco from Virginia. During the 1650s, the planters changed to sugarcane cultivation.

The origin of the sugar industry on the island, according to the Caribbean historian and planter Bryan Edwards, can be traced back "chiefly to the enterprising spirit and extensive views of Christopher Codrington of Barbados." According to Edwards, "This gentleman removing to this island about the year 1674, applied his knowledge in sugar planting with such success that others, animated by his advice, and encouragement, adventured in the same line of cultivation."[22] Codrington, whose first plantation was called Betty's Hope (one of seven sugar plantations), had a major impact on the sugar industry.

Sugar was the chief commercial trading item for the Caribbean in the eighteenth century. The West African slaves made up a considerable part of the labor force in Antigua. They consisted of Mandingoes, Coromantees or Akan, Pawpaws, Nagoes, Mocoes and Ibos, together with slaves from Angola and the Congo.[23] In the early eighteenth century, the Coromantees were the ethnic group the planters in Antigua preferred to have working for them. This is clear from the writings of the island's governor-general, Christopher Codrington, who wrote, "There is a difference between them and all other Negroes beyond what 'tis possible for your Lordships to conceive. There never was a rascal or coward of that nation, intrepid to the last degree, not a man of them but will stand to be cut in pieces without a sigh or groan, grateful and obedient to a kind Master, but implacably revengeful when ill treated."[24]

The Coromantees seemed suited for the oppressive and suppressive Antiguan plantations, where, according to John Newton, "it was seldom known that a slave had lived above nine years."[25] But, as the Antiguan plantocracy discovered, the slaves' intrepidity could manifest itself in ways that did not always benefit the planters. This was evident in the slave uprisings in the early eighteenth-century plantation society.

One such revolt came after the speaker of the House of Assembly, Major Samuel Martin of Greencastle, was killed by his Coromantee slaves. In 1701 Major Martin was murdered by his slaves for withholding the statutory three-day holiday at Christmas. Fifteen new Coromantee slaves had taken on the role of negotiators. When the negotiations reached a stalemate, the slaves cut off Major Martin's head. The governor, Codrington, was told how the murderers "cut off his head which we afterwards took up in the grass, where they had washed it with rum, and triumphed over it."[26] Given what we know of the African dance tradition, I wonder if the celebrations included any dance. If so, what kind of dance?

The governor accused the major of being "guilty of some unusual act of severity" because the Coromantees "are not only the best and most faithful of our slaves, but really all born heroes."[27] Yet, in 1729, another localized Coromantee revolt occurred on Crump's plantation. It too failed, resulting in the banishment of the conspirators.[28] In 1736, an even bigger scheme to transform Antigua into a West African kingdom was planned. As David Barry Gaspar has pointed out, the Court/Klass revolt was significantly different from most slave revolts.[29] It was not the usual spontaneous revolt by overworked, oppressed and ill-treated field hands. The conspirators were supposedly the crème de la crème of the slave society, or so some historians argue.[30] They were mainly domestics and slaves who were artisans and had better jobs than the field hands. They dressed differently from other slaves, and they stayed in the main house or the factory as opposed to being out in the hot sun. They were given easier tasks and had greater privileges, especially in terms of movement within a very restricted slave society.

In 1736, the group of Coromantees involved in the Court revolt planned to blow up Government House. Their intention was to kill all the whites and institute black rule. The rebels paid dearly. In less than four months eighty-eight slaves were executed. Of these, five slaves were broken on the wheel, six were gibbeted (hung up alive), and seventy-seven were burned. Among those executed were three waiting men, fourteen carpenters, eight coopers, one coppersmith, one sugar boiler, two masons, one butcher, twenty-seven slave drivers, three coachmen, one millwright, three fishermen, one "head field negro," and one drummer. The occupations of the other rebels were not given.[31] The leader of the revolt, Court, was beheaded. His head was stuck on a pole at the door of the jail and his body was burned. Other slaves were burned alive or were gibbeted at the marketplace in St. John's until they were near the point of death, at which point they were removed, executed and their heads displayed on poles, either on the plantation or before the jail.[32] Moreover, the trade in Coromantee slaves was suspended.

King Klass, alias Court/Tackey, had been one of the prime movers in the revolt.[33] The plan had been to blow up the governor and the chief planters who had been expected to attend an annual ball commemorating the coronation of George II in St. John, a ball scheduled to be held on October 11, 1736. At the same time, a fighting vanguard was to seize the forts and ships in the harbor while, on a signal, the slaves would rise up on all the estates, killing and burning, before converging on the capital. But the ball was postponed for two weeks because of the illness of the governor's son, the plot was discovered, and three traitors informed on their leaders. Court and ten other ringleaders were condemned and executed. What is fascinating here is that as part of the preparations for the uprising, Court and the other leaders had openly staged a "military dance and shew"—to be precise, a war dance (which they called "akem" or "ikem"). The purpose of this was to find out how many followers were prepared to take part in the rebellion. Two thousand slaves had attended. Even though it was viewed by many unsuspecting whites as a dance entertainment, for the many slaves it held a binding significance, for it was the same dance as that performed by the Coromantee king in Africa in front of his captains once he had decided on war. Court danced the role of the king in Antigua. As part of this war dance, aiding the king were his "brasso," or marshal, and "asseng," or chamberlain. In October 1736, the music and ceremonies slowly built to a crescendo when Court made and received a sacred oath.

"Tomboy was the greatest General," reported the published account, "to whom the Ceremony of the Oath in the Coromantee language was addressed by Court, the bystanding Slaves huzzaed three times, the Coromantees knowing, but the creoles not understanding the engagement they entered into by it. For to some who knew it, things appeared so audacious and terrible, that some of the Coromantees endeavored by means of jumping among the Dancers and Spectators, and otherwise endeavoring to prevent it being performed, apprehending the Meaning of it might be discovered; being nothing could be intended by it less than a Declaration of War, and that of necessity against the Whites."[34]

Again, what is important here is not the rebellion itself so much as the ceremony that preceded the declaration of war. Court was not only dressed in the full traditional Coromantine war costume but, even more importantly, he was able to perform the "ikem" dance with such proficiency that some of his countrymen tried to stop it. Apparently, two elders were his principal advisors.[35] The intriguing aspect about the whole event is that it clearly showed that the African dance tradition was very much alive in Antigua in 1736. It shows that the older slaves remembered their cultural traditions and that even though some slaves came to the plantations at a very young age, their cultural heritage had not been entirely lost. In Ghana, the Ashanti (the Coromantees of the slave ships) now call it the "asafo" dance and these days it is used for ceremonial purposes rather than as a preparation for war. David Barry Gaspar has helpfully described the "ikem" dance in Antigua that survives to the present day.[36] What nobody seems to have noticed is that the same dance, movement detail for movement detail, still exists in Ghana. This brings fresh evidence to the information conveyed by David Barry Gaspar. In 1736, therefore, the weight of evidence suggest that rebellious slaves were using a dance which was well known in West Africa, and which has survived there to the present.

In his thoughtful analysis of the revolt, David Barry Gaspar has pointed out the chasm that existed between the white judges' understanding of the affair, and the ways the black participants interpreted events for themselves. What can be noticed in passing is how lax and permissive many Antiguan planters had become in their relations with their slaves. Many of the prohibitions on slaves' behavior were violated or ignored seemingly at will. Court, the leader of the revolt, had his own horse and was allowed to move around the island as he pleased by an indulgent owner who not only had great confidence in him but also had offered him his freedom. This offer had been refused, a refusal that can best be understood in terms of Court's own mental attitude. Court saw himself as a highborn member of Akan society on the Gold Coast, taken from there to Antigua by force. He was treated as their leader by the large number of Akan slaves in Antigua. As a leader, according to Gaspar, his manhood required him to take his freedom back by force because he had been robbed of it by force.

The double lives seemingly led by black slaves, especially men, has already been discussed. One way of life was restricted to their relations with the world of the whites. Their other way of life was jealously guarded by them from any intrusions by whites, so much so that whites had no knowledge at all of what was going on in the black secret world which existed around them.[37] The judges in the trials of the accused noted that Court, leading the largely African-born Akan ethnic group, made an alliance with a black slave, Tomboy, who was generally recognized as an important leader of the growing creole ethnic group on the island. The judges interpreted this alliance in terms of expediency, and it certainly made sense in those terms. Gaspar points out that it was much more than that. The Akan and the creoles were not separate and distinct ethnic groups, since creoles were themselves descended from African-born slaves. In the secret world of slave society in Antigua, kept strictly guarded from any white knowledge, the African-born Akan tended to seen as elders, wise ones, whereas the creoles tended to be seen as the young men, representing strength and energy. This was a direct reflection or imitation of Gold Coast society, and showed how, in the relatively early days of slavery, many African attitudes and assumptions persisted, unknown to the whites.

Among the ten main ringleaders of the plot, Court was African-born, and eight were creole, while one seemed to have arrived in Antigua as a child. Court was thus explicitly assuming the role of an African chief while his "generals" were recruited from the young men. Over a period of at least a year and probably more, the ringleaders recruited adherents to the plot by appealing largely to the sense of manhood and honor of those recruited, which could be restored by winning back freedom. This made the ceremony of the war dance particularly apposite. It was carried out, as were so many secret activities of the black slave world, in full view of the whites, with the black participants confidently secure that the whites would remain blissfully ignorant of what was going on — in effect a traditional declaration of war by a chief against his enemies.

According to the official report quoted above, the Coromantees understood what was going on but many creoles, while prepared to "huzza" three times, did not really understand what was involved. This seems unlikely. As we have already noted, there was a secret world among black slaves about which whites were kept ignorant. Once the revolt had failed, it would be sensible and politic for creoles to claim that they had not understood what was happening. Yet they were there, taking a full part in the ceremony when it happened. Is it not more likely that in a cross-cultural way, even though they were not Akan themselves, they were sufficiently versed in their African cultural heritage to have a reasonable grasp of what was involved? It would be easy to deny this in any subsequent questioning by the whites, since the slaves were quite accustomed to hiding a secret world which included the dance of the shout as well as the Akan war dance, the "asafo," from any white questioning.

In the same way, those recruited to the plot were bound by an equally potent African ritual ceremony of oath taking, in which drinking liquor mixed with cock's blood and dirt taken from the graves of buried slaves made it religiously important, backed by the presence of an Obeah man embodying the old African religion.[38] In these ways African dance, African music and African religion had clearly not only survived the Atlantic crossing but were also seen as crucial in the secret world making up attitudes and assumptions that were kept from the whites. The whites present indulgently watched a ceremony about which they understood nothing and did not care. For the world of the black slaves, so adept at keeping their secrets safe from white understanding, the dance was both a link with their past and a terrible way of announcing to themselves their fearsome intentions. There is yet more relevant evidence to add to David Barry Gaspar's information. A series of watercolors will be analyzed in detail in chapter 5. It is sufficient here to note that they provide evidence that the solo danced in the "ikem" war dance has not only survived in Antigua to the present day, but also is still regularly danced in Ghana — and, even more interestingly, seems to have been used in one of the improvised sets of the quadrille as it was performed by black dancers in London in 1820.

After the 1736 revolt, Antigua was more or less calm. According to Samuel Martin in his *Essay upon Plantership*, this was because "an insurrection can never be successful in these islands, while Britain has such ample power to suppress and take vengeance upon the rebels."[39] The creation of the naval dockyard at English Harbour in 1725, later called Nelson's Dockyard after Lord Horatio Nelson, symbolized the planters' power. Although the job of the squadrons stationed there was to defend the English colonies from French, Spanish, and Dutch attacks, another function was to suppress any revolts among the slaves. The very existence of the naval dockyard must have been intimidating for the slaves themselves.

According to John Horsford, the Antiguan plantocracy were renowned as being the most progressive and compassionate in the Caribbean.[40] They were clearly surprised by the African uprising and showed some ferocity in suppressing it, in spite of this supposed reputation for compassion. They had showed even less compassion in 1710 when they had murdered the governor, Colonel Daniel Parke. His harassment and condescending treatment of influential individuals in the community had not endeared him to the planter class. So they murdered him. The governor's house was burnt down and his murderers were never brought to justice. Granny Sarah, a slave, remembered "perfectly well the rejoicing on Bacra's (which is what blacks called the planters) being let out of gaol, who killed Governor Parke."[41] The whole incident helps to highlight many of the complex issues these small societies had to face.

Parke had been a greedy individual. He had been single-minded and blinkered in amassing a small personal fortune at the expense of the planters. He did not take the time or make the effort to know or understand the unwritten rules that permeated the way the whites in Antigua lived. At the time of the murder, according to Richard Sheridan, Antigua was a "family-centered society where the great families (65 such families) were units of considerable permanence and power." He adds: "It was the rare outsider who made a fortune without also adding his name to the pedigree of a local family of prominence."[42]

In 1672 there were 1,052 white men compared to 570 blacks in Antigua.[43] The slave population in 1734 was 24,408,[44] compared to a local defense force of only 1,373 men, 1,223 of whom belonged to the militia, while the remaining 150 were soldiers stationed on the island.[45] By 1810, there were 3,000 whites to 37,000 blacks.[46] It must be remembered that in Antigua at least fifty-two of planter families were away from the island for long periods. In the years 1730–75, these included twenty London–West Indian merchants, twelve M.P.'s, nine titled persons, and one Lord Mayor of London.[47] The planters did not travel alone to London. They took many of their house servants with them. It must be remembered that numbers of slaves as well as their owners were accustomed to spending long periods of time both in London and Antigua. This would mean that black Londoners were well aware of what was happening in the Caribbean. This is not supposition, although it would be common sense to assume that slaves who came with their masters to London stayed with them and accompanied them when they returned back to Antigua. The literature of the time provides plenty of examples of this. Beef was the servant of the magistrate John Baker, who resided both in England, where he served as a barrister of the Middle Temple, and on St. Kitts in the Leeward Islands, where he was Solicitor-General. Baker kept a diary of entries for over twenty years, beginning in St. Kitts at the end of 1751.[48] Most of the entries describe business, but they also provide hard evidence of the journey back and forth from England to the Caribbean. In fact, the journeys of Beef to the Caribbean lasted for three years at a time.[49]

Similarly, Olaudah Equiano, who experienced slavery in what is now the U.S. South and the Caribbean spent much of his life in England. For instance, he tells us that "in the year 1783 I visited eight counties in Wales."[50] In the spring of 1784 he sailed to New York,[51] and returned to London in January 1785.[52] During March 1785, he was in Philadelphia[53] and returned to London in August.[54] In October 1776 he arrived in Jamaica.[55] In November he was bound for England.[56] During March 1788, he says, "I had the honor of presenting the Queen with a petition on behalf of my African brethren."[57]

A third and later example was Mary Prince who in 1831 was the first black British woman to escape from slavery and publish a record of her experiences. Prince was a servant in Antigua from 1814 until 1827 when she escaped and worked as a servant in London.[58] The movement was in both directions. Slaves returning from visits to London talked with fellow slaves about what they had experienced in London. The privileged class among the slaves, the house slaves, made these journeys. Just as Equiano discussed the conditions of his "brethren" in the Caribbean, so the "brethren" in the Caribbean were aware of the house slaves' experiences in London.

In Antigua, house slaves and field slaves took part together in the same social functions. Sunday was market and recreation day.[59] It was also a day to dance — the slaves danced together at least once a week. Even as late as 1844, it is interesting to discover, Antiguans were still dancing their own native dances, using their own musical instruments. In his book *Antigua and the Antiguans: A Full Account of the Colony and its Inhabitants*, published in 1844, Frances Lanaghan wrote: "Africans are content with their own native dance, and their music of the Bangoe and Tum-tum. Christmas is the principal season for these assemblies, although there are subscription balls held once or twice a week, in some of the small houses at the back of the town ... some of the Christmas balls or 'quadrille parties' are however, conducted upon a very grand scale."[60] It is clear from what Lanaghan writes, that when black Antiguans came together to dance, they apparently danced their own African dances to their own music and European dances, like the quadrille, to European music. It would be appropriate here to remember the minuet congo mentioned in chapter 2. Although a mention is all we have of it, it would seem reasonable to assume it represented some combination of European and African dance.

In 1814, Jane Austen published her novel *Mansfield Park*. Edward W. Said makes much of the visit in this novel of Sir Thomas Bertram to Antigua as an example of the way England's upper class increasingly depended for its wealth on colonial exploitation. What should be noted here is that in this novel, Sir Bertram spends most of his time in England and only visits Antigua when his plantations are in difficulties and require his personal attention. Like the planters in real life, he spends as much or more time in England as in Antigua.[61] Yet for the 37,000 blacks in Antigua in 1810, the great majority of whom were working in the plantation fields, life remained hard and exhausting.

The busiest time on the sugar plantation was during crop time. The gangs of slaves cut, bundled and then transported the cane to the factory where it was processed by skilled labor into crude muscovado sugar. These skilled slaves were boilers, masons, carpenters, blacksmiths, wheelwrights and coopers. The season lasted from January until July. Once the crop was harvested, the most difficult job was holing, which was the preparation of the ground for planting.[62] The slaves were also assigned to mend roads, see to any factory repair work and clear ponds. This they referred to as the "dull season." When the crop was dealt with there were the usual harvest festival ceremonies in which dance played a major part. These harvest festivals and the dance in them are described in *A History of Antigua, The Unsuspected Isle*, by Brian Dyde.[63]

Sunday was the one day off on the plantations, where slaves could be seen dancing in the afternoons when the great market was over. In 1788, according to John Luffman,

> Negroes are very fond of the discordant notes of the banjar and the hollow sound of the toombah. The banjar is somewhat similar to the guitar; the bottom, or under part, is formed of one half of a large calabash, to which is prefixed a wooden neck, and it is strung with catgut and wire. This instrument is the invention of, and brought here by the African Negroes, who are most expert in the performance thereon, which are principally their own countries' tunes, indeed I do not remember ever to have heard any thing like European numbers from its touch. The toombah is similar to the tabor, and has gingles of tin or shells; to this music I have seen a hundred or more dancing at a time, their gestures are extravagant, but not more or so than the principal dancers at your opera house, and, I believe, were some of their steps and motions introduced into the public amusements at home, by the French or Italian dancers, they would be well received.[64]

Luffman here shows admiration but little technical understanding of the African dance he is watching. In the same way, he assumes that dancers in the London opera house would be French or Italian. In fact, at this time most of the dancers in the London opera house were English, trained in ballet schools long established in London.[65] Luffman shows little understanding of the steps and motions of either African dance or European ballet and is unaware of the technical problems involved if either were to attempt to incorporate steps from the other.

In 1791, William Young writes of a dance at his Old Road plantation ("in the evening we had a very smart well dressed Negro ball in the hall of my old mansion") and describes how he and his companion "both impartially allowed the Negroes, young men and girls, to dance better in step, in grace, and correctness of figure, than our fashionable, or indeed any couples at any ball in England; taking that ball generally, there is no one negro dances ill. I danced a country-dance with old Hannah, and a minuet with Long Nanny. Not a complaint remains at the old road."[66]

The two quotations above illustrate two different but important aspects of cultural survival. The first describes African music and African dance in Antigua in 1788. The second describes black slaves taking part in European social dances in 1791. It is fascinating to see that African dance and African musical instruments had survived so vigorously in Antigua. But it is also fascinating to see how in a negro ball in Antigua, European dances are performed with such grace and correctness. These are vivid examples of the process of creolization described in chapter 1. In a modern carnival in Antigua, one can see that elements of both African dance and European dance have survived. Antiguans are still dancing a version of the quadrille and they are still dancing at least a solo from the asafo, the Akan war dance. Both these elements are now incorporated in a new creole identity, of which Antiguans are justly proud. One element is clearly African in origin and one element is clearly European in origin. But both are now firmly part of a creole Antiguan identity. Both these aspects have to be borne in mind when we discuss the attitudes to dance of the blacks in London and the kinds of dances they adopted.

Before doing so, there is one further example to be analyzed. In 1733 a serious slave revolt occurred in South Carolina, part of the then English colony of West Virginia. Richard Cullen Rath has discussed it in detail.[67] Unfortunately when Rath came to deal with the jig, as part of his analysis of the revolt, he seemed unaware of the long history this dance form had in European dance and theater, certainly from the Middle Ages onward. (The origins of the jig are discussed in chapter 2.) He quotes, seemingly with approval, a recollection written in 1876 by Henry W. Ravenal harking back to childhood and maintaining: "The jig was an African dance, and a famous one in old times."[68] The jig is not an African dance but an established European dance form, which was adopted along with so many other forms by black slaves imitating the behavior, music and dance of their masters. Yet at the same time there can be no doubt that Rath's analysis of the musical element of the jig as a vivid example of the practice of creolization was perceptive. The European form of the jig was transformed into a series of coded messages for its black slave hearers, incorporating and paraphrasing the drumming they were forbidden to do by planter society. As Rath commented: "It was no coincidence that two of the most-frowned-upon activities in which a coastal lowlands slave could engage after 1740 were reading and particular forms of music — namely, the loudest forms, drums and horns."[69]

Rath was enlarging here on a notice in the *South Carolina Gazette* in 1733 offering a reward for the return of a runaway slave, one Thomas Butler, known as "the famous Pushing and Dancing Master."[70] Rath thought it unusual and ironic that the notice should refer to a slave as a master. Here he again showed little appreciation of eighteenth-century language. In the eighteenth century, almost everybody knew what a dancing master was and all gentlemen of means employed them to teach not only how to dance but how to behave generally, how to bow, how to sit and how to eat. It is a pity that Rath should seem to betray some ignorance about this common eighteenth-century usage. When Lord Chesterfield wrote to his son to emphasize the importance of dancing, he was taking it for granted that a dancing master was teaching his son.[71] Nevertheless, Rath did point out that this runaway slave was famous, according to the notice, for teaching "pushing and dancing."

Quite rightly, Rath wanted to know what this "pushing and dancing" represented. What was pushed and what was danced? He cleverly extrapolated from Angolan and Congolese warrior dances in Africa to the capoeira dance still popular in Brazil where it is called capoeira de Angola.[72] The "pushing and dancing" is a form of dance that comes close to actual physical combat. It is done to the music of bowed stringed instruments. Rath suggested that the origins of this dance form's popularity may well have depended on there having been no weapons available and drums being forbidden. The planters who forbade the drums might well have been unable to understand the significance of the percussive element of the music. The bows were in fact substitutes for drums.[73]

Rath produced a splendid example of creolization. A dance form that existed in Angola and the Congo was adopted to suit the conditions of slavery and yet retained much of its African punch and vigor. As danced in Brazil it still does retain this, even though it has long dropped out of use in the Caribbean and in Carolina. As the dance scholar Nathaniel Hamilton Crowell Jr. has pointed out, many Congolese dance forms still survive in Caribbean dance.[74]

Three years before the failure of the uprising on the Caribbean island of Antigua in 1736 where West African dance played a vital part, something similar occurred in South Carolina. A group of at least twenty slaves, all from central Africa, "Surpriz'd a Warehouse belonging to Mr. Hutchenson, at a Place called (Stono); they there killed Mr. Robert Bathurst and Mr. Gibbs, plunder'd the House, and took a pretty many small Arms and Powder."[75] This created a dangerous crisis. Unarmed slaves had taken over a warehouse stocked with guns and ammunition. Possibly they managed to overthrow any guards with the very "pushing and dancing" described above. Marching south, beating forbidden drums as they did so, their numbers rising rapidly to somewhere between sixty to one hundred, the insurgents stopped outside Charleston and "set to Dancing, Singing and beating Drums."[76] Obviously the drums were sending encoded messages that most Africans would have understood. White planters had no chance of decoding their messages, although they had feared the drums sufficiently to ban them. The planters gathered their forces and — in a pitched battle — more than twenty whites and twenty slaves died before the slaves finally ran away. Runaways were captured and shot in the following weeks but the uprising was not suppressed for at least a month.[77]

Rath carefully analyzed the role of the drumming. It was to be expected that if any African culture survived, drumming was an integral part of a protest that equally used singing and dancing to express itself and to arouse its adherents. Rath rightly sees this as an example of creolization. The fighting, the protest and the uprising were all the direct result of slavery that belonged to black experience in a white world. The manner of assembling forces and triumphantly celebrating the power of rebellion through drumming, singing and dancing were all essentially African. As Rath says, "by shifting the focus of the inquiry to the path between underlying structures and concrete cultural expressions, it becomes possible to discern how Africans from diverse regional backgrounds came to understand each other in ways that were broadly 'African' rather than 'Coromantee,' 'Mende,' or 'Angolan.'"[78] This supports one of the major contentions stated here, that the main characteristics of African dance were cross-cultural throughout the many regions displaying the rich variety of dance in Africa.

Summary and Conclusion

What has been shown in this chapter is the way music and dance were — and still are — not only inextricably intertwined in African society, but that most of the implicit assumptions about them survived the Middle Passage. Their influence pervades the Caribbean and the black communities in the United States in so many ways that it would be absurd to maintain as Frazier did, that African culture more or less perished in the crossing. The African contributions to western musical and dance culture have been considerable. But all this chapter has attempted to do is to show that when the slaves left the Caribbean for London, they carried with them as part of their mental baggage, not only the European culture into which they were forcibly immersed, but also a great deal of the African culture from which they had been torn.

4

The Importance of Dance for the Black Community in London and Its Growth and Development in the Seventeenth, Eighteenth and Nineteenth Centuries

In order to understand the importance of dance for the black community in London, it is necessary to first examine the growth and development of that community. It has been argued that although there were a surprising number of blacks in London in the eighteenth and nineteenth centuries, their aims were largely submerged within the general aims and movements of the working class as a whole.[1] This was not so. Obviously, black members of the working class shared many of the grievances and disadvantages of the working class as a whole. Yet, it is significant that subtle racial differences still tended to keep whites and blacks apart. Not only did the black community develop a strong sense of its own identity and continue to use music and dance as it always had done, as an important way of dealing with the issues which affected it, but blacks also did not find it easy to identify themselves with a white working class which itself continually reminded them of the fact that blacks were inferior and different.

In dealing with this widespread prejudice against them, blacks had little chance but to develop a collective sense of their own identity. Perhaps the most important single phenomenon which enabled them to feel different from — even equal or superior to— the majority, was their response to music and dance. It is significant that when blacks came together, they did so not to listen to speeches, set up committees, and pass resolutions, so much as to enjoy making music and dancing.

I have described how important music and dance continued to be in the slave societies in the Caribbean. It is not surprising therefore, that dance continued to be the cement which did much to hold the black community together in London. Blacks were far from being submerged in the general working-class movements of the eighteenth and nineteenth centuries. They could not have joined those movements even if they had wished to do so. Racial prejudice herded them into a ghetto. It was their resilience in the face of this prejudice which gave them a strong sense not only of their own grievances, among which the very fact of slavery was prominent, but also of their own identity.

London was the center of black activities in England, according to Peter Fryer, Gretchen Holbrook Gerzina and Folarin Shyllon, until emancipation in 1834.[2] Black people in London during the seventeenth, eighteenth and nineteenth centuries appear to have succeeded in retaining a community life in which dance played an important role. While there are plenty of individual examples of black men making their presence felt in London, it is difficult to estimate the numbers of black people in London at any time during the eighteenth and nineteenth centuries. Even contemporary observers could only make guesses, which appear to have been based largely on the numbers of black people seen by individuals. In *The Gentleman's Magazine* in 1764, it was stated that "the number in (London) only, is near 20,000." Samuel Estwick, a West Indian agent, in a tract published shortly after the Somerset case in 1787, gives the figure as 15,000, adding, "scarce is there a street in London that does not give many examples" of blacks being part of the everyday scene.[3] But according to the authoritative Folarin Shyllon in his book *Black People in Britain, 1555–1833*, this figure (15,000–20,000) seems too high. Shyllon writes, "The black population during the eighteenth century was in a constant state of flux. While some blacks were arriving from the West Indies and America, others were returning. Ill-treatment, starvation, disease, and poverty took their toll among those who formed the 'permanent' black population." He concludes: "After weighing all these factors carefully, it seems that the black population in Britain throughout the eighteenth century at any given time could not have exceeded 10,000."[4]

It was in 1801 that John Rickman completed and published a census of the population of England, undertaken at the order of the House of Commons. The census returns revealed that the population of England and Wales was 9,168,000.[5] London, the largest city in the western world, contained 900,000 people. It has been estimated that the population of London in 1750 was 676,250.[6] If the population of England and Wales throughout the eighteenth century expanded from five to ten million, and if there were probably no more than ten thousand black people in England and Wales during the same period, then it is possible to estimate how many there were in London. On the reasonable assumption that the masters of black slaves tended to belong to the upper classes who were more likely to congregate in and around London, then the black population in London in 1730 at the lowest estimate would have been around three thousand, but was more likely to have been between five to seven thousand. The African population in London during the period was made up of two groups: the free and the slaves. Until the Somerset case in 1772 it would seem that the great majority were slaves. From then onward, the number of free blacks increased until 1834 when black slaves in both Britain and the colonies were emancipated. Gretchen Holbrook Gerzina makes this clear: "Up until 1783 Britain's black population consisted mainly of servants and former servants, musicians and seamen. Suddenly, with the end of the war with America, England felt itself 'overwhelmed' by an influx of black soldiers who had served the loyalist cause and who crossed the Atlantic for their promised freedom and compensation."[7]

From the sixteenth century onward, a growing body of black people formed a community in London. Continuity within an even larger black community was maintained from the seventeenth century. It will be important to examine how Africans got there, to investigate how the white majority regarded them and also how Africans tried to establish their own sense of identity and observe their continuing links with both Caribbean and African culture.

David Bygott states, "The first blacks in Britain may have been those who came here 2,000 years ago with the Roman Imperial Army, long before Anglo-Saxons arrived. Most of these blacks were Berbers or Moors from northern Africa. Some of them were personal servants or slaves (along with many whites). Other blacks were soldiers. Roman records refer to a body of 'Moors' defending Hadrian's wall, for example, in the far north of England."[8]

After the Roman occupation ended, some Romans may have stayed on, living in Britain permanently. Could any of these new inhabitants have been black? Did they intermarry with the many whites here? If so, did their children become the first black British-born people? There is very little evidence. Bygott, however, mentions that there are "some male skeletons found in a Roman-British cemetery in Yorkshire (that) have proportions which, some think, indicate African descent"[9] and that "the same is thought of a young girl buried in the ninth century in Norfolk."[10] Even if this is so, no lasting black presence resulted from the Roman invasion of Britain.

It is not until the end of the fifteenth century that we can be certain of a continuous black presence in Britain. Black musicians played at the royal courts in England in the early part of the 1500s. Bygott states that the name of "the black trumpeter who played for Henry VII and later Henry VIII is given in the wages accounts of 1507 as John Blak." He also mentions the Queen's two black servants, Ellen and Margaret. The court records show that in 1513 "gifts of ten French crowns were made to 'the twa blak ledeis.' Clothes bills refer to 'blak Margaret' and 'Elen More,' and in 1527 a payment was made to 'Helenor, the blak moir.'"[11] It is quite clear that the women being referred to here are of African origin.

The increasing evidence of black people in Tudor Britain comes from an age in which great advances in technology were being made. Better ships that could sail on the open ocean and better navigation meant that the previously unexplored could be conquered. At the same time the Portuguese and Spanish started to ship African slaves to Europe. They had set out to explore the coastline of Africa in search of a sea route to the spices of the East and to Ethiopia for gold. In 1441, a ship returned with twelve slaves from West Africa, followed by 235 slaves three years later. An eyewitness, Gomes Eannes de Azurara, recalled the suffering of the slaves.[12] Pope Nicholas V authorized the Portuguese to conquer and enslave any other heathens in Guinea.

According to Martha Warren Beckwith, the first blacks in England were slaves brought to Britain in 1440.[13] In 1555, John Lok brought five "blake" men from West Africa to England to learn English, so that on their return to Africa, they would "be a helpe to Englishmen" as interpreters. Cedric Dover states that "the first slaves sold in the English market were two dozen West Africans who were knocked down to curious English gentlemen in 1553."[14]

Among the first English sea captains to engage in the slave trade was John Hawkins in 1562. His voyage consisted of three stages (which were to become the traditional "three stages" of the future British slave trade). First, he sailed to Sierra Leone with a cargo of goods from England that he thought would appeal to Africans. According to Richard Hakluyt,

Hawkins "stayed some good time and got into his possession, partly by the sworde, and partly by other means, to the number of 300 negroes at the least."[15] The slaves were then transported to the second stage of Hawkins's voyage across the Atlantic to the Caribbean. Here, Spanish colonists wanted more laborers for their expanding plantations and were willing to pay a high price for them.[16] Their money allowed him to buy a third cargo—cane sugar, spices, hides and pearls—all wanted by people in Europe. This was the third stage. On each stage of the "Atlantic triangle," Hawkins made a profit. Everyone he traded with in Africa, America and Europe gained too.

Yet the English slave trade remained marginal until the establishment of British colonies in the Caribbean and until the introduction of the sugar industry in Barbados after 1640, and the setting up of the Royal African Company in 1662. When the political and social upheavals of the civil war period came to an end, England was ready to embark wholeheartedly on a branch of commerce whose importance to the English sugar and tobacco colonies in the New World was crucial. An English monopoly in this slave trade was granted to the Royal African Company in 1672. Between 1680 and 1686 the company transported an annual average of 5,000 slaves, mostly to the Caribbean. In 1698, the Royal African Company lost its monopoly, and free trade in black slaves was established. Most of Britain's slave ships sailed from Liverpool and Bristol, but many also sailed from London.[17]

The major contract for the trade in Africans was the "Asiento" or agreement of the King of Spain to the importation of slaves into Spanish colonies. The Papal Bull or Demarcation of 1493 debarred Spain from African possessions, so Spain made a contract with other nations for slaves. This contract was held by the Portuguese in 1600; in 1640 the Dutch received it, and in 1701 the French. The War of Spanish Succession brought this monopoly to England as part of the Treaty of Utrecht. The Asiento of 1713 meant England had a monopoly on the Spanish colonial slave trade for thirty years. England engaged to supply the Spanish colonies within that time with at least 104,000 slaves at a rate of 4,800 per year.[18]

It has to be remembered that the French also set up a triangular trade similar to the British, and so to a lesser extent did the Portuguese, the Danes and the Dutch. Nantes in France played the same role that Liverpool and Bristol played in the English slave trade, becoming steadily more affluent and important. From Nantes, the merchants sent ships packed with manufactured goods—knives, tools, trinkets, glass and gunpowder—to Africa. These goods were exchanged for slaves who were then transported in conditions just as bad or even worse than in English ships. The slaves who survived were then sold to plantation owners in the Caribbean in exchange for tropical products. The ships, then laden with sugar, tobacco, coffee, cotton, cocoa, indigo and other commodities, returned to Nantes and sold their goods at huge profits, ultimately financing splendid public buildings and luxurious mansions that are still the pride of the city.

Along the River Loire, factories making sweets, chocolates and preserves sprang up to take advantage of the incoming West Indian sugar, which made up nearly 60 percent of imports into the Nantes port; cotton was the other major import. In 1814, Louis Say founded Beghin-Say in Nantes, which is still refining 120,000 tons of cane sugar annually in France to this day. Slavery was abolished in French colonies in 1794, reestablished by Napoleon in 1802 and finally ended in 1848.[19]

The result of the 1713 Asiento meant that England became the leading slave trader and slave carrier of the world. While British ships were engaged in transporting large numbers of Africans in the Middle Passage, either to die en route or to end up in servitude, oppressed on the sugar, rice, cotton, and tobacco plantations of the West Indies and elsewhere in America, a sizeable number of blacks were landed on the English shores to be kept in bondage in England. Gretchen Holbrook Gerzina, writing that "others, depending upon the year and the source, put the figure somewhere between 10,000 and 30,000," puts the proper figure as "probably closer to 15,000."[20] It was the norm to allow captains of slave ships to transport a few "privilege slaves" in each cargo for their personal gain, and these slaves tended to complete the third leg of the journey and be sold by their captain owners. In Bristol in 1715, in the will of a ship's captain named Nightingale, "the proceeds of his two boys and girls, then on board his ship" were among his bequests.[21] In October 1718, a merchant named Becher Fleming left to Mrs. Mary Becher "my Negro boy, named Tallow."[22] Many West Indian planters also brought slaves with them when they moved back to England. As John Latimer points out, "It was doubtless through this custom that so many slaves were brought to England, lived, and died here in servitude."[23]

Black people began to appear in England from the sixteenth century and it seems realistic to say that the black man was a familiar sight in London from then until the middle of the nineteenth century. Clare Tomalin writes of this black presence in her biography of Samuel Pepys. She tells us that "in his diary on 27th March 1601, Samuel Pepys records Charles II has a dancer and had brought over French dances with him. Although what most struck Pepys that first evening was not any display of French dancing, but the skill of a black servant, Mingo, invited to show what he could do."[24] Tomalin later informs us that "Pepys himself owned and sold two slaves in 1670s and in the 1680s."[25] In the early nineteenth century, in the famous painting by David Wilkie, *Chelsea Pensioners Reading the News of the Battle of Waterloo,* unremarkably and taken for granted, there is a black man.

English captains of slaving vessels that went to Africa on slaving adventures would often be entrusted to take the sons and daughters of chiefs and kings to England to be educated.[26] It was in the interest of both parties that such visits to England took place. For Africans it was a way of learning about the foreigners who were playing an increasing and threatening part in their own lives. For ships' captains, the advantage was that these children often acted as hostages for the safety of the captain and his crew. In *The Atlantic and Slavery,* H. A. Wyndham had this to say on the subject: "The trading, which was the main object of Western enterprise in Africa, depended upon the good will of the coastal chiefs; nor were the Europeans able to rely on force to secure it."[27] David Eltis has provided an impressive analysis of the failure of European attempts to use African labor in Africa, which was one of the main reasons why the slaves were shipped across to the Caribbean and to the Americas, where they could be exploited as labor much more successfully.[28]

For those slaves brought to London, the London newspapers of the last quarter of the seventeenth century and the eighteenth century contain scores of "hue and cry" advertisements. The most distinguishing mark of a ship's captain in the streets of London was the black servant who attended him. The taste for black servants spread, until it became fashionable among the nobility to have such black servants, which in turn brought an increase in the population of black people to London. In 1714, when George I arrived in the metropolis to ascend the English throne, he brought with him two black servants. The blacks thus brought into Britain were treated little different from slaves. They were forced to wear collars like dogs, were bought and sold and beaten. Slaves in the Caribbean were treated at least as badly as this in the eighteenth century. When their owners brought them to England, the evidence of the "hue and cry" advertisements makes it clear that they continued to treat blacks in the same way. We know they had to wear collars.[29] We know they were bought and sold. We know they were beaten.

There can be no doubt about the horrors endured by those unfortunate enough to experience servitude. In a "hue and cry" advertisement in *The*

London Gazette for March 1685, a Colonel Kirke advertised the fact that his black servant boy of about fifteen years of age, called John White, had absconded: "He has a silver collar about his neck upon which is the colonel's coat of arms and cipher; he has upon his throat a great scar."[30]

There had always tended to be social unrest among the lower classes of London society. We have evidence of the socio-political change that was taking place in London from a black perspective, in the form of the black literary figure Ignatius Sancho. In his retirement, Sancho spent his last years writing letters. From his grocery in Charles Street, Westminster, Sancho watched the Gordon Rioters, and his letters in those early days of June 1780 provide something of a brief running commentary on the activities of the rioters.[31]

It was ironic that one of the commodities Sancho sold to the public was tobacco produced by the oppression of black slaves. Also, although some of the illustrations of the day depict blacks on the street taking part in the riots, Sancho identified so clearly with other London middle class shopkeepers that he was horrified by the Gordon Riots. One might have expected that as a member of perhaps the most exploited minority in London, the black community, he might have been on the side of those rioting against the establishment, but he was not. All the same it is clear that for him, as for the whole black community, Lord Mansfield was a hero (from his judgement in the Somerset case) which is why the burning of the Mansfield house is equated with martyrdom. Obviously the black community in London echoed and imitated the social hierarchies of London society. It contained some middle-class shopkeepers like Sancho and it would also have contained many more members who were straightforwardly working class. At a time of social crisis, such as the Gordon Riots, different groups within the black community would have tended to respond according to the social class in which they perceived themselves to be. It was their misfortune that in spite of the ways in which they identified with a majority white social class, at the same time they always felt excluded from that class because of their color. Sancho expressed the same response as other shopkeepers, but at the same time felt different from other shopkeepers. Among the working-class rioters there were black members of the working class as well as white, but they too faced much the same prejudice from their white fellow rioters. Dorothy George's investigative review of the Old Bailey Sessions Papers confirmed that from the records of people on trial for their alleged involvement in the Gordon Riots in 1780, at least one was black.[32]

That same year, on December 14, Sancho died in his shop and was laid to rest in Westminster.³³ Sancho had been a prolific writer, and one of his friends, Miss F. Crewe, gathered his letters and published them two years later in two volumes titled *Letters of the Late Ignatius Sancho, an African*, with a preface written by Joseph Jekyll M.P. in the form of a memoir on Sancho.³⁴ Some contemporary writers on Sancho, such as Paul Edwards, after studying Sancho's *Letters* concluded, "It must be acknowledged, in spite of occasional hints of tensions and ironies, that Sancho's letters point clearly to his almost complete assimilation into eighteenth century English society."³⁵ But the evidence contained within Sancho's *Letters* suggests otherwise.

Sancho was well acquainted with the literary figure Laurence Sterne, and the two became friends after Sancho read Sterne's sermons and *Tristram Shandy*, with the latter's compassionate position on subjugated Africans. Sancho asked him to "consider slavery—what it is—how bitter a draught—and how many millions are made to drink it." Moreover, he specifically pointed out that "of all my favourite authors, not one has drawn a tear in favour of my miserable black brethren—excepting yourself."³⁶

Sancho watched the Gordon Rioters from his shop. His commentary on the rioting makes it clear that he was identifying with other white members of the middle class, and to that extent he had certainly been assimilated into English society. Yet it is clear from his many other writings that he was well aware that being a black African meant that he would always be different, and that he fully identified himself with the plight of the black Africans in London as a whole. In a letter he wrote, "I am not sorry I was born in Afric."³⁷ In another letter he called himself "a poor Blacky grocer."³⁸ And in a letter to the fop Julius Soubise he wrote: "Look round upon the miserable fate of almost all of our unfortunate colour—superadded to ignorance—see slavery, and the contempt of those very wretches who roll in affluence from our labours."³⁹ This extract alone is evidence to refute Edward's claim that Sancho's letters "point clearly to his almost complete assimilation into eighteenth century English society." They make the opposite point. And there is further evidence. Brycchan Carey, writing perceptively about Sancho, notes, "On one occasion, he reflects with relief that he and his family 'were gazed at—followed, etc. etc.—but not much abused' on a day out, which suggests that racial taunting was a regular occurrence in their lives."⁴⁰

The presence of blacks during the Gordon Riots prove that they were not only concerned with fighting for their own cause but also were taking part in working-class white protests. At least two blacks are shown in an anonymous print depicting the riots, a work in the collection of the Walker Art Gallery in Liverpool.[41] Peter Linebaugh and Marcus Rediker note that two years earlier an anonymous eyewitness noted that multiethnic American sailors "were among the most active in the late tumults" of London in 1768. They were "wretches of a mongrel descent," the "immediate sons of Jamaica, or African Blacks by Asiatic Mulatoes."[42] It should be noted that the anonymous eyewitness described these "wretches of mongrel descent" firstly by their race, secondly by their nationality. Only after they have been described in this way was their occupation or class mentioned at all. As was undoubtedly the case with Sancho, they were seen first as being different because they were black. Whatever their place in the social hierarchy, a black man was clearly always aware that he could never fully assimilate into the London world, because that London world saw him first and foremost as a black man, as a member of an ethnic minority, and as inferior because of it. Blacks in London would be reminded of this in endless slights and insults endured probably daily. To suggest that black people assimilated so well that they lost their sense of a black community and of a black solidarity is to ignore the repeated evidence of what they themselves wrote. Some of them were middle class like Sancho, some of them were working class like those who took part in the Gordon Riots, but they were first and foremost aware that they were part of a black brotherhood, an ethnic minority, in a larger society that looked down on them because of their race.

This is made all the more clear by Peter Fryer in his book *Staying Power: The History of Black People in Britain*. In his chapter titled "The Black Radicals: The Everyday Struggle, 1787–1833," Fryer states:

> It is hardly surprising that, of the black people living in Britain in this period whose names are known, so many were fighters of one sort or another: political activists or prize-fighters. Everyday life was a grim struggle for all poor people in those days. Whoever did not learn this lesson was liable to become a victim. One such victim, chained to his master's table like a dog, was rescued ... from a house in Long Acre, in the heart of London, in 1814. According to the master, the lad he had chained up and 'otherwise ill treated' was his apprentice, whom he had brought from the West Indies two months before and who had cheated him of money and stolen his wine. No, he could not produce the boy's indentures. No, he had not paid him any wages. He had been going to send him back to the West Indies by the next fleet and had chained him up to stop him running away.[43]

This quotation makes two things very clear. It highlights the appalling conditions in which black slaves had to exist. It also makes clear that this

4. The Importance of Dance for the Black Community in London 113

particular slave was prepared to struggle against injustice. If he was not chained up his master knew that he would run away.

An indication of the political and social life of the blacks of London is the following news item in *The London Chronicle* from February 17, 1764: "Among the sundry fashionable routs or clubs that are held in town that of the blacks is not the least. On Wednesday night last, no less than fifty-seven of them, men and women, supped, drank, and entertained themselves with dancing and music, consisting of violins, and other instruments at a public-house in Fleet street, till four in the morning. No whites were allowed to be present, for all the performers were Blacks."[44] This news item warrants some detailed observation. First we should consider the social framework in which the dancing of the blacks took place.

In August 1773, two black men were committed to Bridewell for begging in the streets of north London. *The General Evening Post* of August 28, 1773, reporting the arrest of the Africans, considered them "common impostors" since they were making enough money from begging to support their wives in some comfort. According to the paper, while they were detained at Bridewell they were not only "visited by upwards of 300 of their countrymen," but also the solidarity that existed amongst the black community meant that their brethren "contributed largely towards their support during their confinement."[45] There could be no better evidence than this that there was at this time a black community bonded together working for each other. The management and administrative skills needed to mobilize the 300 visitors at Bridewell and the arrangement of financial assistance demonstrate the efficiency of the black community's strong networking mechanisms. Jean J. Hecht has made this point clear. In his view the black community had its own leaders who planned and arranged the political and social agenda. It was focused in certain taverns and public houses that were solely run by blacks.[46]

In order to understand what was happening in these taverns and public houses, it is helpful to remember the dance historian Robert Hinton's points about the 1793 slave uprising in Haiti. After the uprising, the French planters moved their slaves to Louisiana, the French colony in North America. Hinton tells us:

> One of the many factors leading to the Haitian Revolution was that the majority of the slaves there were Africans who remembered a life before slavery. Those Haitian slaves unfortunate enough to be brought to Louisiana brought with them the Afro-Haitian culture they had synthesized from their various African origins.... With the smells of the Haitian Revolution still fresh in their nostrils, the planters of Louisiana feared that

any large gathering of blacks was potentially revolutionary and in 1817 the City Council of New Orleans passed a law limiting slave gatherings to Sundays and designated Place Congo (Congo Square) as the site where blacks could dance under strict surveillance.[47]

The fact that the slaves were only allowed to "dance under strict surveillance" suggests that the planters recognized the potential of the black dance vocabulary to communicate resistance. This may well have been what Philip C. Yorke, diarist and former solicitor-general of the Leeward Islands, had in mind when recording certain aspects in the life of Jack Beef (John Baker's black servant). Yorke wrote: "The watering-places (in London) were much frequented by the West Indians. They formed a social circle of their own and were bound together ... by common interests ... of which the foundations had been laid in the West Indies, where the English families, owing to their small numbers, and the dangers which threatened them in common, from the rising of the blacks...."[48]

We must return to the news item in *The London Chronicle*, February 17, 1764: "[N]o less than fifty-seven of them, men and women, supped, drank, and entertained themselves with dancing and music, consisting of violins, and other instruments at a public-house in Fleet street, till four in the morning. No whites were allowed to be present, for all the performers were Blacks."[49] The fact that the blacks were able to enforce the no-white color bar suggests that the public house was at least managed, if not owned, by a black publican. The enforcement of the color bar in itself suggests that the blacks had some political clout in the first place. The public house may well have been one of the lively African centers mentioned by Philip C. Yorke.[50] Yorke also tells us that the servant of Jack Baker, a year before his death in 1771, a black named Jack Beef, was "on friendly terms with the white servants, and accompanies them to the theatres in London besides attending 'balls of blacks.'" Edward Long in 1772 described with some bitterness these black social circles which were very much bonding centers for black servants newly arrived from the Caribbean. "Upon arriving in London," Long wrote, "these servants soon grow acquainted with a knot of blacks, who having eloped from their respective owners at different times, repose themselves here in ease and indolence, and endeavour to strengthen their party, by seducing as many strangers into the association as they work to their purpose."[51] To illustrate this point further one need only turn to the peevish Phillip Thicknesse, who may have had a similar thought in mind when he wrote in 1788 that "London abounds with an incredible number of ... black men, who have clubs to support those who are out of place."[52]

An instance of this black political solidarity and the gathering of blacks for social and racial affinity and identity through dance was exhibited during the Somerset case. Blacks in London closely followed the proceedings of the case of their compatriot. As Granville Sharp wrote, "The cause of Somerset the Black continued from time to time, according to the convenience of counsel and the court, running through months, and occupying different days in January, February, May, down to the 22d June 1772, when judgement was finally delivered."[53] At each hearing there had been a core black group present. So the news of the day of judgment must have circulated quickly through black community. "A great number [of blacks] were in Westminster-Hall," according to *The Middlesex Journal* the following day, "to hear the determination of the case and went away greatly pleased."[54] In a more detailed report in the *London Chronicle* we read: "Several [blacks] were in Court to hear the event of the above case so interesting to their tribe, and after the judgment of the Court was known, bowed with profound respect to the Judges, and shaking each other by the hand, congratulated themselves upon the recovery of the rights of human nature, and their happy lot permitted them to breathe the free air of England. No sight could be more pleasingly affecting to the mind, than the joy which shone at that instant in these poor men's sable countenances."[55] A couple of days after the landmark judgment of James Somerset, the black community held a celebratory dance, a ball. "Near two hundred blacks, with their ladies," the *London Packet* reported, gathered "at a public house in Westminster, to celebrate the triumph which their brother Somerset had obtained over Mr. Stewart his master. Lord Mansfield's health was echoed round the room, and the evening was concluded with a ball. The tickets to this Black assembly were 5s. each."[56] There was an even greater involvement by the black community in all the issues which permeated the ever-more-powerful movement aimed at the legal abolition of slavery in the British colonies. When this was finally achieved in 1834, there were probably a whole series of elaborate black balls to celebrate the occasion.[57]

Eugene D. Genovese in his influential book on slavery in the Americas, *Roll Jordan, Roll: The World the Slaves Made*, has produced arguments that are almost as applicable to the black minority in London as they are to conditions in the Americas, even though it does mean leaping to urban London blacks at the end of the eighteenth century from American plantation slavery in the first half of the nineteenth century. Genovese carefully notes the stratagems and methods by which slave society managed to construct a sense of identity and to resist, albeit often passively, the oppression under which they suffered. The religion, the music and dance, and the folk culture which gradually emerged in the syncretism of creole culture were in Genovese's view, largely palliative in the long run.[58] An important group of scholars, including O. Nigel Bolland, Philip Morgan, Richard Follett, Christopher Morris and David Brion Davis have all examined the rebellious inclinations bringing master and slave into structural conflict, and have gone so far as to suggest that religion, dance and music in creole culture in effect tended to dissipate rather than underpin tendencies to revolt.[59] Religion, dance and music made life easier and more bearable, but they did not really change the social structures in any crucial way.

Here what was happening in London tended to part company with what was happening in the Caribbean. Until emancipation, slavery in the Caribbean was a given, a depressing fate from which there were few ways out. In London things were different. In the early days of slavery in the Caribbean islands, there had been a tendency for adventurous and rebellious slaves to disappear into inaccessible forests and mountains and swamps, in order to try to set up societies on their own. As the plantations became more organized, these hidden fastnesses tended to be either eliminated or strictly controlled, so that escape was much more difficult, making islands like Jamaica and Haiti, where hidden fastnesses continued to operate, the exception rather than the rule.[60] In London the process was different. Blacks who had run away from their masters set up complex and efficiently organized communities within the city slums, ones that not only looked after themselves, but looked after newcomers. For a slave being maltreated in London, there was an alternative, as we shall show. He or she could disappear into a black ghetto where not only was a welcome awaiting, but help and care as well.

Richard Follett in his perceptive *The Sugar Masters: Planters and Slaves in Louisiana's Cane World, 1820–1860*, makes very clear the oppressive systems in which slaves on the sugar plantations found themselves.[61] The slaves' only escape from the system was in building their own social structures, including religion, the all-important music and dance, and attempting to trade on their own outside the system.

It could be argued that in the early days of industrialization workers in the early factories found themselves in conditions not so very different from the kind of slavery that developed in some of the more enlightened plantations. Additionally, London blacks, where they were members of the working class (and almost all of them inevitably were) knew in much the same situation as their fellow whites. It should be remembered that Karl

Marx, living in London in the nineteenth century, was forming his ground-breaking theories about the inevitability of class conflict between the exploited and oppressed working class and an increasingly prosperous bourgeoisie, while observing what was happening around him in the city.[62] Anti-abolitionists often used the very arguments about the similarities between workers in the early factories and workers in the plantations, but the degradation and horrifying physical abuse of actual slavery made the differences between industrial workers and plantation slaves too great for such arguments to be effective.

Fortunately for London's black community, dance is an empowering experience, and in spite of the appalling conditions in which they found themselves black slaves were able to experience "fragments of autonomy," as Rebecca Scott has put it, through dance and music.[63] Eugene Genovese would consider these "fragments of autonomy" as effecting little change in the real structures of slave society.[64] The dynamics of black-white power in the plantation world were, all too often, depressingly paralleled in Britain's early factory systems. The black community in London were even more exploited, perhaps, than their white class peers since they were all too often seen as somehow inferior because of their color. Undoubtedly in industrial England, the centripetal forces of industrial and agrarian capitalism led to class alienation, and in the case of the black community, doubtless racial alienation too. When Sancho was reflecting the attitudes of his fellow bourgeois shopkeepers to the Gordon Riots, he obviously lacked the analytical tools that enable a Marxist historian to set the Gordon Riots in a wider context of inevitable class struggle. Cultural resistance in any Marxist analysis is not so much experiential and cognitive as a material result of the inevitable class conflict produced by the struggle for economic power and domination.

Yet there is a case to be made for the experiential and cognitive assumptions and attitudes of London's black community. Peter Way in his *Soldiers of Misfortune: New England Regulars and the Fall of Oswego, 1755–1756* gave a strikingly different analysis of the military disaster of Oswego from that of most historians. He looked at the dynamic role played by the rank and file in the making of this historical event. Regular soldiers, both European and colonial, fought authority through insubordination, desertion and mutiny, so making a military garrison ineffective. In pursuing their sense of what was right and just and their due, they in effect sabotaged a whole military operation, almost doing the enemy's job.[65] This is a good example of a set of individuals whose experiential and cognitive approaches, when added together, produced collective results that were very different from what the military commanders involved had intended.

Elsewhere, Way also examines the historiography of class and ethnicity in nineteenth-century America and distinguishes two tendencies among historians, one favoring a cultural model that accentuates the role of laborers in the construction of their own class, while the other tends to a more Marxist view of workers, particularly unskilled workers, very much at the mercy of economic forces over which they have little or no control. The black community in London found itself embedded in a class structure, enduring the stresses and strains of the particular class element in which they found themselves. Yet, at the same time they also had an additional sense of identity forced upon them by their different appearance. If any group was likely to construct their own sense of class and identity, it was likely therefore to be a black community which had a sense of their difference forced upon them by the majority of the whites around them.[66]

Lawrence T. McDonnell in his *October Revolution: Communism's Last Stand* has analyzed the processes that led to the storming of the Russian parliament in October 1993, and sees the event as one which can be analyzed in terms of social and political conflict.[67] The same can be seen in Way's *Oswego*. Individuals' experiential and cognitive behavior produced results which were unexpected by the politicians in charge. It would be equally possible and equally profitable to discuss the various ways in which black London society in the eighteenth and nineteenth centuries organized itself at least partly for cultural resistance, in terms of a Marxist analysis of the social forces at work. Let's look at the case of William Davidson, who was arrested by the police as one of the Cato Street conspirators. Davidson, one of the eleven men tried in April 1820 for the conspiracy, maintained in court that the jury would be against him because of his color.[68] The judge assured him: "You may rest well perfectly assured that with respect to the colour of your countenance; no prejudice either has or will exist in any part of this court against you."[69] Acting on the judge's noble and glorious sentiment of equality, the jury found Davidson equally guilty with the rest and Davidson was among the five who was hanged.

No doubt a Marxist analysis would explain the Cato Street conspiracy in terms of the economic structure of society and the inevitable class conflicts it produced. McDonnell has pointed out the ways in which the laws of the marketplace tended to eradicate differences between free men and slaves when one was buying or selling something to the other.[70] Yet what is more important is Davidson's state of mind during the trial. His statement is almost a cry of anguish at the injustice of the way he and his brethren were treated by the white majority. There has to be a sense of

4. The Importance of Dance for the Black Community in London 119

personal agency and cognition in any attempt to understand not only how he felt, but also how he and his fellow blacks organized themselves as a result of similar feelings they all shared. Admittedly, in the long run, the black balls, the social clubs and organizations that blacks in London so carefully structured, were to mean remarkably little in the light of history. Black communities were lost in a few generations and simply disappeared into the gene pool of the majority.[71] In any Marxist analysis, with its emphasis on the dictatorship of the proletariat, economic determinism and the interpretation of history as class war, in a process leading toward social amelioration, they would count for very little. Yet, for those taking part in them they counted a great deal. They provided a sense not only of identity, but also a sense of honor and self-respect.

The currently fashionable term "infrapolitics" in studies of racial minorities and economically exploited social groups applies with striking resonance to the black minority in London during the nineteenth century. James Scott, Robin Kelly and Walter Johnson have all explored a relatively new area in the understanding of how oppressed and exploited minorities function.[72] They suggest that "beneath the veil of consent, lies a hidden history of unorganized, everyday conflict."[73] It is no longer just a question of finding historical and cultural evidence of resistance to class and racial domination. Both Scott and Kelly want to change the ways in which scholars interpret resistance and quiescence among the black working class who do not appear to be engaged in formally or politically organized resistance. They both look at how scholars use concepts of power, politics and domination. Kelly in particular places great emphasis on forms of protest and even rebellion, in music, song and dance.[74] Although music and dance play an all-embracing part in African culture, producing attitudes, at least some of which survived in the process of creolization in the Caribbean and from there to London, they play a significant part in almost *every* known culture. And obviously dance, music, and other forms of popular culture serve multiple purposes, expressing everything from love to anguish, betrayal, individual hatred, and resistance to oppression. Examples can be drawn from a variety of cultures to show that the tendency to satirize, to caricature and even desecrate those wielding power, is a widespread human tendency. Francois Villon from medieval France, Shakespeare in Renaissance England, Sembene Ousmane of Senegal and Kabuki theater in Japan, although widely separated in time and geography, all share the same tendency.[75] It is a tendency I will note in the way the quadrille was used in black balls. To understand London blacks' use of the quadrille, Mikhail Mikhailovich Bakhtin's concepts of "degradation and grotesque realism" in *Rabelais and His World* are helpful. In a much-quoted passage, Bakhtin says that "to degrade is to bury, to sow, and to kill simultaneously in order to bring forth something more and better ... grotesque realism knows no other lower level; it is the fruitful earth and the womb. It is always conceiving."[76] Clearly cultural criticism of the powerful expressed in areas where the powerful do not necessarily dominate, is not only an example of resistance and dissent, but a way of expressing views quite outside the political process of dominant groups. The quadrille as danced in the black balls in London was a striking embodiment of this mode of political articulation.

Just as in the process of creolization black slaves in the Caribbean adopted the quadrille, but then subverted it and used it for their own purposes, so much the same process can be observed in the way that creole culture adopted the carnival. Bakhtin, in his study of Rabelais, devotes considerable space to the European carnival, and since his work was translated into English in 1968, a wide range of scholars from cultural studies, anthropology and literary criticism have tended to write of carnival as a liberating social ritual without equal, a systematic denial and reversal of the structures and hierarchies that normally order society. In the carnival, the oppositions of high and low, inside and outside, male and female, and so on, are riotously subverted in an apparent orgy of play, satire and ungovernable sexuality and pleasure.[77] Richard D. E. Burton devotes a whole chapter of his book *Afro-Creole: Power, Opposition and Play in the Caribbean* to the carnival in the Caribbean. He suggests that where the carnival is seen as subverting the status quo or reinforcing it, or indeed managing to do both simultaneously, it is all too often seen as an interruption, which upsets the smooth flow of normality for a brief period of happy riot and disorder, and then withdraws, leaving normality either undermined or reinvigorated according to the particular bias of the scholar writing about it. Burton suggests that carnival both challenges and reinforces the status quo, and quotes Roger Sales describing it as "a vehicle for social protest and the method for disciplining that process."[78] Burton then suggests that what happens in the few days of carnival are "not fundamentally at variance with what happens during the remaining 360-plus days of the year."[79] In his view, carnival merely intensifies attitudes which are either hidden, controlled or restrained at other times.[80] For blacks from the Caribbean in London, there were very few opportunities to indulge in the riotous overturning of the usual conventions, which European carnival involved. It was in the ribaldry and satire with which London blacks subverted the quadrille in their balls that a strong element of

4. The Importance of Dance for the Black Community in London 121

Bakhtin's "degradation and grotesque realism" surfaced.

As John Rule makes clear in his book *The Labouring Classes in Early Industrial England, 1750–1850*, "The old plebeian pursuits had been tamed by a process of suppression (counter-action) and then had been replaced (counter-attraction) by more acceptable (from the capitalist viewpoint), respectable, less dangerous 'rational' uses of non-work time."[81] The last bull to be baited was in 1811 and Rule quotes an old man regretting that such amusements had largely passed away among young men in 1849, along with skittle-playing, quoits and football: "There is less fighting now than in my day, for the young men now-a-days have not courage to fight as they used to do."[82] Yet, as both Rule and E. P. Thompson in his *The Making of the English Working Class* make clear, the early years of the industrial revolution "saw a growth in provincial pride and self consciousness." "As the new factory discipline encroached ... so self-consciousness was sharpened by loss," and this "conscious resistance to the passing of an old way of life" was "frequently associated with political radicalism."[83] Just as the black community found in dance an outlet for some of their frustration, so the survival of folk customs and leisure pursuits became a kind of resistance, too, in the early industrial revolution. This gives the black balls more importance. It is not suggested here that the total overturning of conventional behavior to be seen in the carnival can be seen in black balls, yet some of the irrepressible desire to satirize and send up dominant authority, which was so marked a feature of the old European folk carnival, was undoubtedly one of the many elements that made up the pleasure of coming together as blacks did, in setting up and organizing their dances.

There were other elements involved in the black balls. Peter J. Wilson, in his perceptive *Crab Antics*, analyzes the English-speaking but Colombian-owned island of Providencia which he regards as typical of some social and cultural patterns across the English-speaking Caribbean in the twentieth century. He discerns two distinct but complementary value systems at work, to which he gives the names "Respectability" and "Reputation."[84] "Respectability" represents the value system put forward by the churches, adhered to by a small middle class, and more generally by women of all social classes, for whom the church acts as "the principal public domain of sociability" and who tend to be more "devout" than their male partners. The key values are marriage, the home, self-restraint, work, education, economy, and respect for social hierarchies. "Reputation" is seen as a structure of values depending on the street and the rum shop where males gather to drink, play games, and talk noisily, competitively, with a sense of style that tends to turn everything into small drama. In the rum shop, Wilson writes, "conversations are uninhibited, animated and intimate, full of banter, joshing and confidence, quite unlike the style of conversation in the home."[85] It is a questionable jump in time, to go back from creole culture in the modern Caribbean to creole culture in the eighteenth and nineteenth century Caribbean. Yet most observers agree about the tenacity and long-lasting elements in Caribbean creole culture. The quadrille is still being danced in the Caribbean, particularly in Jamaica and Antigua. Given Peter Wilson's perceptive analysis of basic modern attitudes in the Caribbean, which he regards as common across the whole of the English-speaking Caribbean islands, just as the quadrille has persisted, it is likely that Wilson's basic attitudes have also persisted too, and in fact stretch back to an earlier century. It is then reasonable to assume that these two value systems, complementary but conflicting across the male/female gender divide, accompanied Caribbean creoles arriving in London. What is interesting about London's black community is that in its ability to organize, it reflected much of the organizing power of the church and the community back in the Caribbean, and thus could be seen as "Respectability." Yet the coming together of this organized community for a black ball involved both males and females in roughly equal numbers, since dances like the quadrille require an equal number of men and women to take part in them. The males in their desire to show off, to be competitive, and to do things in style, represented the set of values Wilson lumps under "Reputation." Thus the black balls represented a rare combination of the "Respectability" and "Reputation" sets of values. For many of the women, the black balls had elements strongly similar to a church social event. They would doubtless have brought food and drink which they had prepared in advance, and this would have been part of the careful organization which preceded the balls themselves. It would have been a relatively rare occasion when women in their leisure time ventured outside the home. The men, on the other hand, would have been accustomed to congregating outside the home, and showing off to each other in the ways covered by the term "Reputation." Apart from church services, they would not have been accustomed to social events outside the home where women were present in equal numbers. This would have made the ball an important, special and different occasion. The ball would also have represented a rare chance to express some of the subversive and satiric elements that were to become such an important part of creole carnivals.

Difficulties of Assimilation

The three hundred people who visited the two black men in prison in Bridewell in 1773 have already been noted. They provide striking evidence of an organized black community.[86] Bridewell was packed with working-class poor people. It is unlikely that many of them were visited by three hundred people. The fact that two blacks were supported in this way was sufficient for the *General Evening Post* to make it a news item. What paper was marvelling at was the way in which an oppressed minority had so managed to organize itself.

Their need for a collective sense of identity had been forced upon them by the way in which the majority of white people looked down on black people due to skin color. Blacks knew that they were considered inferior. Bearing in mind the different ways in which the white community perceived the black minority, all these differences obviously impinged on the black community and affected the way they perceived themselves and their relations with whites. Every time they were treated differently, they would inevitably be pushed into a stronger sense of belonging to a black community that was different from the rest. The injustice of many of the ways in which they were treated would also give them a shared sense of resentment. The very process of existing as a black minority within a much larger white majority would have helped to reinforce a sense of black community.

As a result of this widespread prejudice, it was seldom possible for a black person to identify completely with a political issue or any movement strongly felt within the working class as a whole. This illustrates Homi K. Bhabha's view of the diasporic imagination as being consistently caught between the existential quandary of being "neither one nor the other" and shows the ambiguity and "doubleness" of self that can be seen to characterize Caribbean blacks in London.[87] As W. E. B. DuBois puts it, a member of the black minority always feels "twoness ... two warring ideals in one dark body."[88] In order to understand why dance and black balls played such a vital part in reinforcing a collective sense of black identity, it should be enough to look at the careers of two black political activists. Each in turn makes clear their awareness that being black cut them off from the majority of those involved in the very causes for which they were struggling.

These black political activists were Robert Wedderburn and William Cuffay. The radical Robert Wedderburn was born in 1762 in Kingston, Jamaica, the son of an African-born woman and a father who was a sugar planter who sold his mother when she was five months pregnant with Robert. Deemed free from birth by his mother's new owners, Robert was baptized an Anglican and given a decent schooling. He joined the Royal Navy before arriving in Britain in 1778 and became a skilled tailor until 1813 when he became a licensed Unitarian preacher. In 1819 he joined the revolutionary group of Arthur Thistlewood and formed a new group in Soho which became a center for political discussion. He managed to avoid being involved in the Cato Street conspiracy since he had been arrested for blasphemous libel the month before and was still in prison. In May 1820 he was given two years further imprisonment. Four years later he published his autobiographical *The Horrors of Slavery* and other writings. Wedderburn was responsible for the awareness of slavery among London artisans and radicals.[89]

Wedderburn makes his own position as a revolutionary—fighting the working-class cause, but still feeling different as a black man—defiantly clear: "Oh, ye Africans and relatives now in bondage to the Christians because you are innocent and poor; receive this the only tribute the offspring of an African can give, for which, I may ere long be lodged in a prison. For it is a crime now in England to speak against oppression.... I am a West-Indian, a lover of liberty, and would dishonour human nature if I did not shew myself a friend to the liberty of others."[90] This gives a harrowing picture of a man who even while fighting in the radical cause feels alienated from his fellow radicals, by his birth and the color of his skin.

Our second radical, William Cuffay, was born in Chatham, Kent, and was baptized there in 1788. His father came from St. Kitts and was a cook on a British warship. His mother brought him up. After becoming a journeyman tailor in his late teens, he stayed in that trade for the rest of his working life. He took part in the 1834 strike of London tailors for shorter hours, and this resulted in his being sacked from his job. In 1839 he joined the Chartist movement and helped to establish the Metropolitan Tailors' Charter Association. Two years later he was elected to the metropolitan delegate council and later appointed president of a five-man interim executive, after the arrest of the movement's national leaders. In 1844 he was on a committee opposing a bill which would have given magistrates power to imprison a worker for months merely on an employer's oath. Two years later Cuffay was elected one of the ten directors of the National Anti-Militia Association and he also became a member of the Democratic Committee for Poland's Regeneration. In 1847 he was on the central registration and election committee. In the following year he was one of the three London delegates to the Chartists' national convention and was appointed to chair the committee for managing the procession that on April 10 was to accompany the Chartist petition to the House of Commons from a mass meeting on Kennington Common. When this procession was banned and then called off, Cuffay protested strongly. He became a member of the Ulterior Committee that was planning an uprising in London. On August 15, eleven members, plotting to set fire to certain buildings as a signal for the rising, were arrested at the Orange Tree Tavern, Bloomsbury, and Cuffay was arrested at his lodgings the next day. He was convicted at the central criminal court on September 30, for levying war on the queen. After a defiant speech, Cuffay and two comrades were sentenced to transportation (deportation to a penal colony) for life.[91]

Cuffay was noted for his militancy. He was attacked by the press who made a point of referring to his blackness. *The Times* referred to London's Chartists as "the Black man and his party" and Cuffay was ridiculed in *Punch* and in the *Illustrated London News* in 1848, the latter writing of Cuffay's "nigger humor."[92] Both these examples make it very clear that even while fighting for their fellow white workers, blacks still felt alienated from the majority.

This chapter has concerned itself with demonstrating that throughout the period between 1730 and 1850, there was a sizeable black population in London. Against considerable prejudice and oppression this community established a sense of its own particular identity and worked together as a group. The black community was an undoubted presence in London and was recognized by contemporary commentators. It was greeted with distrust, suspicion and often downright hostility by many of those whites who wrote about it. Fortunately for the black community, and largely through dance, they were both able to reinforce their sense of identity and continue to struggle against the place in society so arbitrarily imposed upon them. It is now time to examine that dance in detail.

5

Interpreting the Visual Representation of Black Dance in London During the Nineteenth Century

It is important to use visual evidence to establish what kinds of dance were performed at black balls in London at the end of the eighteenth century and the beginning of the nineteenth. Blacks in an alien environment had dances and music that helped bond them together. They had emerged from an African culture where dance played a more significant part than it did in European culture and was significant in cementing group cohesion. Clearly, after the process of creolization, they cherished what remained of their African culture and at the same time were greatly affected by the new culture in which they found themselves. This dichotomy can be discerned in a set of prints which will be analyzed in this chapter. They will make clear that besides providing social enjoyment, which was the main purpose of the exercise, blacks also used dance as a means of bonding together, and by satirizing the behavior of the whites who surrounded them, they asserted not only a collective sense of their own identity, but also found a means of struggling against the oppression of the white majority.

So great was the cultural conditioning in Africa, in both rhythmic music and the dance that accompanied it, that even after the process of creolization an inherited, cultural predisposition to music and dance stayed with them, as I've shown. The black community knew and could see that they responded more sensitively to rhythms than the white people who were oppressing them. Understandably they clung to the last vestiges of their African culture; it helped to make them feel different and special. They shared a cultural knowledge of some dance steps and movements from Africa and they shared the old sense of the importance of music and dance. Inevitably, as the process of creolization took place, they found themselves more and more involved in the music and dance of the class that dominated and owned so many of them, yet their approach to it was bound to be different. There were harshly practical reasons why the process of creolization involved the slaves copying the dances and amusements of the Europeans. My great-grandmother, Rebecca James, herself a slave in Barbuda, told my father that slaves were banned from practicing their own African dances because increasingly the planters came to fear that they might lead to the sort of revolt that had been planned in Antigua. Only by adopting the dances of the Europeans were slaves able to congregate in large numbers. Often indeed, undercover, they were still then able to plan their revolts without the planters suspecting anything.[1]

Norman C. Stolzoff suggests that African musicians and creole house servants learned European music and dance and took these to the slave quarters where, to a certain extent, they transformed them by combining European elements with African traditions such as the traditional mento form. "The fifth figure of the quadrille, the finale, was the most popular and was typically performed in 2/4 mento form or 6/8 time."[2] Black slaves also used the dance to express some of their resentment at those whites who obviously felt superior to them, and yet who tended to move so badly and to miss out on so much of what the music had to offer. They could actually make fun of the clumsiness and arrogance of the whites attempting to dance, by caricaturing and satirizing that clumsiness. This was one of the few areas where they could see and feel how much better it was to be black, and they made the most of it. And what were the dance forms they had available in the new and alien culture in which, for better or worse, they were condemned to live? Before examining the series of prints, the origins of the quadrille, as set out in chapter 2, should be remembered.

Most of the blacks in London would have recalled the European dances that as house servants they would have danced in the Caribbean. The plantation system in the Caribbean developed an "us and them" situation among the slave population. The house servants believed that they were superior to the field hands.[3] This mattered when they came to learn European dances. Ex-slave Austin Steward, who was a Caribbean slave until 1817, recalled: "House servants were of course 'the stars' of the party: all eyes were turned to them to see how they conducted (themselves).... The field hands ... look to the house servants as a pattern of politeness and gentility. And indeed, it is often the only method of obtaining any knowledge of the manners of what is called 'genteel society'; hence, they are ever regarded as a privileged class; and are sometimes greatly envied."[4] The difference between house servants and "outer" servants, that is, those responsible for the gardens, the horses, and the carriages, although still a hierarchical division among servants in London, was a good deal less marked than those between house servants and plantation workers in the Caribbean. The quadrille was extremely popular in the Caribbean and was danced at all major social occasions held at the great houses in the islands. It was copied by the slaves and subsequently went through a process that one ethnomusicologist called "Afro-Caribbean transformation."[5] The "monthly or quarterly balls" included just one of the few forms of amusement for the planters in Jamaica, particularly for the wives.[6]

That dances like the quadrille, the cotillion and the minuet were performed in London by nonwhites, much as they had been in the Caribbean, is made apparent from the series of prints examined in this chapter. Some of these are by one "RFW," which would seem to refer to Robert F. Watson, a landscape and marine painter who exhibited from 1845 through 1866 at the Royal Academy. These watercolors would seem to have been early works.[7] Included, with one verse that appears under an image of a male central figure lying in state, with six figures supporting him. He is black, and wearing a red tailcoat with gold braiding, and tan trousers. Some of the figures probably represent aspects of his career; one is a sailor dancing a hornpipe, another an officer in red tailcoat, another a black gentleman. The other three are white—two men and one woman who look like musicians and artists. The verses that accompany the picture provide a number of tantalizing clues to the identity of the picture's subject. They suggest that he ended his life with a well-managed "cash and ledger," that he was skilled at writing "profuse panegyric in *Herald* or *Post*," and refer to his charges which "might well have astonished a Jew." All this implies some sort of journalistic skill, writing for cash, and expecting clients to pay heavily. There are also military references. It is a "Brigadier's breath" that "death has arrested," and he's referred to as "Captain." He would also appear to have served in Mauritius and in Spain.

Opposite: "RFW" watercolor sketch and verse, London, 1820, by Robert F. Watson. (Courtesy of Michael Graham-Stewart)

Hic Jacet

Nauta, Mercator,
Miles, Speculator,
Cheull Spectator.
Chas — —

Pause! Passenger, Pause! Ere your way ye pursue
Pay the tax of a tear, for the tribute is due
Here rest the remains of a right honest fellow,
Who's dropp'd from Life's tree like a pear that is mellow;
None abler than he to exorcise a Ghost,
By profuse panegyric in Herald or Post.
For a Guinea or two, he'd have made ye subscriber
To Charities reaching from here to the Tiber,
With a Garnish of "Talented" "Honor'd" "Respected,"
& your Widow as cheerful as might be expected.
An extra half Crown would have sent ye above
To Continue your well commenc'd labor of love.
So kind & so good was this Tenant of dust,
That is, He had been, had you chanc'd to die first.

"Ah G—r, how often together we've toil'd,"
"Well ice'd in the Winter, in Summer par-boil'd."
"All Business undaunted, with plenty to do,
"My Charges might well have astonish'd a Jew."
"& methinks, had a Viper attack'd such a File"
"As yourself, he'd have felt his Teeth ache a long while."
But Flesh is but Grass, & the venom of Death
Hath arrested sans mercy, the Brigadier's breath.
No more shall he visit the shady Mauritius,
For Curious Sharks & Sea serpents Nutritious,
No more shall the Trumpet of sunny-less Spain
Awaken the Captain to glory again.
& his well manag'd Cash & his Ledger unite
In Mutual Love & Esteem for the Night
For G—r reposes, his Glories are set
Let us hope when he rises, it mayn't be
              in Debt

CORONAT FINIS OPUS

"RFW" Verse Transcription

Hic Facet
Nauta Mercator
Miles Speculator
Eheu!! Spectator
Aetat —
Pause! Passenger, pause! Ere your way ye pursue
Pay the tax of a tear, for the tribute is due.
Here rest the remains of a right honest fellow,
Who's dropped from Life's Tree like a pear that is mellow.
None abler than he to exorcise a Ghost,
By profuse panegyric in Herald or Post.
For Guinea or two he'd have made ye subscriber
To Charities reaching from here to the Tiber,
With a Garnish of "Talented" "Honor'd" "Respected,"
& your widow as cheerful as might be expected.
An extra half Crown would have sent ye above,
To continue your well commenc'd labor of love.
So kind & so good was this Tenant of dust,
That is, He had been, had you chanc'd to die first,
Ah G_____r, how often together we've toiled,
"Well iced in the winter, in summer par-boiled."
"At business undaunted, with plenty to do,
"Thy charges might well have astonish'd a Jew,"
"& methinks, had a viper attack'd such a File"
"As yourself, he'd have felt his teeth ache a long while."
But Flesh is but Grass, & the venom of Death
Hath arrested sans mercy the Brigadier's breath.
No more shall he visit the shady Mauritius,
For curious sharks & sea serpents nutritious,
No more shall the Trumpet of pennyless Spain
Awaken the Captain to glory again.
Or his well manag'd Cash & his Ledger unite
In mutual Love & Esteem for night.
For G_____r reposes, his Glories are set
Let us hope when he rises, it maynt be
in Debt.

5. Visual Representation of Black Dance in London 131

Above and following page: "RFW" watercolor sketches, London, 1820, by Robert F. Watson. (Courtesy of Michael Graham-Stewart)

Britain captured Mauritius from the French in 1811, and the Duke of Wellington's Peninsular War ran from 1809 to 1814. It would seem that our subject might well have been a black officer involved in both these campaigns. J. D. Ellis, author of a thesis titled *The Visual Representation, Role and Origin of Black Soldiers,* has stated in a private letter, "I have never seen any direct reference to black officers in the Peninsular, but have heard anecdotally of one serving with the 28th Foot."[8] From the references to business and toiling in the winter and summer together with the writer of the poem, the subject might well have been connected with the supply of provisions to the army. The Latin at the head of the poem implies that not only was he a sailor as well as a soldier, but a pun may be intended on the word "speculator." The verse also makes clear that its writer served in Mauritius and in Spain with the dead man he is lamenting: "How often together we have toiled, in winter, in summer." Who the subject "G — r" is must remain a mystery. It has not been possible to track him down in army records of the period. What is plain from both verse and picture is a light-hearted, playful mood, and this should be borne in mind when looking at the pictures of the dances. It is highly probable that the funeral is really a mock ceremony, a private joke between the painter and his subject. It would be unlikely to adopt such a light-hearted attitude in the face of a real death.

The most important "RFW" illustration shows a ball with figures dancing. Two musicians are accompanying the dance. The piano is of a type made in the 1820s, although only a few were made in England.[9] The costumes too date from this period.[10] In this watercolor the figures are dancing the quadrille. Another illustration shows a man and a lady companion walking past a genuflecting man who bows in front of a cage with two monkeys in it. Another depicts a couple retreating from a man who doffs his hat. Yet another portrays the central figure as a dancer; his arms and fingers are held in an attempted ballet "fifth" position with the legs in a fouetté.

The monkeys in the cage are significant and give us a clue as to the ethnic identity of the dancers. They are black.[11] One of the common ways of seeing black people in the seventeenth and eighteenth centuries was as apes or monkeys.[12] There is also a possible contrast intended between the behavior of the figures in the front of the cage and the behavior of the monkeys in the cage. The black man dressed in the military uniform of an officer, approaches a black figure who is positively kowtowing, not merely bowing. The monkeys in the cage could be seen as mirroring this. One of them is upside down, while the other is upright, but turns away. Is there a suggestion in the picture that there is something monkeylike about the humans in front of the cage? There is another, perhaps even more distant and recondite connection between blacks and monkeys. Slaves were also made to play with monkeys in the slave pens in order to keep them free of lice and ready for sale at the auction block. This is apparent in the following description given by an ex-slave from Memphis, who remembered, "We stayed in there (slave-pen) three or four weeks. They would fix us all up and carry us in a great big old room and circle us all around every morning and every evening. They would have us up in the show room to show us to the people. They would hit us in the breast to see if we was strong and sound. Monkeys would play with us and see if any boogies (lice) was in our heads. They would do pretty well if they found any, but if they didn't they would slap us. They had the monkeys there to keep our heads clean. They made us dance and made us take exercise all the time we was there."[13]

John Gardner Kenneys wrote in a pro-slavery pamphlet published in 1783: "Every planter knows that there are negroes, who ... cannot be humanized as others are, that they will remain, with respect to their understanding, but a few degrees removed from the orang-utan (i.e. the chimpanzee and gorilla); and from which many negroes may be supposed, without any very improbable conjecture to be the offspring.... The Colonists of the West Indies are instrumental in humanizing the descendants of the offspring of even brutes ... to the honour of the human species, and to the glory of the divine being.... If the control we maintain over them is proved to be for their good, and to the welfare of society; that it is, probably, taming of brutes ... theirs (*sic*) and our rights will appear in very different points of view."[14]

Melville and Frances Herskovits noted that there were "'retentions' of Africanisms in Trinidad where the blacks exhibited motor behavior while singing, such as swaying of the body, and the manner in which handclapping is done with cupped hands rather than with flattened palms ... is African."[15] These subtleties of motor behavior can be seen clearly in the watercolors. They are depicted in the black dancing bodies. The traditional European aesthetic when dancing is notably the erect spine. The torso is held still and the knees straight, as discussed in chapter 2. European dancing requires that dancers' limbs move away from and return to a vertical center, with gestures that move upward and outward. This style of dancing is not visible in the print. Instead we see black dancers who have their body weight pitched slightly forward: there is a grounded feel and an apparent earthy quality to their movement, a "gettin' down an' wid it" quality that looks very much like Robert Farris Thompson's notion of "African art in motion" which characterizes the "Africanist" aesthetic.[16] Thompson is referring to aspects of movement that are more common to African dance than to European, such as a tendency to crouch rather than remain upright, a tendency to push the body forward on an inclined and not vertical plane, and a tendency to make the rhythm of the dance a counterpoint to the rhythm of the music.

The crouching position of the male dancers is obvious. And although they are all supposedly at the same point in the dance, each dancer is making his or her own individual variation on the movement. Arms and legs are doing subtly different things that represent the individual dancer providing unique rhythmic variation to the basic rhythms of the quadrille. While the dancers are all recognizably dancing the same dance, each dancer is adding something of his or her own, which is the "Africanist" aesthetic to which Thompson refers.[17] A closer look reveals that the dancers have reached a point in their particular quadrille where they are called on to improvise. Ellis Rogers says that in "the quadrille called 'Le Pastourell' a solo dancer has to improvise for eight bars of the music. In another set of quadrilles, known as Paine's 12th set, both a man and his opposite lady are asked to improvise for eight bars each."[18] They have deserted the usual positions of the quadrille and each is giving their own interpretation in a dance that looks far more African than European. Of the four men dancing in the central section of the watercolor, each is doing something quite different from the others. This looks far more like the shay-shay African dance still introduced in Jamaican performances of the quadrille.[19] As a result of the process of creolization, this is what we would have expected, an African dance, or something very similar to an African dance, introduced into a formal European structure. In the seventeenth century, when Samuel Pepys admired a black dancer's contribution, something similar was probably what he was admiring. We do not know how Doctor Johnson's black servant and his white wife danced, but he may well have introduced something similar when called on to improvise. It would be these moments in the dance when blacks in London would feel collectively different from and superior to the Europeans whose dance forms they were adopting and adapting.

There is more to observe in the other watercolors. It is clear there is an overall exaggeration in their dancing, even gesticulation. They stoop too low. They curtsey too low. The man in the broad-brimmed hat lifts it too high. The single male dancer has his leg raised too high for this type of dancing during the period.[20] How do we know? Fortunately there exists a wide range of textbooks on European dance from the period that make clear how precise movements in social dancing had to be. A close look at the illustrations from *Le Maitre a Danser (The Dancing Master)* should make this clear. It was written by Pierre Rameau, a distinguished dancing master, and dedicated to Elizabeth Farnese, the second wife of Philip V of Spain (1700–1746). This book provides one of the most valuable records of eighteenth-century technique. It is early in our period. But later textbooks all make it clear that the basic positions of dances like the minuet and the cotillion were rigidly adhered to.[21] A movement was either correct or it was wrong, and everybody knew what was correct. Rameau lays great emphasis on the exact angle at which arms should be held, the right depth for a plié or bent knee, the exact position of the feet and the hands, and gives detailed illustrations making the correct positions clear. He gives no less than six illustrations of the correct way to bow.[22]

The exaggerated movements depicted in the watercolors are intended to be satirical, in the same way as the verse that accompanies them. In fact there are two kinds of satire. The artist is white. He is intending to make fun of the black people he is painting. Whether or not he realizes it is unclear, but he is depicting black dancers who are themselves making fun

24	25
Premiere tems pour oster le Chapeau	*Deuxieme attitude de l'exercisse du Chapeau*
	32
La maniere de tenire son Chapeau a côté de soi	*Reverence de côté, saluant du costé gauche*

Above and opposite: **The Dancing Master,** by Pierre Rameau. Published London, 1725.

5. Visual Representation of Black Dance in London 137

Premier mouvement du Contreté

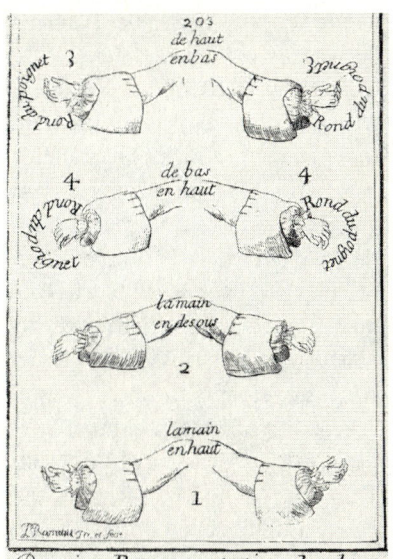

Premiere Representation des bras pour le mouvement des Poignets

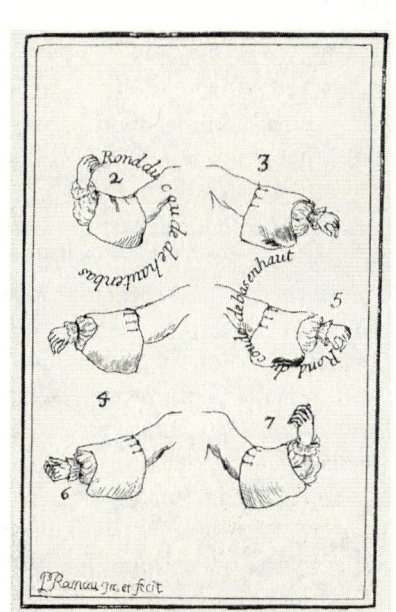

Demonstration du changement de l'oposition

Premiere Figure des saillies ou pace chapée

of the way the quadrille is normally danced. They stoop too low, as can be seen by comparing them with Rameau's illustration. The single male dancer has his leg raised too high. The arms and hands are hopelessly wrong. The artist probably knew all this. What he would not have known would have been why black dancers were so different from white dancers performing the same steps. Looking back at chapter 1, where we considered Savigliano's concept of the "colonizing gaze," it is interesting to see that even in the early nineteenth century the "colonizing gaze" already saw black dance, even when blacks were performing European steps and movements, as somehow alien and exotic. Black dancers were not altering the dance from lack of skill. On the contrary, they were deliberately Africanizing movements that were originally European.

The "RFW" watercolors provide an insight into the way in which black dance was more than just a social dance, but had also became politicized. The work of "RFW" provides revealing insight into the way blacks used dance as both social and political satire. The dancers are not just dancing a European quadrille; they are reinterpreting it. As Shane White and Graham White say in *Stylin'*: "Even if slaves were performing European dances such as the quadrille, the cotillion and the schottische, differences in style, the rhythmic complexity, the persistent improvisation, suggested that different cultural values underlay the performance."[23]

St. Lucia has set dances like the quadrille as part of its history. The quadrille was probably first introduced there in the 1820s after the English took control there in 1814. The St. Lucian "kwadril" is understood as quintessentially European, as linked with political and social power, as something born out of the plantocracy, which the locals now participate in openly and freely.[24] In Jamaica, it is clear that the quadrille was used for enjoyment. As an exhilarating social dance, called "katreel" or "kachriil," the quadrille is danced in many of the parishes, with different emphases. Five or six figures are danced within each set, and many include a framework drawn from the vocabulary of European dances, steps, and figures, including the waltz, polka, schottische, mazurka, and promenade. What is extraordinarily important is that local dances of African origin such as mento or shay-shay are often used as the last dance in the set.[25] Here we have striking evidence of the way African dance, combined with European dance, was danced to an "Africanized" form of European music played by black fiddlers but with a greater emphasis on drumming than would have been the case in Europe. Even more importantly, there are two quite separate forms in Jamaica: the "ballroom style," which is European, and the "camp style," with two lines of dancers, which is a sturdy

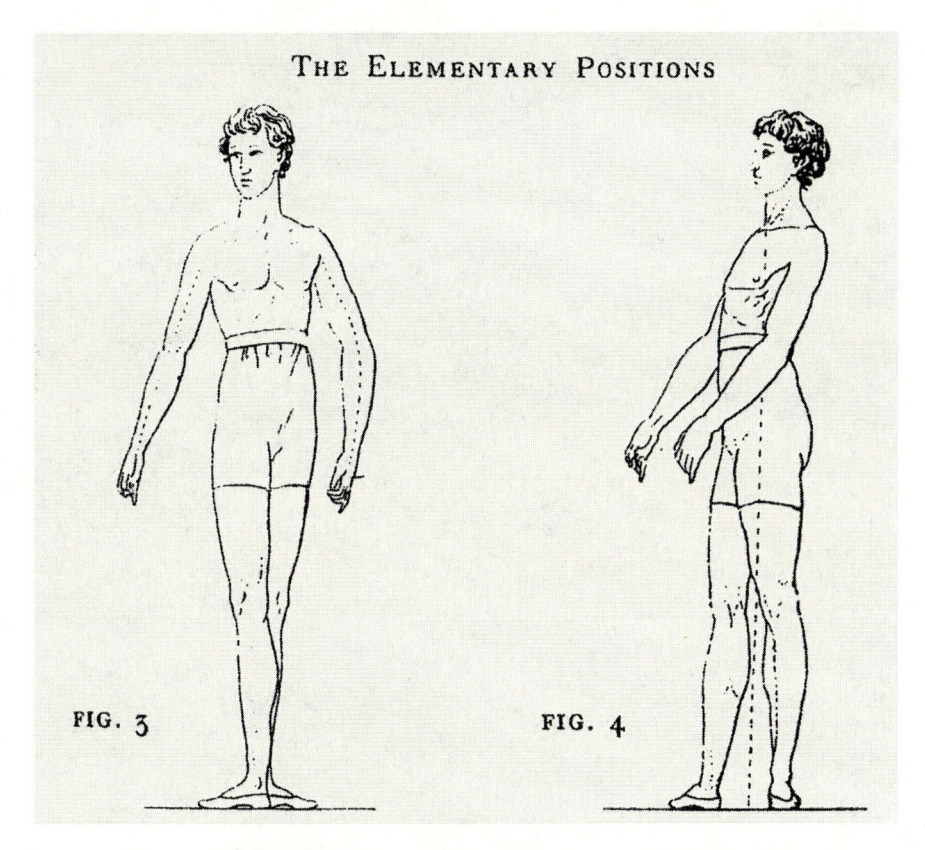

5. Visual Representation of Black Dance in London 139

THE ELEMENTARY POSITIONS

FIG. 3 FIG. 4

An Elementary Treatise upon the Theory and Practice of the Art of Dancing, by Carlo Blasis. Published Dover, 1820.

survival from the days when the quadrille was used to make fun of the slave owners.[26] This use of black dancing style was another contributing factor to both the continuity and the reinterpretation of African dance traditions in London. That the blacks in London in the eighteenth and nineteenth century continued this practice should be clear from the illustrations shown later in this chapter, particularly those published by G. S. Tregear. It is in this context of black expression that Albert J. Raboteau has succinctly noted: "Perhaps the most obvious continuity between African and Afro-American religions is the style of performance in ritual action. Drumming, singing and dancing are essential features of African and Afro-American liturgical expression."[27] Partly they did this because the remnants of their own culture had instilled in them a different approach to movement and music. Partly they used the dance as a way

of reminding themselves how badly Europeans danced and how much better Africans managed it.[28] And partly they were reinforcing in these ways their own sense of black solidarity, of black consciousness, and reminding themselves that they belonged to a visible community which may have been despised by Europeans but which they themselves felt was not only the equal of the European majority, but was in some ways superior to it. As a character later on in this chapter will claim, "when you comes to reg'lah dancing, niggers leaves 'em way behin'!" What the watercolors show us is black dance as a means of expressing a sense of collective identity and also as a means of making statements about the white majority, which reinforced the blacks' own sense of identity and defiance. Given the topicality of slavery during the slave trade abolition debates and the large black population in the London ports, it is not surprising to see that such watercolors as these exist.

A lithograph published in 1833 is a patronizing example of the way that whites in London viewed the struggle for emancipation. Published in London, the sketch by "HB" is titled *New West-India Dance, to the Tune of 20 Millions*. The humor comes from the idea that if the slaves are allowed to be free, then who will compensate their former owners? The man on the left, offering his hat to the man on his right, says, "As you called for the dance sir, I hope you won't have any objection to pay the Piper."

The man on the right, John Bull, representing England[29] replies: "Eh!. O. Yes. All to oblige the big Gentleman in the broad brimmed hat. Go to him."

The man in the broad-brimmed hat is the popular figure whom everybody associated with the fight for emancipation, William Wilberforce, though long since dead in 1833.[30] He was so well known that his face did not even have to be shown in the cartoon. Sadly the artist seems unaware of the way black people in London held their own series of balls and danced European dance forms. He shows black people as most English people in his day thought of them, as a set of primitive savages dancing a crude example of the earliest dance form, known as the ring dance.[31] The joke, if there is one, is all about money, confirming Napoleon's view of the British as a nation of shopkeepers. "*L'Angleterre est une nation de boutiquiers.*"[32] The other, nobler issues that William Wilberforce was at pains to express are here ignored. Worse still, there is no acknowledgement in

Opposite: *New West-India Dance, to the tune of 20 Millions*, HB Sketches No. 269. Published by Thomas McLean, London, June 18, 1833. (Courtesy of Michael Graham-Stewart.)

the cartoon of the sizeable black community in London, also working hard to promote emancipation. The role that dance actually played in Africa, in the West Indies, and for the black community in London, was apparently outside the artist's comprehension altogether.

In 1834 the London engraver and publisher, Gabriel Shire Tregear, who called his business "A Humorous and Sporting Print Shop," published *Tregear's Black Jokes: Being a Series of Laughable Caricatures on the March of Manners amongst Blacks*. For this W. Summers made a series of colored, numbered and titled caricatures to mock the social life of the newly emancipated slaves, taking its origins from Edward Williams Clay's series of prints *Life in Philadelphia*, published in America a few years earlier. A series derived from Clay's prints appeared in the *New Comic Annual*, published in London in 1831, which: "coincided with the rearguard action fought by anti-abolitionists which prompted the publication of a number of satirical prints in England."[33] Tregear expanded this series when he issued his *Black Jokes* just a year after the House of Commons passed the abolition bill in 1833.

Writing in 1989, Hugh Honour, in his survey *The Image of the Black in Western Art*, wrote of these engravings, "The 'jokes' in question were childish puns (of a type peculiarly popular in early nineteenth-century England) on the word 'black' as in black-ball or black tea, illustrated respectively as a dance and tea party attended by blacks. As there were virtually no black aspirants to middle class at this date in England, the popularity of the series can have been due only to the notion that blacks were figures of fun. Incongruity provides mirth; to the English a modishly dressed black may well have seemed incongruous. The prints that had begun as satires on fashionable affectations but acquired more serious, if fortuitous, implications as a result of mounting racial tension in Philadelphia, had been transformed into a series of coarse jokes at the expense of blacks, and perhaps Americans."[34]

The evidence would seem to contradict this assertion. First, as we have seen, a visible if small number of free blacks in London owned and ran businesses, mixed with aristocracy, and socialized with politically influential white men and women. The whites could see their upwardly mobile aspirations. There certainly were "black aspirants to middle-class at this date in England." Second, Honour has missed the point that blacks may well have been satirizing the whites in the prints he writes about. This is not really surprising, since the whites that were being satirized also missed the point when watching black dance itself. Like them, Honour has taken the prints at face value. Jean and Marshall Stearns, in their book *Jazz Dance:*

A Story of American Vernacular Dance, quote an elderly actor who remembered his seventy-year-old nurse explaining the point to him, about American slaves dancing in the early 1820s: "Us slaves watched white folks parties ... where the guests danced a minuet and then paraded in a grand march, with the ladies and gentlemen going different ways and then meeting again, arm in arm, and marching down the center together. Then we used to mock 'em, every step. Sometimes the white folks noticed it, but they seemed to like it; I guess they thought we couldn't dance any better."[35] He is referring, of course, to American slaves, not to British slaves, but a great deal of evidence has already been provided about the tendency to satirize and indeed the need to satirize, in an oppressed people.

Honour's view that these prints have transformed what in America were satires into coarse jokes for Londoners seems to miss the point, in much the same way as white observers missed the point when watching blacks making fun of Europeans in their dance. Entry to London black balls could on grand occasions cost as much as five shillings, not a sum readily available to the poor, although one shilling was the more normal charge. According to *Harris's List of Covent Garden Ladies*, in 1787 these black balls were also referred to as "an innocent amusement, vulgarly called 'black hops,' where twelve pence will gain admission."[36] London blacks were relatively prosperous. They could pay anything between twelve pence and five shillings to enter their own "black hops." The black community as a whole seemed to have supported those who were not prosperous; this implies both organization and financial resources.[37] Obviously the majority of black slaves could not have had much money at their disposal, but increasingly the black community of freed, former and runaway slaves, who made up the majority of those present at black balls, would have earned wages that put them on a par with other London workers, who were attending their own similar entertainments.[38] Phillip Thicknesse has stated that black clubs supported those who were "out of place." This made clear that the majority of those in the clubs were not "out of place" but had a place and were earning wages. Clearly the series of prints by Tregear intended to make fun of black people, but perhaps they also indicate that white people, while enjoying the prints, failed to see that much of the black behavior depicted in them had an element of satire of white people, which only black people understood and enjoyed. Hesketh J. Bell, writing of "West Indian life and character" in the 1890s, gives a vivid description of the steps danced at the black balls in the Caribbean that would also have been used in London, something Tregear's prints help make clear:

The negro has a remarkable capacity for observing and taking note of any laughable peculiarity or oddity noticeable in their employers or others of the upper classes, and any one listening to these belairs would be surprised to find what trifles attract their notice, and how mercilessly they lay bare the little *faiblesses* of their superiors. To replace these barbarous dances (belairs) the blacks were taught how to dance European steps, and many of them are very good waltzers. The upper class of black and coloured people now give what are called quadrille parties, and invitation cards are sent to their friends and acquaintances something in the style of one I came across in the kitchen the other day — "Mister Cudjoe requests the pleasure and company of Mister and Mistress John Bull, Esq., to a quadrille party on the 19th ultimo. 'Gentlemen, a candle; ladies, a dish ... In the ball-room ... the host or one of the guests is appointed Master of Ceremonies and is endued with supreme authority; which he sometimes exercises with the utmost disregard of *les convenances*. I have seen one of these gallant personages, like Beau Nash of old in the Pump Room at Bath, suddenly stop the music while a quadrille was going on, merely, as he said, to 'show his tority.' The music generally consists of a fiddle, scraped with the utmost disregard to tune or time, in conjunction with a tambourine, beaten *con furore*, and accompanied by a performer on the triangle, chosen, I believe, on account of the size and weight of his feet, with which he thumps the time on the floor, and which is really the *motif* to which the assembly cuts the fantastic toe, and a very fantastic toe it is, too. At the wedding of a man who was working for me, I was requested to open the ball in the first quadrille with the bride, an immense and most maternal-looking lady. But, alas, for my presumption! I had always considered the first figure simple enough, and flattered myself I would get through it without much bungling; I however, gave myself up for lost when I saw our *vis-à-vis* going through such an amount of 'chassez' and 'balance' fancy steps, pirouetting and flying up and down the room, as would distract even a ballet master. This pas de deux must have lasted full ten minutes, when I found I was expected to perform the same antics with my blooming partner. Summoning up all my courage, I endeavoured to put a bold face on it, and tried my best to imitate some of the contortions I had once seen at a Bal de l'Opera, but with small success, as could be seen by hardly concealed contempt entertained for my dancing by the assistants, who plainly thought but little of my energetic performance. Hastily resigning the bride to some partner more worthy of her, I looked on to admire the wondrous mazes of this interminable quadrille, which must have lasted full an hour; not more to the enjoyment of the performers than to the delight of the lookers-on, who testified to their approval and admiration of any extra complicated step by loud cries of 'Superior, superior,' or 'First class' until reduced to more subdued approbation by the stentorian 'Silence' of the Master of the Ceremonies.[39]

According to the introduction to his book, Bell's description was written "and strung together during a sojourn of some years in the colonies, and treat principally of Grenada, which may be taken as a fairly representative type of a West Indian colony." He published his book in 1889 in London. Even though this was over a half a century after emancipation, nothing much seems to have changed since 1834 and Tregear's prints in the way black balls were used both to satirize the whites and as a means of social bonding.

There were fundamental differences between European dance and African dance. These differences were so great that most Europeans, faced with African dance, found it largely incomprehensible. And what they did see they tended to describe as indecent, largely because of its occasional semi-nudity and the overtly physical nature of the movements. In African culture, music and dance are inextricably intertwined. The music, too, is largely hidden from European ears, because it requires a sophisticated and sensitive set of responses to rhythms which Europeans tend to lack.[40] In African traditional dance, not only does the drumming play a major part but the drumming itself incorporates an impressive complexity of different rhythms. Africans' first response to their dance is to see it as adding a fresh layer of rhythmic complexity to the drumming. The dance itself has a contrapuntal addition to the rhythms of the music. Only secondly is the dance seen as a set of physical movements in their own right, and the physical movements themselves have a very different basis from European dance movements. African traditional dancers tend to have their feet apart and parallel, with their knees bent. The body weight moves slightly forward. To European eyes this looks almost like a crouch. But to African eyes it gives the movement a grounded feel and an earthy quality. Arms and legs can be doing different things at the same time, each working to a different rhythmic pattern. To European eyes this has a tendency to look uncoordinated. To African eyes it adds to the subtlety of the rhythmic complexity and can seem very sophisticated indeed. As the main rhythms of the drumming change, and these rhythms are the center point of the dance, so do the rhythms of the dancer's body alter in response.

European dance throughout its history has shown little response to rhythmic complexity. European dance music tends to concentrate much more on melody than on rhythm, and the dance is seen as a response to the melody while tending to echo the relatively simple rhythms of the music. The stance of the dancer is very different from that of the African dancer. Europeans value the straight back as the basis for most dance movement and this verticality is emphasized in the springing nature of their dance, constantly defying gravity and jumping in the air, while the more the body is controlled throughout every movement and coordinated to create a set pattern, the better the dance is thought to be. There is a tendency to turn the feet away from each other, not to have them in parallel, thus giving the feet a better spring when jumping in the air and greater control when landing. Remaining upright and keeping careful control in a coordinated pattern of movement between legs, arms and torso has always been at the center of European folk dance, as well as in social and theatrical dance.[41]

Until the nineteenth century, neither European nor African social dance involved much lifting of other dancers, nor was there a tendency for dance couples to face each other in a *danse à deux*, but dances were seen as done in lines, diagonals, circles or by groups of dancers creating a pattern by the group actions. Only in the nineteenth century did the action of two dancers facing each other and holding onto each other emerge, as part of European social dance, with the waltz.

What is apparent from the illustrations reproduced above is that blacks in London brought with them something inherently African in their dance movement, even when adopting a European form of dance. Their bodies tend to look a little freer, a little less coordinated in set patterns than do those of Europeans. They tend to pitch the body slightly forward and the physicality of their dance retains more of a response to rhythm than is altogether usual in European dance. When they wish to do so, by exaggerating some of the movements, they can caricature the way European dancers hold themselves. They somehow manage at times to find this invigoratingly funny. European dancers tend not to realize they are being satirized, because the differences are subtle. Where there is room for improvisation, and in the quadrille this is certainly the case, the African dancer can happily incorporate some of his or her own dance moves which have distinct African overtones. The body will pitch further forward, the arms and legs will do different things and fresh rhythmic layers will be added to the simple rhythms of the quadrille. As Hesketh J. Bell reminds us, "In the time of slavery, if the owner of a plantation did not allow his slaves to dance on his estate, they would think nothing of walking eight of ten miles on Saturday nights to some place where a dance was to be given, and many of the outbreaks and rebellions of the slaves were no doubt concocted under cover of these gatherings."[42]

The Antiguan Akan rebellion is an example. Over 2,000 blacks were present for the Akan dance there which was intended to presage the rebellion. The same dance, now called asafo, is still performed on ceremonial occasions in Ghana to this day.[43] A version is performed during carnival in Antigua to this day as well, and there are striking similarities with the version that is danced in Ghana.

An interesting comparison may be made between the way the black community used dance and the way the white working class used dance. As seen in chapter 2, eighteenth-century aristocrats considered it important to dance well, but dance lost its importance for the aristocracy in the nineteenth century. Conversely, more and more dance halls were built in the nineteenth century for the lower middle class and more prosperous elements in the working class. According to A. H. Franks, "The many buildings given the title of assembly rooms which sprang up towards the end of the century were of quite a different nature, being erected to satisfy the demands of more and more people.... Where the aristocracy regarded it more and more as bad form to dance well, the people now began to put dancing England once more on the map."[44]

These developments meant that while blacks were dancing in black balls from which whites were largely excluded, their equivalents in the white working class were also dancing for enjoyment and entertainment in their own dance halls. Clearly this had an effect on the popular dance of the day. In the white dance halls that were largely working class, a simpler form of the quadrille emerged, known as the lancers and described here by Franks:

> A set dance favoured at popular assembly rooms for many years was the albert quadrilles, more commonly known as the alberts. It comprised the first figure of the quadrilles, the second of the caledonians, the third of the lancers, the fourth of the waltz cotillion and the fifth of the quadrilles. This arrangement was originated by Charles d' Albert, a Frenchman who was at one time ballet master at Covent Garden. Later he settled, of all places, in Newcastle, and composed a fair amount of dance music. A form of lancers much in favour right at the end of the century and into the twentieth was known as the kitchen lancers. In this version, which at times became extremely boisterous, the ladies were frequently swung off their feet. Presumably it acquired the 'Kitchen' in its title because of the less genteel behavior required for its performance. Be that as it may, in more than one rich establishment, if not in noble ones, this form was at party time just as popular above as below stairs.[45]

It was noted earlier that the white working class, in the early days of industrialization, tended to cling to folk dance forms, partly from nostalgia and partly as a way of asserting their own identity in the face of the rapid social changes taking place around them. Mainly, no doubt, they danced to enjoy themselves, but the reestablishment of popular dance halls in industrialized society no doubt involved many of the same issues as were involved in the "black hops." The establishment of trade unions and political pressure groups became inextricably linked with working-class leisure activities. Blacks in their balls were using dance in just the same way. They danced for enjoyment, they were political, and they established a sense of solidarity. Dance was also a potent weapon of satire. Yet any attempt to suggest that black interests were somehow assimilated in and submerged by the larger issues of the whole of the working class in England would be misguided. The black community was conscious of its differences from the rest of the working class and often used dance as a way of emphasizing those differences.[46] Hilary S. Carty asserts that the slaves adopted the quadrille "as a means of mimicking the master."[47] Just as blacks in the Caribbean used European dances for their own purposes, so the black balls in London continued to do so in their own ways which were different from those of the white working class. No doubt that white working class had its own ways of sending up and making fun of their betters in the social hierarchy, but that is not our concern here.

A good example of black dance as mimicry and satire is provided by the two prints from *Tregear's Black Jokes*, the first entitled *The Route*, and the second entitled *The Breaking Up*. The whole series of *Black Jokes* prints is drawn in the style of most caricatures of the time, of which perhaps prints by James Gillray are best known.[48] Another example is the caricature drawings that accompany William Makepeace Thackeray's lampoons of social and theatrical dancing.[49] As discussed above, the *Black Jokes* series was loosely based on Edward Williams Clay's prints, *Life in Philadelphia*. They are drawn in a popular fashion by a white European for a white European audience, considering black people as inferior and generally something to be laughed at. Watching black people behave as Europeans do had for this audience much the same appeal as humans sometimes find when watching chimpanzees dressed up and supposedly having a tea party. The blatant racism of the cartoons is their sole justification and the appeal to racial prejudice is what sold the pictures to the public.

As we know, the black community in London at this time was holding balls and dancing the sort of dance caricatured in both *The Route* and *The Breaking Up*. We know that they exaggerated some of their movements and some of their behavior in some of these dances deliberately to make fun of whites. There is therefore a peculiar irony about these two prints. They show blacks supposedly trying hard to ape the behavior of their white superiors. This is obvious in the language within the dialogue balloons of *The Breaking Up*: "Shall I hab de happiness to present you wid an Ice, Mrs. Leonard." The print's jokes are the sort we no longer find very amusing

From *Tregear's Black Jokes: Being a Series of Laughable Caricatures on the March of Manners amongst Blacks.* Hunt after Summers. Published by G. S. Tregear, London, c.1834. (© National Maritime Museum, London)

but which people in the nineteenth century obviously did. The real humor of the print rests in the idea of black people trying to be as formal as white people and to adhere to the same social etiquette as the white aristocracy was supposed to maintain.

What must have given the prints a layer of additional meaning for the black viewer was the knowledge that when blacks behaved anything like this, it was probably because they were themselves setting out to satirize and make fun of the whites. This is something the whites never seemed to have grasped. James Stewart, for example, published in London in 1823 an account of black dance in the Caribbean which, while reluctantly conceding they displayed "some skill in performance," asserted that the slaves did not really understand the dances they were attempting to imitate so closely and that it was "laughable to see with what awkward minuteness they aim at such imitations."[50] What he did not seem to understand was that the awkwardness he commented on was a far from subtle send-up of the way whites danced.

The very words "black jokes" would have meant different things for a white viewer and a black viewer. The white viewer would have found anything the blacks did almost automatically funny, simply because they were different and black. But the words for a black viewer would have been loaded differently. They might well have suggested jokes made by blacks about whites. It follows therefore that for a black viewer the semiotic interpretation of these prints would have been wildly different from the interpretation of a white viewer. A white viewer would have seen black people behaving absurdly when trying to imitate whites. A black viewer would have seen black people behaving in such a way that they highlighted the absurdities of white behavior. These prints therefore make clear, firstly, the racial prejudice that surrounded the blacks of the day, and secondly that whites found the incongruity of black people trying to behave as whites a source of humor. Thirdly, they show that when black people made fun of white people it did not need to be behind their backs, because white people seemed to have been crassly ignorant about what was going on. Fourthly, the same picture viewed by a white person and a black person could bear astonishingly different interpretations according to the social background of each viewer. Fifthly, the prints make clear how little real understanding there was between whites and blacks. How can we know this? We have seen and repeated the evidence from dancers in the Caribbean and in the United States as to the way dance was used to make fun of the plantation masters. We have also noted the fact that the masters remained oblivious. The exaggerations in the prints would have had much the same effect for a London black viewer. A white viewer would have remained oblivious.[51]

Although largely concerned with literary criticism, Henry Louis Gates, Jr.'s Africanist theory of interpretation and its origins is relevant here. The second half of his book *The Signifying Monkey* uses the trickster figures of Esu and the Signifying Monkey as a guide to twentieth-century African-American literature and to help explore contemporary black vernacular culture. According to Gates the monkey suffered a "sea change" as a result of the Middle Passage, emerging as the African-American "signifying monkey." The monkey embodies oral practices involving double-voiced trickery through indirection that can involve innuendo, needling and ridiculing. The very same qualities can be observed as Africans adopted, interpreted and altered European dance forms like the quadrille for their own purposes. Gates's theories would seem to be just as appropriate to the Caribbean and to the eighteenth- and nineteenth-century black community in London as they are in the United States.[52]

The dancing figures in both prints have their body weight forward and in something of a crouched position which is associated with African dance. According to Jean and Marshall Stearns, African dance has six basic characteristics. It is danced on the naked earth with bare feet, often flat-footed, favoring gliding, dragging or shuffling steps; it is frequently performed with knees flexed and body bent at the waist like a hunter crouched for the kill; it imitates animals in realistic detail; it places great importance upon improvisation, allowing freedom for individual expression; it is centrifugal, exploding outward from the hips; and it is performed to a propulsive rhythm, which gives it a "swinging quality."[53] This definition is important because it spells out the different use of body weight between the two cultures.

In *The Breaking Up*, when the fiddler asks the young women, "Why you not turn your Toes out you little Black Niggress?" the white viewer might well have found this all of a piece with the posture of the dancers, highlighting another example of how black people had not properly adapted to European social dance. The black viewer might well have seen something quite different, black people enjoying pointing out the oddities of white behavior. Much the same applies to *The Route* which has the central couple dancing a minuet. The essence of this dance is that the dancers are hand in hand. The dancers watched the company and the company watched them, as described by Rameau and Tomlinson in their dancing manuals, both for their own enjoyment and for that of onlookers. The dance begins with honors to the company and then to the partner. The man offers the woman his right hand with his palm facing upwards. The woman accepts by placing her left hand on his with her palms facing down. For white viewers the idea of a black couple leading the minuet, roles reserved for very important personages at a ball, would have seemed particularly ludicrous.

The pen-and-ink *Terpsichore in the Flat Creek Quarters, Pea Ridge* is not only outside our period, but unfortunately for our purpose, set in America rather than in the Caribbean or in London. It would appear to date from about 1860. All the same, it so aptly illustrates the point we have been making that it is worth including here. The drawing shows a sense of fun, and so is slightly exaggerated. All the feet for example are rather too large. What the artist wants to convey is a sense of energy and excitement that pervades a set of dancers giving themselves wholly to the quadrille. The drawing and the poem that accompanies it seem to be by the same person, who also seems to have been black. There is a light-hearted element of satire, not only in the drawing, but even more so in the poem. The verse is delivered by the caller seated on the right of the sketch. He urges the group of dancers, all of whom are black, "Do your lebbel best an' stomp it like you used to do [in Africa]!" and asserts, "De white folks come in mighty handy, walzin roun' so nice & fine; But when you comes to reg'lah dancing, niggers leabes 'em way behin'!"

Even though based in America, this verse is relevant to London because it suggests one of the motives for the way that black people chose to glory in their dance. It can be connected back to London because its depiction of blacks relates to a series of contexts including the European representation of race and dance. The sketch could draw on the heritage of anti-slavery propaganda and black dance as a means of coping with minority oppression. The all-important words "But when you comes to reg'lah dancing, niggers leabes 'em way behin'" make clear that the black dancers think they dance better than white dancers. And it does more than that. The speaker has already referred to African culture as a folk memory which black dancers have ever present in their minds. This key sentence now deliberately sneers at "white folks ... so nice & fine," by comparing them explicitly with black dancers who dance so much better. The sneer is reinforced by the use of "behin'," which in colloquial Caribbean and Black English has a scatological connotation. Many blacks would appreciate the subtleties of this remark, whereas whites, who do not know the slang, miss this additional layer of meaning completely.[54] The visuals reinforce this statement.

The stance of the dancers varies astonishingly. The man closest to the

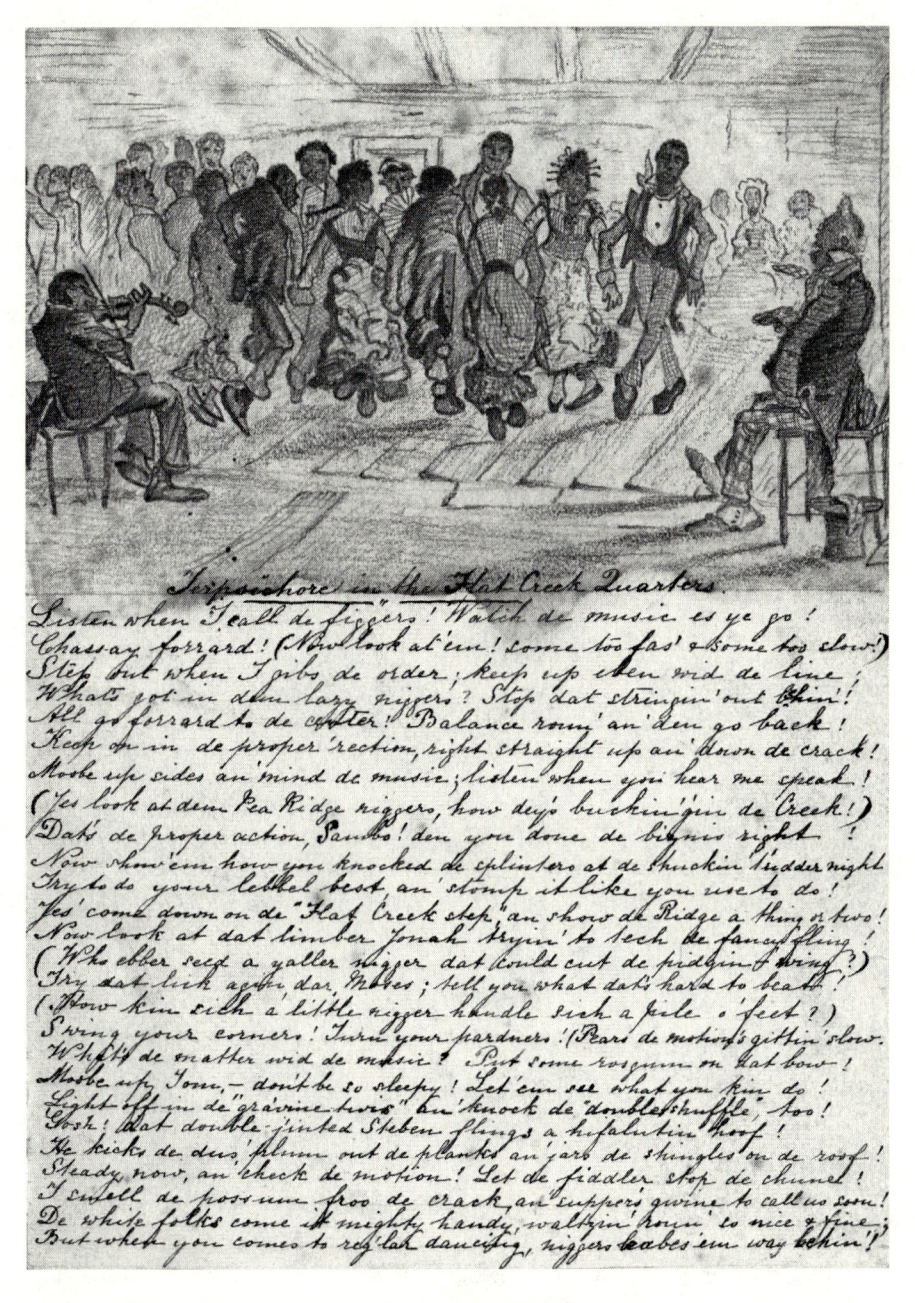

Terpsichore Flat Creek Quarters, Pea Ridge. Unknown artists, c.1860. Print from a pencil sketch. (© National Maritime Museum, London)

caller is upright, pointing his feet, and his arms are approximately in the right position for the quadrille. But what about further down the line? Some dancers are high in the air, some are on the ground, and some are hunched forward. The feet show an astonishing variety of different positions. In other words, the quadrille has been Africanized. Within the framework of the dance, individuals are interpreting it in their own way, each bringing something special to their own interpretation. This is exactly what we would have expected to see in a black ball in London within the period we have discussed. Much the same would no doubt have applied to the music accompanying the dance, and we have stressed in chapters 1 and 2 their interdependence. In interpreting the visual evidence, we have in this chapter restricted ourselves to the dance element since unfortunately no written music accompanies the dance, even though musicians can clearly be seen. The most significant lines from the accompanying manuscript poem read:

> Listen when I call de figgers! Watch de music es ye go!
> Chassay forward! (Now look at 'em! Some too fas' & some too slow!)
> Step but when I gibs de order; keep up eben wid de line;
> What's got in dem lazy niggers? Stop dat stringin' out behin'! ...
> Steady now, an' check de motion! Let de fiddler stop de chune!
> I smell de possum froo de crack an supper's gwine to call us soon!
> De white folks come in mighty handy, waltzin roun' so nice & fine;
> But when you comes to reg'lah dancing, niggers leabes 'em way behin'!

The popularity of the quadrille among the slave community grew just as it did in London.[55] It has to be remembered that there was a not-inconsiderable interchange between the sugar plantations in the Caribbean and London society. Some black house servants and freed slaves would have been as accustomed to one place as to the other.

The black community in the Caribbean danced at local gatherings, celebrations and on holidays such as Christmas, Easter and Crop-Over. When the slaves were brought over to London as servants, many of them took part in the festivities of their masters. In 1775, Hester Lynch Piozzi, in her book *Anecdotes of the Life of the Late Samuel Johnson*, mentions that she invited her friend Johnson's black manservant, Francis Barber, to a birthday celebration: "On the birth-day of our eldest daughter, and that of our friend Dr Johnson, the 17 and 18 of September, we every year made up a little dance and supper, to divert our servants and their friends, putting the summer-house (in Streatham) into their hands for two evenings, to fill with acquaintance and merriment. Francis and his white wife were invited of course."[56] In a middle-class world, servants, even black servants, were often treated with a rough-and-ready sense of equality as members of the family.

This was not new. We have already noticed that Samuel Pepys referred to the way a black dancer was admired on an equivalent social occasion in the seventeenth century. This was a process that was to result in the complete assimilation of blacks into the white gene pool by the end of the nineteenth century. In a BBC 4 television program on June 28, 2006, the direct descendent of Doctor Johnson's black servant Francis Barber was interviewed. He looked completely white and a typical Englishman, a clear example of black assimilation into the gene pool.[57] The separate black community that we have observed making strenuous dance efforts to keep a special sense of identity, in fact ultimately disappeared.

Another example of this process can be seen in the black music tradition. In 1796, John Gabriel Stedman, in his book *Narrative of a Five Years' Expedition, against the Revolted Negroes of Surinam and Guiana,* mentioned the vocal melody, music, and dancing of Africans, which he believed was perfectly timed. He then talked about the letters of Ignatius Sancho, saying that Sancho's letters "would not disgrace the pen of an European."[58] Sancho studied and composed music, and is said to have written and published a theory of music which was dedicated to the Princess Royal.[59] His compositions were clearly written to accompany dance. Sancho was obviously aware of the introduction of the quadrille in society. He even mingled with members of the aristocracy such as the Duchess of Queensberry, moved in artistic circles, and was painted by Thomas Gainsborough.[60] Here a former black slave, composing within the European musical tradition and dance of the day, brought to his creations an awareness of black dance music tradition as well. He mixed with members of the black community, like the poet Phillis Wheatley and the well-known fop Julius Soubise. Europeans in their turn also danced to his music in their own balls.

When slavery was legally ended throughout the British Empire on August 1, 1834, the strong abolitionist movement and the black community in London held celebratory "balls of blacks," just as they had after the judgment about James Somerset. There was a difference. In 1843 their black brother and fellow abolitionist Ignatius Sancho might well have composed some of the music to which they were dancing.

That whole black community seems to have become merged into London's gene pool, and to have disappeared as a group with a separate identity. It was perhaps ironic that when there was a fresh influx of black people into London from the 1950s onward, they should have brought with them the selfsame dance, the quadrille, which both they and those earlier blacks in London had used to satirize their masters.[61] My parents, for example, both immigrants from Antigua, danced the quadrille (which they called the "kachriil"), with knowledgeable enthusiasm.

President George W. Bush, in Liberia on July 8, 2003, affirmed that "the captive slave[s] endured an assault on their culture and their dignity, but the spirit of Africans ... did not break."[62] Watching a quadrille still being danced by people of Afro-Caribbean descent in parts of South London such as New Cross, as it is still danced in Jamaica, it is clear that both the spirit and dignity have survived untarnished.[63]

Dance has helped maintain a special sense of cultural identity for Afro-Caribbeans in London. As an oppressed minority, they have used dance as a way of reminding themselves that they were different and special, even when they were using the dance forms of the majority. They also consciously used European dance forms like the quadrille and minuet to satirize and caricature the white majority. The two forms of the quadrille that still exist in Jamaica, the "Ballroom" and the "Camp" styles, remain as evidence of this widespread activity. As Eileen King-Dorset says, "The movement in the 'Camp' style begins from the hips and is very grounded and makes use of improvisation and is multi-rhythmic. The 'Ballroom' is more formal and the movement quality is a lot more contained."[64]

Conclusion

In the literature on the black presence in London, the capital has been presented as a place where the black community "married and were absorbed into the white population. Their children are now white, with no inkling of their African blood and ancestry."[1] This is true, but no longer applicable to the twenty-first century. In the 1950s a fresh influx of blacks from the Caribbean and from Africa have brought back both African and Caribbean dances which originally helped to bond together that early black community in London in the eighteenth and nineteenth centuries. And elements of African dance persist, even in twenty-first century London.

The evidence showing how blacks in London danced in the eighteenth and nineteenth centuries makes clear that some of the criteria used to measure what survived from Africa in the process of creolization are seriously flawed. Survival theorists, especially in the early years of studies on African "retention" in the Caribbean, frequently linked the disappearance of African cultural traditions to plantation slavery which they believed destroyed African dance. The evidence would seem to contradict this. Ethnographers and anthropologists agree that African music and dance pervaded every facet of African life. It was so basic to their sense of cultural identity that it even survived plantation slavery in the Americas. Herskovits claimed that dance was "a fundamental element in aesthetic expression everywhere in Africa," adding, "dancing takes multitudinous forms, and all who have had firsthand contact with the area of our special interest speak of the many varieties of dances found there. These may be ritual or recreational, religious or secular, fixed or improvised, and the dance itself has in characteristic form carried over into the New World to a greater degree than almost any other trait of African culture."[2]

Evidence has been provided to show that some African dance, as part of the quadrille, survived in London up to the nineteenth century. This book shows that a number of factors probably contributed to this situation. Data has been presented sequentially to show that certain events on both sides of the Atlantic led to the situation in London. For instance, on the African continent, the role that African dance played in community life before the chaos and anarchy of the slave trade was an experience so strong that it withstood the impact of slavery.

Once the slaves had negotiated the Middle Passage, their dances had to survive in a hostile and oppressive society. Drumming and other cultural practices—even religion—were often banned altogether, along with some music and dance. Even so, some of the slaves' sacred dances managed to evoke many of the ideas and associations that had originally been part of their banned religions.

Social dance—"black balls"—were clearly a catalyst in helping London's black community bond together with a common sense of identity. The fact that when two of their number were in prison in Bridewell they were visited by over three hundred of their fellows and that the black community supported them financially is amazing evidence of how well organized and how strong this sense of a common identity must have been.[3]

If it were possible to go back in time to a black ball in 1835, what would be seen? The first impression would be of a large group of people, men and women, not only with a common sense of identity, not only with a shared cultural heritage, but where each person would personally know and like many of those present. They would have come together to enjoy themselves and they would be experiencing a shared joy of movement to music. What kind of movement? What kind of music? Superficially, both would appear to be European, but it would be European with a difference, an African difference. Some of the sets in the quadrille would actually be taken over by dance steps and movements that came from Africa via the Caribbean. Some of the rhythmic emphasis in the music would be more congenial to African ears. At certain points in the dance a deliberate attempt would be made to make fun of the way white people moved to music. Any white people watching would probably have remained unaware of what was going on and attributed the exaggerations to black people's inability to dance properly. For black people these moments would have been full of humor, as they, an oppressed minority, asserted a reassuring sense of dance superiority over the majority.

Newcomers would bring candles, if they were men, and food, if they were women. Here were people acting as a community, bonded together by a shared knowledge of the dance and music they loved so much. It had seen them through the horrors of slavery, the growth of some sort of independence in London, and finally the emancipation from slavery of all their Caribbean brethren, toward which they had worked so hard, together with white liberals and Quakers. The dances from 1835 onward must have been triumphant indeed. So a number of factors contributed to the persistence of some elements of the African dances in London in the eighteenth and nineteenth centuries. Paradoxically, these dances have surfaced again in London in the twentieth and twenty-first centuries. To what extent will they persist? Essentially there are still major differences in style between the way black people and white people dance the same musical steps.

It is difficult in a written analysis to describe what Herskovits called "subtleties of motor behavior." It has been even more difficult to analyze the ways in which blacks danced in London as part of their fight for emancipation in the eighteenth and early nineteenth century. Yet it would be almost impossible to overemphasize the important role dance had played, and would continue to play, for the black minority attending a "black hop" in 1835. It is only in the context of their particular situation in London at that time that the importance of dance for them can be fully appreciated.

Chapter Notes

Preface

1. Melville J. Herskovits, *The Myth of the Negro Past* (Boston: Beacon Press, 1958), 11. The first edition of Herskovits's book was published in 1941; Frazier and Herskovits were in some ways reacting against DuBois's pioneering synthesis. W. E. B. DuBois, *The Souls of Black Folk* in *Three Negro Classics* (New York, Avon Books, 1965)
2. Herskovits, *The Myth of the Negro Past*, 13–14; Sandra T. Barnes, "The Many Faces of Ogun" in *Africa's Ogun*, ed. Sandra T. Barnes (Bloomington: Indiana University Press, 1989), 9.

Chapter 1

1. Ira Berlin, *Many Thousands Gone: The First Two Centuries of Slavery in North America* (Cambridge, MA: Harvard University Press, 1998), 55.
2. Richard Price and Sidney W. Mintz, *The Birth of African-American Culture* (Boston: Beacon Press, 1976), 9–10, 20–12, 52–53.
3. Folarin Shyllon, *Black People in Britain 1555–1833* (Oxford: Oxford University Press, for the Institute of Race Relations, 1977), 159–160.
4. Shane White and Graham White, *Stylin': African American Expressive Culture from Its Beginnings to the Zoot Suit* (Ithaca: Cornell University Press, 1998), 79.
5. Terry Harnan, *African Rhythm, American Dance: A Biography of Katherine Dunham*, (New York: Alfred A. Knopf, 1974), 55–60.
6. Herskovits, *The Myth of the Negro Past*, 13–14.
7. Ibid., xiii–xiv, 13–32.
8. Ibid., x–xi.
9. Ibid., 6–9.
10. Ibid., 16.
11. Ibid.
12. Ibid., 16–17.
13. David Eltis, "The Volume and Structure of the Transatlantic Slave Trade: A Reassessment," *William and Mary Quarterly*, 3rd ser., 2, no. 1 (January 2001), 17–46.
14. Herskovits, *The Myth of the Negro Past*, 53–87.
15. Ibid., 76.
16. Herskovits, *The Myth of the Negro Past*, 297.
17. Ibid.
18. Edward Franklin Frazier, *The Negro Family in the United States* (Chicago: University of Chicago Press, 1939, reprinted 1966), 7.
19. Stanley M. Elkins, *Slavery: A Problem in American Institutional and Intellectual Life*, (Chicago: University of Chicago Press, 1959); Kenneth M. Stampp, *The Peculiar Institution: Slavery in the Ante-bellum South* (New York: Alfred A. Knopf, 1956); Daniel Patrick Moynihan, "Social and Economic Conditions of Negroes in the United States," *Bureau of Labor Statistics and Bureau of the Census BLS Rpt. No. 332 and Current Population Report*, Series No. 24 (Washington, DC., 1976), 23.

20. Edward Franklin Frazier, *The Negro Church in America* (New York: Alfred A. Knopf, 1964), 1–16.
21. Sterling Stuckey, *Slave Culture: Nationalist Theory and the Foundations of Black America* (New Haven: Yale University Press, 1985), 3–97.
22. Ibid., p.24.
23. Ibid.
24. Ibid., p.31.
25. Joe Nash, "Talley Beaty" in *African American Genius in Modern Dance*, ed. Gerald E. Myers (American Dance Festival, 1993), 3–5.
26. Stuckey, *Slave Culture*, 31.
27. White and White, *Stylin,'* 76.
28. Ibid.
29. Ibid.
30. John W. Blassingame, *The Slave Community: Plantation Life in the Antebellum South*, (Oxford: Oxford University Press, 1972).
31. Herbert George Gutman, *The Black Family in Slavery and Freedom, 1750–1925* (New York: Pantheon Books, 1976).
32. Richard Price and Sidney W. Mintz, *Birth of African-American Culture* (Boston, Beacon Press, 1976), 9–10, 20–12, 52–53.
33. Richard Price and Sidney W. Mintz, "An Anthropological Approach to the Afro-American Past: A Caribbean Perspective," in *2 ISHI Occasional Papers in Social Change* (Philadelphia, Institute for the Study of Human Issues, 1976), p. 1.
34. Jane C. Desmond, "Embodying Difference: Issues in Dance and Cultural Studies" in *Meaning in Motion: New Cultural Studies of Dance*, (Durham: Duke University Press, 1997); Helen Thomas, *The Body, Dance and Cultural Theory* (Houndmills: Palgrave Macmillan, 2003); Lawrence W. Levine, *Black Culture and Black Consciousness: Afro-American Folk Thoughts from Slavery to Freedom* (New York: Oxford University Press, 1977), ix.
35. Thomas, *The Body, Dance and Cultural Theory*, 128.
36. Ibid., 129.
37. Ibid., 126.
38. Ibid.
39. Ibid.
40. Ibid.
41. Ibid., 127.
42. Ibid.
43. Ibid.
44. Ibid., 128.
45. Ibid.
46. Ibid., 129.
47. Ibid., 135.
48. Desmond, "Embodying Difference," 36.
49. Ibid., 37.
50. Winthrop D. Jordan, *White over Black: American Attitudes Toward the Negro 1550–1812* (Chapel Hill: University of North Carolina Press, 1968), 5–47.
51. Desmond, "Embodying Difference," 37.
52. Ramsay Burt, *The Male Dancer, Bodies, Spectacle, Sexualities* (London: Routledge, 1995), 130.
53. Barbara Browning, *Samba: Resistance in Motion* (Bloomington: Indiana University Press, 1995), 20.
54. Ibid., 21.
55. Ibid.
56. Ibid., 22.
57. R. Bickell, *The West Indies as They Are; or a Real Picture of Slavery, but more Particularly as it Exists in the Island of Jamaica* (London: Printed by R. Taylor, 1825), 226.
58. Browning, *Samba*, 92.
59. Ibid., 95–96.
60. Ibid., 96.
61. Martha E. Savigliano, *Tango and the Political Economy of Passion* (Boulder: Westview Press, 1995), 32.
62. Ibid., 69.
63. Ibid.
64. Ibid.
65. Ibid., 70.
66. Ibid., 74.
67. Ibid., 75.
68. Ibid., 75–76.
69. Mungo Park, *Travels in the Interior Districts of Africa: Performed under the Direction and Patronage of the African Association in the Years 1795, 1796 and 1797* (London: Printed by W. Bulmer for the author, and sold by G. and W. Nicol, 1799), 66; Thomas Edward Bowdich, *Mission from Cape Coast Castle to Ashantee, with a Statistical Account of that Kingdom, and Geographical Notices of Other Parts of the Interior of Africa* (Glasgow: Khull, Blackie, 1819), 32.

70. Richard A. Long, "The Mission of Black Modern Dance" in *The Black Tradition in American Dance*, ed. Gerald E. Myers (Durham: American Dance Festival, 1988), 18.
71. Charles W. Joyner, *Down by the Riverside: A South Carolina Slave Community* (Urbana: University of Illinois Press, 1984), xvii–xviii.
72. Ibid., xviii.
73. Ibid., xix.
74. Levine, *Black Culture and Black Consciousness*, xi.
75. Ibid.
76. Ibid.
77. Joyner, *Down by the Riverside*, xiii.
78. DuBois, *The Souls of Black Folk*, 207–390.
79. Dena J. Epstein, *Sinful Tunes and Spirituals: Black Folk Music to the Civil War* (Chicago: University of Illinois Press, 1977), 139.
80. Ibid., 346.
81. Peter H. Wood, "Gimme de Kneebone Bent: African Body Language and the Evolution of American Dance Forms" in *The Black Tradition in American Dance*, ed. Gerald E. Myers (Durham, American Dance Festival, 1988), 8.
82. Ibid., 7.
83. Ibid., 8.
84. Elizabeth Johns, *Winslow Homer: The Nature Observation* (Berkeley: University of California Press, 2002).
85. Katherine Dunham, *Katherine Dunham's Journey to Accompong* (New York: Henry Holt, 1946); Katherine Dunham, "The Dances of Haiti," *Acta Anthropologica* 2, no. 4 (November 1947), 53.
86. Long, "The Mission of Black Modern Dance," 19.
87. Ibid.
88. Marshall Stearns and Jean Stearns, *Jazz Dance: The Story of American Vernacular Dance* (New York: Macmillan,1966); Lynne Fauley Emery, *Black Dance in the United States from 1619–1970* (Dance Books, 1988).
89. Thomas F. DeFrantz, *Dancing Many Drums: Excavation in African American Dance* (Madison: University of Wisconsin Press, 2002), 13.
90. Robert Farris Thompson, "Dance and Culture, an Aesthetic of the Cool," *African Forum* 2 (Fall 1966), 85–102.
91. Ibid., 88.
92. Long, "The Mission of Black Modern Dance," 19.
93. DeFrantz, *Dancing Many Drums*, 15.
94. Ibid., 16.
95. Christy Adair, "Phoenix Perspectives: African American Influences on a British Dance Company," in *Embodying Liberation: The Black Body in American Dance*, ed. Dorothea Fischer-Hornung and Alison D. Goeller (Hamburg: Lit Verlag, 2001), 127.
96. Ibid., 129.
97. Brenda Dixon-Gottschild, "The Afrocentric Paradigm," in *Design for Arts in Education*, January/February 1991, 15–22.
98. White and White, *Stylin,'* 75.
99. Ibid.
100. White and White, *Stylin,'* 83.
101. Ibid.
102. Ibid.
103. Ibid., 84.
104. Paul Gilroy, *The Black Atlantic: Modernity and Double Consciousness* (Cambridge: MA., Harvard University Press, 1993), 73.
105. Ibid., 74–75.
106. Edouard Glissant, *Caribbean Discourse: Selected Essays*, trans. J. Michael Dash, (Charlottesville: University Press of Virginia, 1989), 248; John Baugh, *Black Street Speech* (Austin: University of Texas Press, 1983).
107. Antonio Benitez-Rojo *The Repeating Island: The Caribbean and the Postmodern Perspective* (Durham: Duke University Press, 1996), 12.
108. Ibid.
109. Ibid.
110. Ibid., 12–16.
111. Benitez-Rojo, *The Repeating Island*, 61–69.
112. Ibid., 61.
113. Ibid., 62.
114. Ibid.
115. Ibid.
116. Ibid.
117. Ibid., 62–63.
118. Gilroy, *The Black Atlantic*, 82.
119. Benitez-Rojo, *The Repeating Island*, 70–71.

120. Peter Wood, *Black Majority: Negroes in Colonial South Carolina from 1670 through the Stono Rebellion* (New York: Alfred A. Knopf, 1974); Peter Wood, *Economic Beginnings in Colonial South Carolina, 1670–1730* (Columbia: University of South Carolina Press, 1971); Judith Carney, *Black Rice: The African Origins of Rice Cultivation in the Americas* (Cambridge, MA: Harvard University Press, 2001).

121. Margaret Washington Creel, *A Peculiar People: Slave Religion and Community-Culture Among the Gullahs* (New York: New York University Press, 1988).

122. Joyner, *Down by the Riverside*, 130–132.

123. Berlin, *Many Thousands Gone*, 17–63.

124. Richard Cullen Rath, "African Music in Seventeenth-Century Jamaica: Cultural Transit and Transition," *William and Mary Quarterly* 50 no.3 (1993), 700–726. For the demographic, historical, and linguistic factors defining creolization, see Philip Baker and Chris Corne, "Universals, Substrata and the Indian Ocean Creoles," in *Substrata Versus Universals in Creole Genesis: Papers from the Amsterdam Creole Workshop*, April 1986, ed. Pieter Muysken and Noval Smith (Amsterdam, 1986), 165–167; Derek Bickerton, *Roots of Language* (Ann Arbor: Karoma Publishers, 1981), 2–4; Derek Bickerton, *Language & Species* (Chicago: University Of Chicago Press, 1990), 105–129; Jeff Siegal, *Language Contact in a Plantation Environment: A Sociolinguistic History of Fiji* (Cambridge: Cambridge University Press, 1987), 16.

125. Rath, "African Music," 700–726.

126. Ibid.

127. Noam Chomsky, *Syntactic Structures* (The Hague: Mouton, 1957).

128. Randy Allen Harris, *The Linguistics Wars* (New York & Oxford: Oxford University Press, 1993); Noam Chomsky, "A Minimalist Program for Linguistic Theory" in *MIT Occasional Papers in Linguistics* (Cambridge: Cambridge University Press, 1992), 1–8.

129. W. N. Francis, *Dialectology: An Introduction* (London: Longman, 1983), 1–7; Frank Parker, *Linguistics for Non-Linguists* (Austin: Pro-Ed, 1986), 115; Lawrence M. Davis, *English Dialectology: An Introduction* (Tuscaloosa: University of Alabama Press, 1983), 1–3.

130. Jack P. Greene, *Pursuits of Happiness: The Social Development of Early Modern British Colonies and the American Culture* (Chapel Hill: University of North Carolina Press, 1988); Benedict Anderson, *Imagined Communities: Reflections of the Origin and Spread of Nationalism*, rev. ed. (London: Verso, 1991).

131. Edward Brathwaite, *The Development of Early Modern British Colonies and the Formation of American Culture* (Chapel Hill: University of North Carolina Press, 1988); Edward Brathwaite, *The Development of Creole Society in Jamaica, 1770–1820* (Oxford,: Oxford University Press, 1971); Glissant, *Caribbean Discourse*, 91–125.

132. Glissant, *Caribbean Discourse*, 91–125; Orlando Patterson, *Slavery and Social Death: A Comparative Study* (Cambridge, MA: Harvard University Press, 1982).

133. Glissant, *Caribbean Discourse*, 114.

134. Ibid.

135. Edouard Glissant, *Poétique de la relation* (Paris: Gallimard, 1990).

136. Glissant, *Caribbean Discourse*, 114.

137. Ibid., 114–115.

138. Ibid., 115.

139. Patterson, *Slavery and Social Death*, 1–2.

140. Ibid., 8.

141. Ibid.

142. Simon Schama, *Rough Crossing: Britain, the Slaves and the American Revolution* (London: BBC Books, 2005); Folarin Shyllon, *Black People in Britain, 1555–1833* (Oxford: Oxford University Press for the Institute of Race Relations, 1977).

143. Susanne K. Langer, *Feeling and Form: A Theory of Art* (London: Routledge and Kegan Paul, 1953), 169–187.

144. Fred Astaire and Bob Thomas, *Astaire: The Man, The Dancer* (London: Weidenfeld and Nicholson, 1985); John Mueller, *Astaire Dancing: The Musical Films* (New York: Alfred A. Knopf, 1985); Stanley Green and Burt Goldblatt, eds., *Starring Fred Astaire* (London: W. H. Allen, 1974).

Chapter 2

1. Bryan Edwards, *The History, Civil and Commercial of the British Colonies in the West Indies*, Vol. II (London: G. and W. B. Whittaker, 1793), 70.

2. Olaudah Equiano, *The Interesting Narrative of the Life of Olaudah Equiano, or Gustavus Vassa, The African, Written by Himself*, Vol. 1 (New York: printed for the author and sold by Johnson & Co, 1789), 7.

3. David Eltis, "The Volume and Structure of the Transatlantic Slave Trade: A Reassessment," *The William and Mary Quarterly*, 3rd Series, 58, no. 1 (January 2001), 17–46.

4. Philip D. Curtin, *Atlantic Slave Trade: A Census* (Madison, University of Wisconsin Press, 1969).

5. Trevor Burnard and Kenneth Morgan, "The Dynamics of the Slave Market and Slave Purchasing Patterns in Jamaica, 1655–1788," *The William and Mary Quarterly*, 3rd Series, 58, no. 1 (January 2001), 208.

6. Paul E. Lovejoy and David V. Trotman, eds., *Trans-Atlantic Dimensions of Ethnicity in the African Diaspora* (London: Continuum, 2003), 31.

7. David Eltis, *The Rise of African Slavery in the Americas* (Cambridge: Cambridge University Press, 2000), 257.

8. "Analysis of Demographic Data," Vol. I (Accra: Ghana Statistical Service, 1994).

9. "Population and Housing Census Summary Report of Final Results," (Accra: Ghana Statistical Service, 2000–2002).

10. Herbert M. Cole and Doran H. Ross, *The Arts of Ghana* (Los Angeles: Museum of Cultural History, 1977), 4.

11. Mathew Nathan, "Historical Chart of the Gold Coast and Ashanti, Compiled from Various Sources," *African Affairs* 4 (1904), 34–35; Graham Connah, *African Civilizations* (Cambridge: Cambridge University Press, 1994) has evidence of cities and states in tropical Africa long before the colonial ambitions of European peoples transformed that continent; Lerone Bennett Jr., *Before the Mayflower* (Chicago, University of Chicago Press, 2003) traces black history from its origins in the great empires of Western Africa to the civil rights upheavals of the 1960s and 1970s; David Basildon, *Africa in History* (New York: St. Martin's Press, 1991) deals with the history and development of African civilizations; Henry Louis Gates Jr., *Wonders of The African World* (New York: Alfred A. Knopf, 1999), examines civilizations in different parts of Africa.

12. Nathan, "Historical Chart," 34; see also A. E. M. Gibson, "Slavery in Western Africa," *African Affairs* 3 (1903–4), 17–52.

13. James Pope-Hennessy, *Sins of The Fathers: The Atlantic Slave Traders, 1441–1807* (London: Capricorn Books, 1967), 20.

14. Ibid.

15. Nathan, "Historical Chart," 36.

16. William Bosman, *A New and Accurate Description of the Coast of Guinea, Divided into the Gold, the Slave, and the Ivory Coast*, James Knapton and Daniel Midwinter ed. (London: Ballantine Press, 1705).

17. William Bosman, *A New and Accurate Description of the Coast of Guinea, Divided into the Gold, the Slave, and the Ivory Coast*, new ed. with an introduction by John Ralph Willis, notes by J. D. Fage and R. E. Bradbury (London: Frank Cass, 1967).

18. Bosman, *A New and Accurate Description* (1967), 181.

19. Connah, *African Civilizations*, 6.

20. Judith Steeh, *History of Ballet and Modern Dance* (Leicester: Magna Books, 1982), 8; Susanne K. Langer, *Feeling and Form: A Theory of Art* (London: Routledge and Kegan Paul, 1953), 175.

21. Belinda Quirey, *May I Have the Pleasure: The Story of Popular Dancing* (London: BBC Books, 1976), 10.

22. Debra Craine, "My dance is an offering" (interviewed with Akram Khan), *The Times*, April 2, 2005.

23. St. Augustine, *Confessions*, with translation and commentary by James J. O'Donnell (Oxford: Oxford University Press, 1992).

24. Equiano, *The Interesting Narrative*, vol. I, 7.

25. K. A. Opoku, "Choreography and the African Dance: Individual Research Report," *Institute of African Studies Research Review*, New Series, 8, nos. 1&2

(1992), 54; Emmanuel Kingsley Braffi, *The Esoteric Significance of the Asante Nation* (Kumasi: Educational Press and Manufactures, 1984), 7; Peter Fryer, "The 'Discovery' and Appropriation of African Music and Dance," *Race and Class* 39, no.3 (January–March 1998), 5–6.

26. A. M. Opoku, "The Dance in Traditional African Society," *Institute of African Studies Research Review* 7, no. 1 (1970), 4.

27. Ibid., 7.

28. Alphonse Tierou, *Doople: The Eternal Law of African Dance* (Paris: Harwood Academic Publishers, 1989), 13.

29. W. Ofotsu Adinku, *African Dance Education in Ghana* (Accra: University of Ghana Press, 1994), 16.

30. Richard A. Long, "The Mission of Black Modern Dance" in *The Black Tradition in American Modern Dance*, Gerald E. Myers, ed. (Durham: American Dance Festival, 1988), 5.

31. R. M. Stone, "Africa" in *The Garland Encyclopedia of World Music* (New York: Garland Publishing, 1998), 108–109

32. Tierou, *Doople*, 9.

33. Janet Wilks, *Benesh Movement Notation Beginners' Manual* (London: Burke Publishing, 1955), 1–7.

34. Irmgard E. Berry, *Benesh Movement Notation Score Catalogue: An International Listing of Benesh Movement Notation Scores of Professional Dance Works Recorded 1955–1985* (London: Benesh Institute of Choreology, 1986).

35. Rudolf and Joan Benesh, *Reading Dance: The Birth of Choreology* (London: Souvenir Press, 1977), 110–113.

36. Ibid., 121.

37. Rudolf and Joan Benesh, *An Introduction to Benesh Movement Notation* (London: A & C Black, 1956), 54.

38. Equiano, *The Interesting Narrative*, 7.

39. Ibid., 7–9.

40. *The Monthly Review*, June 1789.

41. Vincent Carretta, "Olaudah Equiano or Gustavus Vassa? New Light on an Eighteenth-Century Question of identity," *Slavery and Abolition* 20, no.3 (December 1999), 96–105; Vincent Carretta, "Introduction" in *The Interesting Narrative and Other Writings* (London: Penguin Classics, 2003), x–xi.

42. Olaudah Equiano, *The Interesting Narrative of the Life of Olaudah Equiano, or Gustavus Vassa the African*, abridged and edited by Paul Edwards (London: Heinemann Educational Books, 1967), xv.

43. Richard D. E. Burton, *Afro-Creole: Power, Opposition, and Play in the Caribbean* (Ithaca, NY: Cornell University Press, 1997); Richard Price and Sidney W. Mintz, *The Birth of African-American Culture: An Anthropological Perspective* (Boston: Beacon Press, 1992).

44. Burton, *Afro-Creole: Power, Opposition, and Play in the Caribbean*, 66–82.

45. Rath, Cullen Richard, "Drums and Power: Ways of Creolizing Music in Coastal South Carolina and Georgia, 1730–1790," in *Creolization in the Americas: Cultural Adaptations to the New World*, Steven G. Reinhardt and David Buisseret, ed. (College Station, TX: Texas A&M University Press, 2000), 100.

46. John Gabriel Stedman, *Narrative of a Five Years' Expedition against the Revolted Negroes of Surinam, in Guiana, on the Wild Coast of South America, from the Year 1772 to 1777: Elucidating the History of that Country, and Describing Its Productions, Viz. Quadrupeds, Birds, Fishes, Reptiles, Trees, Shrubs, Fruits, & Roots; with an Account of the Indians of Guiana, & Negroes of Guinea* (London: J. Johnson, 1796), 1.

47. Ibid., 285–287.

48. Hans Sloane, *A Voyage to the Islands Madera, Barbados, Nieves, S. Christophers and Jamaica with the Natural History of the Herbs and Trees, Four-footed Beasts, Fishes, Birds, Insects, Reptiles, Etc. of the Last of Those Islands; to Which is Prefix'd an Introduction, Wherein is an Account of the Inhabitants, Air, Waters, Diseases, Trade, etc. of That Place, With Some Relations Concerning the Neighbouring Continent, and Islands of America*, Vol. 1 (London, printed by B.M for the author, 1707–25), 11; Richard Cullen Rath, *African Traits in Seventeenth Century Jamaican Music* (Millersville University, unpublished paper, Spring 1990), as summarized by John Kelly Thornton, *Africa and Africans in Making the Atlantic World, 1400–1800* (Cambridge: Cambridge University Press, 1992), 76, 226–7. Sloane wrote that at times Negroes de-

served the worst punishments they received. These included castration, spurs thrust into their mouths, salt and pepper thrust into their wounds, half a foot chopped off, and being nailed to the ground and slowly burnt with fire. Sloane, *A Voyage to the Islands*, 472.

49. Stedman, *Narrative of a Five Years' Expedition*, 289.

50. Ibid., 288.

51. Mungo Park, *Travels in the Interior Districts of Africa: Performed under the Direction and Patronage of the African Association in the Years 1795, 1796 and 1797* (London: John Murray, 1799), 66.

52. Thomas Edward Bowdich, *Mission from Cape Coast Castle to Ashantee, With a Statistical Account of That Kingdom, and Geographical Notices of Other Parts of the Interior of Africa* (Glasgow: Khull, Blackie, 1819), 32.

53. Lilly Grove, *Dancing* (London: Longmans, Guen, 1895), 65–66.

54. K. A. Opoku, "Choreography and the African Dance," 6.

55. Cole and Ross, *The Arts of Ghana*, 19.

56. Ibid., 7.

57. J. H. Kwabena Nketia, *Drumming in Akan Communities of Ghana* (London: Nelson, 1963), 196. (I am greatly indebted to J. H. Kwabena Nketia for his survey of the importance of dance and music throughout society in Ghana.)

58. Ibid.

59. Braffi, *The Esoteric Significance of the Asante Nation*, 48.

60. Ibid., 49.

61. Cole and Ross, *The Arts of Ghana*, 202.

62. K. A. Opoku, "Choreography and the African Dance," 6.

63. Ibid., 23.

64. A. M. Opoku, "The Dance in Traditional African Society," 4–5.

65. Ibid., 3.

66. Tim Cumming, "From One African Legend to Another," *The Independent*, February 22, 2008.

67. Carol Beckwith and Angela Fisher, *African Ceremonies*, Vol.1 (New York: Harry N. Abrams, 1999), 14–124.

68. Cole and Ross, *The Arts of Ghana*, 16.

69. Ibid., 17.

70. J. H. Kwabena Nketia, "The Interrelations of African Music and Dance" in *Studia Musicologica Academiae Scientiarum Hungaricae*, T. 7, Fasc. 1/4 (1965). "The volume contains the papers read at the International Folk Music Council (IFMC) Conference held in Budapest in August 1964."

71. J. H. Kwabena Nketia, *Drumming in Akan Communities of Ghana*, 140.

72. Ibid., 195.

73. Ibid., 198.

74. Quirey, May I Have the Pleasure, 10.

75. Ibid., 67–68.

76. John Miller Chernoff, *African Rhythm and African Sensibility, Aesthetics and Social Action in African Musical Idioms* (Chicago: University of Chicago, 1979), 144.

77. Paulla A. Ebron, *Performing Africa* (Princeton, NJ: Princeton University Press, 2002), 33–52.

78. Gerald E. Mayers, *The Black Tradition in American Modern Dance* (New York: Prion, 1988), 5.

79. *Dance Black America, April 21–24, 1983.* (Brooklyn, NY: Brooklyn Academy of Music, 1983?), 10.

80. Chernoff, *African Rhythm*, 111.

81. Ibid., 87.

82. Ibid., 82.

83. Ibid, 144.

84. R. S. Rattray, *Ashanti* (Oxford: Clarendon Press, 1923), 146.

85. Melville J. Herskovits, *The New World Negro* (New York: St. Martin's Press, 1966), 13–14.

86. Kellom Tomlinson, *The Art of Dancing, Explained by Reading and Figures* (London: published by the author, 1735); Carlo Blasis, *The Code of Terpsichore: The Art of Dancing Comprising its Theory and Practice* (London: E. Bull, 1830); Henri Cellarius, *The Drawing-Room Dances* (London: E. Churton, 1847); Philip J. S. Richardson, *The Social Dances of the Nineteenth Century in England* (London: Herbert Jenkins, 1960).

87. Cyril Beaumont, *A Miscellany For Dancers* (London: Golden Cockerel Press, 1954), 15.

88. Ibid., 16.

89. John Steegman, *Victorian Taste, A*

Study of the Arts and Architecture from 1830–1870 (London: Thomas Nelson, 1970), 50.

90. Jane Austin, *Pride and Prejudice* (London: T. Egerton, 1813), 18.

91. Norbert Elias, *The Civilizing Process*, trans. Edmund Jephcott (Oxford: Basil Blackwell, 1978).

92. Nicholas Dromgoole, *The Playwright as Rebel: Essays in Theatre History* (London: Oberon Books, 2001); Nicholas Dromgoole, *Performance Style and Gesture in Western Theatre* (London: Oberon Books, 2008).

93. Steeh, *History of Ballet and Modern Dance*, 17.

94. Ibid.

95. Ibid.

96. Ibid., 30–71.

97. Claude Manceron, *Men of Liberty: Europe on the Eve of the French Revolution 1774–1778* (London: Eyre Methuen, 1977), 77–78.

98. Gilroy, *The Black Atlantic*, 73–75.

99. André Ernest Modeste Grétry, *Zemire et Azore* (Paris: Duhan et Cie, 1771), 81.

100. C. J. Feldtenstein, *Erweiterung der Kunst nach der Chorographie zu Tanzen*, trans. Lillian Moore (Frankfurt: C. J. von Braunschweig, 1772). Section II, Chapter II.

101. Tomlinson, *The Art of Dancing*, 6–17.

102. Ibid., Vol. II, 127–128.

103. Madeleine Inglehearn, *The Minuet in the late Eighteenth Century* (London: Madeleine Inglehearn, 1998).

104. Feldtenstein, *Erweiterung der Kunst*, Section II, Chapter II.

105. Giovanni-Andrea Gallini, *A Treatise on the Art of Dancing* (London, For the Author, 1772, reprinted 1976), 173.

106. Elias, *The Civilizing Process*, 3–35.

107. Feldtenstein, *Erweiterung der Kunst*, Section II, Chapter II.

108. Moore, Lillian, "M. L. E. Moreau de Saint-Mery and Danse" in *Dance Index* 5, no. 10 (1946), 235–236.

109. Carol G. Marsh, "Passepied," in *International Encyclopedia of Dance*, vol. 5 (New York: Oxford University Press, 1998), 109.

110. Charles Read Baskerville, *The Elizabethan Jig and Related Drama* (Chicago: University of Chicago Press, 1929), 3–4.

111. Margaret Dean-Smith, "Jig," in *The New Grove Dictionary of Music and Musicians*, vol. XIII (London: Macmillan, 2001), 118–119.

112. Meredith Ellis Little, "Gigue," in *The New Grove Dictionary of Music and Musicians*, vol. 7 (London: Macmillan, 1980), 368.

113. Andrew Lamb, "Cotillion," in *The New Grove Dictionary of Music and Musicians* vol. 6, (London: Macmillan, 1980), 828.

114. Ibid., 829.

115. William Creech, *Edinburgh Fugitive Pieces* (Edinburgh: John Fairbairn, 1815), 338.

116. Richard Hudson, "Passacaglia," in *The New Grove Dictionary of Music and Musicians*, vol. 14, (London: Macmillan, 1980), 269.

117. Cuthbert Girdlestone, *Jean-Philippe Rameau: His Life and Work* (London: Cassell, 1959), 190.

118. Tomlinson, *The Art of Dancing*, 83–84.

119. Margaret Daniels, "Musette," in *International Encyclopedia of Dance*, vol. 4 (New York: Oxford University Press, 1998), 481–482.

120. Meredith Ellis Little, "Gavotte," in *The New Grove Dictionary of Music and Musicians*, (London: Macmillan, 1980), 199–202.

121. Philip J. S. Richardson, *The Social Dances of the Nineteenth Century in England* (London: Herbert Jenkins, 1960), 66.

122. Ibid.

123. Ibid., 67.

124. Violet Alford, "The Rigaudon," *Musical Quarterly* 30, no. 3, (1944), 280–281.

125. Meredith Ellis Little, "Rigaudon," in *International Encyclopedia of Dance*, vol. 5, (New York: Oxford University Press, 1998), 352.

126. Quirey, *May I Have the Pleasure*, 50.

127. Ibid., 51.

128. Wendy Hilton, *Dance of Court & Theatre, French Noble Style 1690–1725* (Princeton, NJ: Princeton Book, 1981), 12.

129. Margaret Dean-Smith, "Hornpipe," in *The New Grove Dictionary of Music and Musicians*, vol. 8, (London: Macmillan, 1980), 720.
130. Ibid., 721.
131. Wendy Hilton, *Dance of Court & Theatre*, 12.
132. Meredith Ellis Little, "Bourree," in *International Encyclopedia of Dance*, vol. 1, (New York: Oxford University Press, 1998), 516–517.
133. A. H. Franks, *Social Dance: A Short History* (London: Routledge and Kegan Paul, 1963), 13.
134. Ibid., 153.
135. Ernst H. Gombrich, *In Search of Cultural History* (Oxford: Clarendon Press, 1969), 32–33.
136. Quirey, *May I Have the Pleasure*, 67–68.
137. Ibid., 118–119.
138. Gombrich, *In Search of Cultural History*, 32–33.
139. Desmond F. Strobel, "Quadrille," in *International Encyclopedia of Dance*, vol. 5, (New York: Oxford University Press, 1998), 285.
140. Raoul-Auger Feuillet, *Recueil de Contredanses* (Paris: L'auteur, 1772), 13.
141. Thomas Wilson, *The Quadrille and the Cotillion Panorama* (London: R & E Williamson, 1818), 136.
142. Quirey, *May I Have the Pleasure*, 72–74.
143. Wilson, *The Quadrille and the Cotillion Panorama*, 35–39.
144. Quirey, *May I Have the Pleasure*, 67; Richardson, *The Social Dances of the Nineteenth Century in England*, 58.
145. Blasis, *The Code of Terpsichore*, 497–501.
146. Cellarius, *The Drawing-Room Dances*, 10.
147. Richardson, *The Social Dances of the Nineteenth Century in England*, 78–79.
148. Ibid., 77.
149. Tierou, *Doople*, 13–19.
150. Raymond Williams, *Culture* (London: Fontana, 1981), 33.
151. Horst Koegler, *The Concise Oxford Dictionary of Ballet* (Oxford: Oxford University Press, 1982), 349; Steeh, *History of Ballet*, 23–24.
152. G. B. L. Wilson, *A Dictionary of Ballet* (London: Theatre Arts Books, 1976), 516; W. G. Raffe, with M. E Purdon, *Dictionary of The Dance* (London: Barnes, 1975), 404.
153. Wilson, *A Dictionary of Ballet*, 515–516.
154. Long, *The Black Tradition in American Dance*, 7–9.
155. Rath, "Drums and Power," 115.
156. Peter Linebaugh and Marcus Rediker, *The Many-Headed Hydra: Sailors, Slaves, Commoners, and the Hidden History of the Revolutionary Atlantic* (Boston: Beacon Press, 2000).
157. Moore, Lillian. "M. L. E. Moreau de St.-Mery and Danse." *Dance Index* 5, no.10 (October 1946), 235–236.
158. Gallini, *A Treatise on the Art of Dancing*, 215–216.
159. James H. Sweet, *Recreating Africa: Culture, Kinship and Religion in the African-Portuguese World, 1441–1770* (Chapel Hill: University of North Carolina Press, 2003).
160. Moore. "M. L. E. Moreau de St.-Mery and Danse," 241.
161. Ibid., 232.
162. Ibid., 241.
163. Ibid.
164. Ibid.
165. Ibid.
166. Ibid.
167. John Kelly Thornton, *Africa and Africans in the Making of the Atlantic World, 1400–1800* (Cambridge: Cambridge University Press, 1992), 189.
168. Lawrence W. Levine, *Black Culture and Black Consciousness: Afro-American Folk Thought From Slavery To Freedom* (Oxford: Oxford University Press, 1977), 298–366.
169. David Hector Monro, *Argument of Laughter* (Notre Dame, IN: University of Notre Dame Press, 1963), 13.
170. Daniel E. Berlyne, "Humour and Its Kin," in *The Psychology of Humour*, ed. Jeffrey Goldstein and Paul McGhee (New York, Academic, 1972), 43–60.
171. Monro, *Argument of Laughter*, 24–26.
172. Marcus Tullius Cicero in *De Oratore*, trans. E. W. Sutton and H. Rack-

ham (London: Heinemann, 1942), lviii–lxii.

173. Hans Jurgen Eysenck, *Dimensions of Personality* (London: Routledge & Kegan Paul, 1947).

174. Warren A. Shibles, *Humor: A Critical analysis* (Whitewater, WI: Language Press, 1978).

175. Sigmund Freud, *Jokes and their Relation to the Unconscious* (New York: Basic Books, 1960; first published 1905), 170.

176. Artistotle, *Aristotle: Poetics*, trans. Gerald F. Else (Ann Arbor, MI: University of Michigan Press, 1967), 6, 97–99.

177. Lane Cooper, *An Aristotelian Theory of Comedy, With an Adaptation of the Poetics and Translation of the Tractatus Coislinanus* (Oxford: Clarendon Press, 1924), 225.

178. Levine, *Black Culture and Black Consciousness*, .321.

179. Joel Chandler Harris, *Uncle Remus and His Friends* (New York: Houghton Mifflin, 1892); Levine, *Black Culture and Black Consciousness*, 81–83, 96, 103, 106–120.

180. Levine, *Black Culture and Black Consciousness*, 16–17.

181. Ibid.

Chapter 3

1. See chapter 1 of this book.

2. Lynne Fauley Emery, *Black Dance in the United States from 1619–1970* (London: Dance Books, 1988), 9.

3. Thomas Clarkson, *The History of the Rise, Progress, and Accomplishment of the Abolition of the African Slave-Trade by the British Parliament*, Vol. I (London: L. Taylor, 1808), 111.

4. Daniel P. Mannix and Malcolm Cowley, *Black Cargoes: A History of the Atlantic Slave Trade 1518 – 1865* (London: Penguin Books, 1963), 114.

5. *An Abstract of the Evidence Delivered Before a Select Committee of the House of Commons in the Years 1790–91, on the Part of the Petitioners for the Abolition of the Slave Trade* (London: Printed by James Philips, 1791), 39.

6. George Francis Dow, *Slave Ships and Slaving* (Salem, MA: Marine Research Society, 1927), 177–78.

7. Richard Drake, *Revelations of a Slave Smuggler: Being the Autobiography of Captain Rich'd Drake, An African Trader for Fifty Years, from 1807–1857: During Which Period He Was Concerned in the Transportation of Half a Million Blacks from African Coasts to America* (New York: Robert M. De Witt, 1860), 44.

8. Alexander Falconbridge, *An Account of the Slave Trade on the Coast of Africa* (London: B. White, and J. Sewell, 1788), 23.

9. Drake, *Revelations of a Slave Smuggler*, 59.

10. George Pinckard, *Notes on the West Indies*, Vol. I (London: Baldwin, 1816), 103.

11. Bryan Edwards, *An Historical Survey of the Island of Saint Domingo, Together with an Account of the Maroon Negroes in the Island of Jamaica; and a History of the War in the West Indies, in 1793 and 1794* (London: Printed for John Stockdale, 1801), 268.

12. Ibid., 88.

13. Olaudah Equiano, *The Interesting Narrative*, 205–7.

14. The print title *The Abolition of the Slave Trade* is No. 8079 in the British Museum's *Catalogue of Political and Personal Satires, 1784–1792*.

15. Samuel D. Wilberforce, *The Life of William Wilberforce* (London: J. Murray, 1868), 105–106.

16. Marcus Wood, *Blind Memory: Visual Representations of Slavery in England and America, 1780–1885* (Manchester: Manchester University Press, 2000), 161.

17. Ibid.

18. W. E. B. DuBois, *Darkwater: Voices from within the Veil* (New York: AMS Press, 1969), 172.

19. Michael Porter, *The Conspiracy to Destroy Black Women* (New York: African American Images, 2001), 29.

20. Daniel McKinnen, *A Tour Through the British West Indies in the Years 1802 & 1803* (London: J. White; R. Taylor, 1804), 70.

21. Brian Dyed, *A History of Antigua, The Unsuspected Isle* (New York: Interlink Publishing Group, 2000), 14.

Notes — Chapter 3

22. Edwards, *An Historical Survey*, 348.
23. Richard Sheridan, "The Rise of a Colonial Gentry: A Case Study of Antigua, 1730–1775," *Economic History Review*, 2nd Series, 13 (1960–1961), 347.
24. *Calendar of State Papers*, Colonial (West Indies) Series (1701), 1132.
25. John Newton, *The Works of the Rev. John Newton Published by the Direction of His Executors*, Vol. VI (London: for the author's nephew, 1808), 544.
26. *Calendar of State Papers*, 1132.
27. Vincent T. Harlow, *Christopher Codrington, 1668–1710* (Oxford: Clarendon Press, 1928), 121. See also Codrington Papers for the daily running of the estate and other political matters. Codrington Papers Microfilm:
RP2616 see British Library M2096, British Library
MF375 *S. Redhead to William Codrington*, 1 June 1762 and 25 April 1783
MF375 *Osborn to C. B. C.*, 30 April 1817
MF375 *Winter to C. B. C.*, 26 September 1832
RP 2616 C 12 letter dated 24 November 1780
RP 2616 C14/1 *W. C. to Reynolds*, 30 July 1786
RP 2616 C20/1 *C. B. C. to W. C*, 2 March 1790
RP 2616 C20/2 *C. B. C. to W. C*, 17 June 1790
RP 2616 C24 *J. James to C. B. C*, 10 February 1826
RP 2616 C27/1 *C. B. C. to Hodge*, 21 June and 4 September 1809
RP 2616 C27/1 *C. B. C. to James*, 3 September 1809
RP 2616 C29 *Jarritt to C. B. C*, 6 October 1829
RP 2616 C33 *Martin to C. B. C*, 7 July 1809
RP 2616 E5 *List of Slaves at Betty's Hope*, 1793
RP 2616 E6 *List of Slaves at Betty's Hope*, 1808
RP 2616 E6 *List of Slaves at Betty's Hope* 1817, 1818–1827
RP 2616 E17 *List of Negroes on Island of Barbuda*, 1805
28. *Calendar of State Papers*, 1132.
29. David Barry Gaspar, *Bondmen and Rebels: A Study of Master-Slave Relations in Antigua* (Baltimore and London: Johns Hopkins University Press, 1985), 29–37.
30. Frances Lanaghan, *Antigua and the Antiguans: An Impartial View of Slavery and the Free Labour Systems*, Vol. I (London: Saunders & Otley, 1844), 87.
31. James Walvin, *Slaves and Slavery: The British Colonial Experience* (Manchester: Manchester University Press, 1992), 57.
32. Robert Arbuthnot, "Minutes of the Assembly of Antigua. Report to the legislature, An Act for Better Discovery of Conspiracy, Treason and Rebellion of Slaves," (Antigua, Oct. 15, 1736), 100–109, *Colonial Papers* C O. 9/25; C O 152/153.
33. Arbuthnot, 40–51.
34. Gaspar, *Bondmen and Rebels*, 248.
35. Ibid., 244.
36. Ibid., 29–37.
37. Ibid., 237.
38. Ibid., 244.
39. Samuel Martin, *Essay upon Plantership, Humbly Inscribed to all the Planters of the British Sugar-Colonies in America, by an Old Planter* (London: T. Cadell, 1773).
40. John Horsford, *A Voice from the West Indies, Being a Review of the Character and Results of Missionary Efforts in the British and other Colonies in the Caribbean Sea with Some Remarks on the Usages, Prejudices, Etc of the Inhabitants* (London: Alexander and Heyhen, 1856), 83.
41. William Young, *A Tour through the Several Islands of Barbadoes, St Vincent, Antigua, Tobago, and Grenada in the Years 1791 & 1792* (London: Printed for John Stockdale, 1801), 265.
42. Sheridan, "The Rise of a Colonial Gentry," 344, 355–7.
43. Lanaghan, *Antigua and the Antiguans*, Vol. II, 284.
44. David Barry Gaspar, "The Antigua Slave Conspiracy of 1736: A Case Study of the Origins of Collective Resistance," *William and Mary Quarterly*, 3rd ser., 34, no. 2, (April 1978), 314.
45. Ibid.
46. Lanaghan, *Antigua and the Antiguans*, Vol. II, 284.
47. Sheridan, "The Rise of a Colonial Gentry," 346.
48. Gretchen Holbrook Gerzina, *Black*

London: Life before Emancipation (New Brunswick, NJ: Rutgers University Press, 1995), 20.

49. Ibid., 45.

50. Equiano, *The Interesting Narrative*, 223.

51. Ibid., 224.

52. Ibid.

53. Ibid., 230.

54. Ibid., 229.

55. Ibid., 213.

56. Ibid.

57. Ibid., 243.

58. Mary Prince, *The History of Mary Prince, A West Indian Slave, Related by Herself, with a Supplement by the Editor; to Which is Added the Narrative of Asa-Asa, a Captured African* (London, F. Westley & AH Davis, 1831), 1–11.

59. Mr. Dawes, correspondence in *Church Missionary Society Papers*, CW/0 31/71 (24 April 1826).

60. Lanaghan, *Antigua and the Antiguans*, Vol. II, 107–108.

61. Edward W. Said, *Culture and Imperialism* (New York: Alfred A. Knopf, 1993).

62. Richard Sheridan, "Samuel Martin, Innovating Sugar Planter of Antigua 1750–1776," *Agricultural History* 4 (1960), 126–139, 134.

63. Dyed, *A History of Antigua*, 32–33.

64. J. Luffman, *A Brief Account of the Island of Antigua* (London: Printed by T. Cadell, 1788), 135–137.

65. Richard Ralph, *The Life and Works of John Weaver* (London: Dance Horizons, 1985), 36.

66. Young, *A Tour through the Several Islands*, 283.

67. Richard Cullen Rath, "Drums and Power: Ways of Creolizing Music in Coastal South Carolina and Georgia, 1730–1790" in *Creolization in the Americas: Cultural Adaptations to the New World*, Steven G. Reinhardt and David Buisseret, ed. (College Station, TX: Texas A&M University Press, 2000), 107–109.

68. Ibid., 115.

69. Ibid., 107.

70. Ibid., 109.

71. Cyril Beaumont, *A Miscellany For Dancers*, 16.

72. Rath, "Drums and Power," 109; John Stern Roberts, *Black Music of Two Worlds, African, Caribbean, Latin and Afro-American Traditions*, (New York: Praeger Publishers,1972), pp. 27–28; and John Lowell Lewis, *Ring of Liberation: Discourse in Brazilian Capoeira*, (Chicago: University of Chicago Press, 1992).

73. Rath, "Drums and Power," 109.

74. Susanna Sloat, ed., *Caribbean Dance from Abakua to Zouk: How Movement Shapes Identity* (Gainesville, University Press of Florida, 2002), 11–20.

75. Rath, "Drums and Power," 111.

76. Ibid.

77. Ibid., 112.

78. Ibid.

Chapter 4

1. Peter Linebaugh and Marcus Rediker, *The Many-Headed Hydra: Sailors, Slaves, Commoners, and the Hidden History of the Revolutionary Atlantic* (Boston: Beacon Press, 2000).

2. Peter Fryer, *Staying Power: The History of Black People in Britain* (London: Pluto Press, 1984), 4–9; Gretchen Holbrook Gerzina, *Black London: Life before Emancipation* (New Brunswick: Rutgers University Press, 1995) 33; Folarin Shyllon, *Black People in Britain, 1555–1833* (Oxford: Oxford University Press, for the Institute of Race Relations, 1977), 3–4.

3. See *The Gentleman's Magazine* (1764) and Samuel Eastwick, *Considerations on the Negro Cause, Commonly So Called, Addressed to the Right Honourable Lord Mansfield, Lord Chief Justice of the Court of King's Bench* (London: J. Dodsley, 1773), 94.

4. Shyllon, *Black People in Britain*, 102.

5. H. Plumb, *England in the Eighteenth Century* (London: Penguin Books, 1950), 144.

6. M. D. George, *London Life in the Eighteenth Century* (London: Penguin Books, 1925), 329–30.

7. Gerzina, *Black London*, 136.

8. David Bygott, *Black and British* (Oxford: Oxford University Press, 1992), 9.

9. Ibid.

10. Ibid.

11. Ibid.
12. Ibid., 10
13. Martha Warren Beckwith, *Black Roadways* (Chapel Hill: University of North Carolina Press, 1929), 3.
14. Cedric Dover, *Hell in the Sunshine* (London: Secker & Warburg, 1943), 159.
15. Richard Hakluyt *The Principal Navigations, Voyages, Traffiques and Discoveries of the English Nation 1598* (Glasgow: J. MacLehose, 1903–5), 61.
16. Shyllon, *Black People in Britain*, 6.
17. Eric Williams, *Capitalism and Slavery* (London: Andre Deutsch, 1964), 30–3.
18. W. E. B. DuBois, *The Negro* (London: Williams & Norgate, 1915), 91–110; W. E. B. DuBois, *The Suppression of the African Slave Trade to the United States of America 1638–1870* (Cambridge, MA: Harvard University, 1896), 3, 207–8.
19. Nick Yupp, *The French Millennium* (Koln: Konemann, 2001), 383.
20. Gerzina, *Black London*, 5.
21. John Latimer, *Annals of Bristol in the Eighteenth Century* (Forme: Printed for the author, 1893), 15.
22. Ibid.
23. Ibid., 146.
24. Clare Tomalin, *Samuel Pepys: The Unequalled Self* (New York: Alfred A. Knopf, 2002), 149.
25. Ibid., 179.
26. *The Gentleman's Magazine* (1749), 89–90.
27. H. A. Wyndham, *The Atlantic and Slavery* (London: Oxford University Press, 1935), 59–62.
28. David Eltis, *The Rise of African Slavery in the Americas* (Cambridge: Cambridge University Press, 2000).
29. *The London Gazette*, March 1685.
30. Ibid.
31. Ignatius Sancho, *Letters of the Late Ignatius Sancho, An African*, 5th ed. (London: J. Nichols, 1803), 271–7.
32. M. D. George, *London Life*, 134.
33. *The Gentleman's Magazine*, 1780, 591.
34. Sancho, *Letters of the Late Ignatius Sancho*, 70–1.
35. Ibid., 25.
36. G. Saintsbury, ed. *Letters of the Late Ignatius Sancho, An African*, Vol. I, (London: J.M. Dent, 1894), 130–1.
37. Sancho, *Letters of the Late Ignatius Sancho*, 273.
38. Ibid., 231.
39. Ibid., 31–3.
40. Brycchan Carey, Markman Ellis, and Sara Salih, eds., "'The Hellish Means of Killing and Kidnapping': Ignatius Sancho and the Campaign against the 'Abominable Traffic for Slaves'" in *Discourses of Slavery and Abolition. Britain and Its Colonies, 1760–1838* (Basingstoke, 2004).
41. Bygott, *Black and British*, 24.
42. Linebaugh and Rediker, *The Many-Headed Hydra*, 221.
43. Fryer, *Staying Power*, 227–228.
44. *London Chronicle*, February 17, 1764.
45. *General Evening Post*, August 28, 1773.
46. Jean J. Hecht, *Continental and Colonial Servants in Eighteenth Century England* (Northampton, MA: Department of History, Smith College, 1954), 49.
47. Robert Hinton, *American Dance Festival, The Black Tradition In American Modern Dance*, ed. Gerald E. Myers (Durham: American Dance Festival, Duke University, 1988–90), 6.
48. Philip C. Yorke, ed., *The Diary of John Baker: Barrister of the Middle Temple Solicitor-General of the Leeward Island* (London: Hutchinson, 1931), 49.
49. *London Chronicle*, February 17, 1764.
50. Yorke, *The Diary of John Baker*, 15.
51. E. Long, *Candid Reflections*, 47.
52. Dover, *Hell in the Sunshine*, 159.
53. Prince Hoare, *Memoirs of Granville Sharp*, Vol. I (London: Henry Colburn, 1828), 113.
54. *Middlesex Journal*, June 23, 1772.
55. *London Chronicle*, June 23, 1772.
56. *London Packet*, June 26–29, 1772.
57. Peter Fryer, *Black People in the British Empire* (London: Pluto Press, 1988), 25; Shyllon, *Black People in Britain*, 238.
58. Eugene D. Genovese, *Roll Jordan, Roll: The World the Slaves Made* (New York: Vintage, 1972).
59. O. Nigel Bolland, *The Formation of a Colonial Society: Belize: From Conquest to Crown Colony* (Baltimore: Johns Hopkins University Press, 1977); Philip Morgan, *Slave Counterpoint: Black Culture in the Eighteenth-Century Chesapeake and Low-

country (Chapel Hill: University of North Carolina Press, 1998); Richard Follett, *The Sugar Masters: Planters and Slaves in Louisiana's Cane World, 1820–1860* (Baton Rouge: Louisiana State University Press, 2005); Christopher Morris, *Becoming Southern: The Evolution of a Way of life, Warren County and Vicksburg, Mississippi, 1770–1860* (Oxford: Oxford University Press, 1995); David Brion Davis, *From Homicide to Slavery: Studies in American Culture*, (Oxford: Oxford University Press, 1986).

60. Samuel Martin, *Essay upon Plantership, Humbly Inscribed to all the Planters of the British Sugar-Colonies in America, By an Old Planter* (London: T. Cadell, 1773), 6.

61. Follett, *Sugar Masters*.

62. Karl Marx, *Das Kapital, Kritik der Politischen Oekonomie* (Hamburg: Meissner, 1857); Karl Marx, *Capital, Volume I: A Critique of a Political Economy* (London: Penguin, 1976).

63. Rebecca Scott, *Slave Emancipation in Cuba: The Transition to Free Labor 1860 to 1899* (Princeton, NJ: Princeton University Press, 1995); Rebecca Scott, Frederick Cooper, and Thomas C. Holt, *Beyond Slavery: Explorations of Race, Labor, and Citizenship in Post-emancipation Societies* (Chapel Hill: University of North Carolina Press, 2000).

64. Genovese, *Roll Jordan, Roll*.

65. Peter Way, "Soldiers and Misfortune, New England Regulars and the Fall of Oswego, 1755–1756," *Massachusetts Historical Review* 1 (2001).

66. Peter Way, "Labor's Love Lost: Observation on the Historiography of Class and Ethnicity in the Nineteenth Century," *Journal of American Studies* 28 (1994), 1–22.

67. Lawrence T. McDonnell, *October Revolution: Communism's Last Stand* (London: Staplehurst, 1994).

68. Marika Sherwood, "William Davison," in *Oxford Dictionary of National Biography*, Vol. 14, (Oxford: Oxford University Press, 2004), 331–332.

69. Thomas Howell, *A Complete Collection of State Trials and Proceedings for High Treason and other Crimes and Misdemeanors from the Earliest Period of the Year 1783 with Notes and Other Illustrations Compiled by T. Howell Esq. and Continues from the Year 1783 to Present Time*, Vol. XXXIII (London: T.C. Hansard, 1826), 1461–1462.

70. Lawrence T. McDonnell, "Money Knows No Master: Market Relations and the American Salve Community," in W.B. Moore et al., ed., *Developing Dixie: Modernization in a Traditional Society* (New York: Greenwood Press, 1988), 29.

71. Shyllon, Black People in Britain, 159.

72. James Scott, *Weapons of the Weak: Everyday Forms of Peasant Resistance* (New Haven, CT: Yale University Press, 1985); James Scott, *Domination and the Arts of Resistance: Hidden Transcripts* (New Haven, CT: Yale University Press, 1990), x; Robin Kelly, *Race Rebels: Culture, Politics and the Black Working Class* (New York: Free Press, 1994), 8; Walter Johnson, *Soul by Soul: Life inside the Antebellum Slave Market* (Cambridge, MA: Harvard University Press, 1999).

73. Kenneth W. Goings and Raymond A. Mohl, eds., *The New African American Urban History* (Thousand Oaks, CA: Sage, 1996).

74. Kelly, *Race Rebels*, 9, 146–147.

75. Michael Freeman, *Francois Villon in His Works, the Villain's Tale, Faux Titre 195* (Amsterdam: Rodopi, 2000); Richard Dutton, Jean E. Howard, eds., *A Companion to Shakespeare's Works* (Oxford: Blackwell, 2003); Thomas Cassirer, Reinhard Sander, Ralph Faulkingham and Samba Gadjigo, eds., *Ousmane Sembene: Dialogues with Critics and Writers* (Amherst, MA: University of Massachusetts Press, 1993); Earle Ernst, *The Kabuki Theatre* (Oxford: Oxford University Press, 1956).

76. Mikhail Mikhailovich Bakhtin, *Rabelais and His World* (Bloomington: Indiana University Press, 1984), 21.

77. Richard D. E. Burton, *Afro-Creole: Power, Opposition and Play in the Caribbean*, (Ithaca, NY: Cornell University Press, 1997), 156.

78. Ibid., 157.

79. Ibid.

80. Ibid.

81. John Rule, *The Labouring Classes in Early Industrial England 1750–1850*, (London: Longman, 1986), 214.

82. Ibid.
83. E. P. Thompson, *The Making of the English Working Class* (London: Victor Gollancz, 1963), 448.
84. Peter Wilson, *Crab Antics: The Social Anthropology of English Speaking Negro Societies of the Caribbean* (New Haven, CT: Yale University Press, 1973).
85. Ibid., 26.
86. *General Evening Post*, August 28, 1773.
87. Homi K. Bhabha, *The Location of Culture* (London: Routledge, 1994), 35.
88. W. E. B. DuBois, *The Souls of Black Folk in Three Negro Classics* (New York: Avon Books, 1965), 207–390.
89. Fryer, *Staying Power*, 225.
90. Ibid.
91. Peter Fryer, "William Cuffay," in *Oxford Dictionary of National Biography*, Vol. XIV, ed. H. C. G. Mathew and Brian Harrison (Oxford: Oxford University Press, 2004), 567–568.
92. Ibid., 567.

Chapter 5

1. This is based on personal conversations with my mother, Eileen King-Dorset, and my father, Eric King-Dorset. My mother's grandmother, Rebecca James, was herself a slave who lived to the age of 84, and had clear recollections of her youthful experiences, which my mother has duly passed on to me.
2. Norman C. Stolzoff, *Wake the Town and Tell the People: Dance Hall Culture in Jamaica* (London: Duke University Press, 2000), 26.
3. John Luffman, *A Brief Account of the Island of Antigua, Together with the Customs & Manners of its Inhabitants* (London: Printed by T. Cadell, 1788), 127.
4. Austin Steward, *Twenty-Two Years a Slave, Forty Years a Freeman: Embracing a Correspondence of Several Years While President of Wilberforce Colony, London, Canada West* (New York: W. Alling, 1857), 20–21.
5. Julio Cesar, cited in Norman C. Stolzoff, *Wake the Town*, 24.
6. James Stewart, *A View of the Past and Present State of Jamaica, with Remarks on the Moral and Physical Condition of the Slaves and on the Abolition of Slavery in the Colonies* (Edinburgh, 1832), 202.
7. Christopher Wood, *The Dictionary of Victorian Painters* (London: Jupiter, 1978), 501.
8. Correspondence between private art collector Michael Graham Stewart and historian J.D. Ellis, London, July 2001.
9. Author's interview with Michael Graham Stewart, London, May 2004.
10. Ibid.
11. Ibid.
12. Mia Bay, *The White Image in the Black Mind: African-American Ideas about White People, 1830–1925* (Oxford: Oxford University Press, 2000), 3.
13. Interview with Mr. Chapman by Mrs. Ophelia Settle Egypt, Fisk University, Social Science Institute, in *Slave Narratives: A Folk History of Slavery in the United States from Interviews with Former Slaves* (Washington, DC, 1936–38), 33.
14. J. G. Kenneys, *Free and Candid Reflections Occasioned by the late Additional Duties on Sugars and Rum* (London: Printed for the author and sold by T. Becket, 1783), 72n, 79n.
15. Melville J. Herskovits and Frances Herskovits, *Trinidad Village* (New York: Alfred A. Knopf, 1947), 192.
16. Robert Farris Thompson, *African Art in Motion* (Berkeley: University of California Press, 1974), 5–45.
17. Ibid.
18. Author's interview with Ellis Rogers in 2000. Rogers is the author of *The Quadrille: A Book on the History, Development and Practice of the Dance* (London: C&E Rogers, 2003).
19. Cheryl Ryman, "The Jamaican Heritage in Dance: Developing a Traditional Typology" *Jamaica Journal No. 44*, 11, 13.
20. Pierre Rameau, *Le Maitre a Danse* (Paris: Chez Jean Villette, Rue Saint Jacques, a la Croix d'Or, 1725).
21. Gennaro Magri, *Theoretical and Practical Treatise on Dancing* (Naples: Orsino, 1779); Judith L. Schwartz and Christena L. Schlundt, *French Court Dance and Dance Music: A Guide to Primary*

Source Writings 1643–1789 (New York: Pendragon Press, 1987); Rameau, *Le Maitre a Danse*, 22–29; Carlo Blasis, *An Elementary Treatise upon the Theory and Practice of the Art of Dancing* (New York: Dover Publications, 1968), 13.

22. Rameau, *Le Maitre a Danse*, 46, 48, 168, 186, 203, 212, 258.

23. White & White, *Stylin,'* 79.

24. January 2008 interview with my mother, Eileen King-Dorset, an enthusiastic folk dancer both in Antigua where she grew up and later in England. My mother is the granddaughter of a slave and remembers talking with her grandmother about these matters. I have also seen the Lucianite Dancers, based in Hackney, perform on a regular basis since November 21, 1998, at London-based quadrille dance events, together with DONA (Dominican Quadrille Group), based in Acton, and Hibiscus Quadrille Troupe, based in Stratford.

25. Ryman, "The Jamaican Heritage in Dance," 11, 13.

26. Author's interview with actor/dancer Darren Walker, August 2003, based on his recollections of taking part in performances of the quadrille in Jamaica.

27. Albert J. Raboteau, *Slave Religion: The "Invisible Institution" in the Antebellum South* (Oxford: Oxford University Press, 1978), 35.

28. Equiano, *The Interesting Narrative*, 7–9.

29. Author's interview with Michael Graham Stewart, London, May 2004.

30. Ibid.

31. Quirey, *May I Have the Pleasure*, 60.

32. Bernard Darwin, ed., *The Oxford Dictionary of Quotations* (London: Oxford University Press, 1941), 360.

33. Hugh Honour, *The Image of the Black in Western Art*, Vol. IV, No. II (London: Harvard University Press, 1989), 60.

34. Ibid., 60–61.

35. Jean and Marshall Stearns, *Jazz Dance: A Story of American Vernacular Dance: A History of Dancing to Jazz, from its African Origins to the Present* (New York: Macmillan, 1966), 22.

36. *Harris's List of Covent Garden Ladies, Or Man of Pleasure, for the Year 1788* (London: H. Ranger, 1788), 84.

37. Cedric Dover, *Hell in the Sunshine* (London: Secker and Warburg, 1943), 113.

38. Ibid.

39. Hesketh J. Bell, *Obeah: Witchcraft in the West Indies* (Westport, CT: Negro Universities Press, 1970; first published in London, 1889), 33–36.

40. Chernoff, *African Rhythm*, 82.

41. Quirey, *May I Have the Honor*, 67–68.

42. Bell, *Obeah*, 31.

43. Maxwell Owusu, "Rebellion, Revolution, and Tradition: Reinterpreting Coups in Ghana," *Comparative Studies in Society and History* 31, no. 2 (April 1989), 372–397.

44. Franks, *Social Dance*, 154.

45. Ibid., 145.

46. Peter Fryer, *Oxford Dictionary of National Biography*, Vol. XIV, ed. H. C. G. Matthew & Brian Harrison (Oxford: Oxford University Press, 2004), 567–568. See chapter 4.

47. Hilary S. Carty, *Folk Dances of Jamaica: An Insight* (London: Dance Books, 1988), 47.

48. Marcus Wood, *Blind Memory*, 153.

49. William Makepeace Thackeray, *The Paris Sketch Book* (London: Bradbury, Evans, 1870).

50. James Stewart, *A View of the Past and Present State of Jamaica, with Remarks on the Moral and Physical Condition of the Slaves and on the Abolition of Slavery in the Colonies* (Edinburgh, 1823), 272–273.

51. Ibid.

52. Henry Louis Gates, Jr., *The Signifying Monkey: A Theory of African American Literary Criticism* (New York: Oxford University Press, 1988), 89–97.

53. Jean and Marshall Stearns, *Jazz Dance*, 14–15.

54. Mervyn C. Alleyne, *Roots of Jamaican Culture* (London: Pluto Press, 1988).

55. Bell, *Obeah*, 31.

56. Hester Lynch Piozzi, *Anecdotes of the Life of the Late Samuel Johnson, LL.D, during the Last Twenty Years of His Life*, ed. S. C. Roberts (Cambridge: Cambridge University Press, 1925), 136–7.

57. Helen Scholes, producer and director, *The Black Georgians*. (Broadcast on BBC 4, June 28, 2006.)

58. Stedman, *Narrative of a Five Year's Expedition,* 259–60.
59. Shyllon, *Black People in Britain,* 187.
60. Thomas Gainsborough's portrait of Sancho is now in the National Gallery of Canada in Ottawa.
61. Interview with my mother, Eileen King-Dorset, London, January 2008.
62. *The Times,* July 9, 2003, 1.
63. The Lucianite Dancers have performed at quadrille events in a number of London regions, including Ealing and Clapton.
64. Interview with my mother, Eileen King-Dorset, January 2008.

Conclusion

1. Shyllon, *Black People in London,* 159.
2. Herskovits, *The Myth of the Negro Past,* 76.
3. *General Evening Post,* August 28, 1773.

Bibliography

Primary Sources

Plantation documents (1752), parliamentary papers (1736), and the laws of Antigua (1723) were useful sources of information. Unfortunately, the plantation documents—the Codrington Papers—tended to be about the daily running of the estate or political matters.

London news journals that comprise the Burnley collection (1700–1850) provided valuable information about one aspect of London's African dance heritage. The many white commentators admitted to having problems with the presence of blacks in London, especially with the "black only" club where the black Londoners danced and worked together to form strong community links in the tradition of their forebears. Probably the commentators were blinkered by their own image of black people and their dance and felt compelled to exercise their own insecurities about the dancing body and so projected them onto blacks.

The series of prints that include ones by Isaac Cruikshank (1792) and G.S. Tregears (c.1834), together with the pencil sketches by Thomas McLean (1833), an unknown artist (1850), and watercolors by Robert F. Watson (1820s), also provided valuable evidence. *The Abolition of the Slave Trade* is recorded in the British Museum's *Catalogue of Political and Personal Satires*, by M. D. George, VI, No. 8079, 1784–1792.

Michael Graham-Stewart, New Zealand and London collector of African art, provided me with copies of prints, lithographs and watercolors depicting black people dancing. Dr. Robert Blyth, until 2006 the curator of imperial and maritime history at the National Maritime Museum in Greenwich, provided me with prints and drawings exploring the abolition of slavery. (Prints purchased by the National Maritime Museum from Michael Graham-Stewart.)

The Public Record Office in Kew, London, provided access to the *Robert Arbuthnot Colonial Papers*, Co. 9/25; C O 152/153; "Minutes of the Assembly of Antigua Report to the Legislature: An Act for Better Discovery of Conspiracy Treason and Rebellion of Slaves" (St. John's Antigua, Oct.15, 1736).

Periodicals

Liverpool Papers, British Library, Add. MSS. 38416, fol.134
General Evening Post, August 28, 1773
Gentleman's Magazine, 1749, 1764, 1780
London Advertiser, July 15, 1788
London Chronicle, June 23, 1772; February 17, 1764
London Gazette, March 1685
London Packet, June 26–29, 1772
Monthly Review, June 1789
Middlesex Journal, June 23, 1772
Times, July 9, 2003; April 2, 2005

Microfilm

Codrington Papers Microfilm (RP2616 see British Library M2096), British Library

MF375 *S. Redhead to William Codrington*, 1 June 1762 and 25 April 1783
MF375 *Osborn to C. B. C.*, 30 April 1817
MF375 *Winter to C. B. C.*, 26 September 1832
RP 2616 C 12 letter dated 24 November 1780
RP 2616 C14/1 *W. C. to Reynolds*, 30 July 1786
RP 2616 C20/1 *C. B. C. to W. C*, 2 March 1790
RP 2616 C20/2 *C. B. C. to W. C*, 17 June 1790
RP 2616 C24 *J. James to C. B. C*, 10 February 1826
RP 2616 C27/1 *C. B. C. to Hodge*, 21 June and 4 September 1809
RP 2616 C27/1 *C. B. C. to James*, 3 September 1809
RP 2616 C29 *Jarritt to C. B. C*, 6 October 1829
RP 2616 C33 *Martin to C. B. C*, 7 July 1809
RP 2616 E5 *List of Slaves at Betty's Hope*, 1793
RP 2616 E6 *List of Slaves at Betty's Hope*, 1808
RP 2616 E6 *List of Slaves at Betty's Hope* 1817, 1818–1827
RP 2616 E17 *List of Negroes on Island of Barbuda*, 1805
Church Missionary Society Papers
CW/0 31/71. London, April 24, 1826, Mr Dawes
CMS CW/031/65
CMS CW/031/64a
Calendar of State Papers, Colonial West Indies Series, 1701
Laws of the Island of Antigua, British Library Publication Department, Vol. I, 1668–1790

Interviews

Eileen King-Dorset
Ellis Rogers
Michael Graham Stewart.
Darren Walker

Secondary Sources

Adair, Christy. "Phoenix Perspectives: African American Influences on a British Dance Company." In *Embodying Liberation, The Black Body in American Dance*, edited by Dorothea Fischer-Hornung and Alison D. Goeller. Hamburg: Lit Verlag, 2001.

Adinku, W. Ofotsu. *African Dance Education in Ghana*. Accra: University of Ghana Press, 1994.

Alford, Violet. "The Rigaudon." *Musical Quarterly* 30, no. 3 (1944).

Alleyne, Mervyn C. *Roots of Jamaican Culture*. London: Pluto Press, 1988.

Anderson, Benedict. *Imagined Communities: Reflections of the Origin and Spread of Nationalism*, rev. ed. London: Verso, 1991.

Aristotle. *Aristotle: Poetics*. Translated Gerald F. Else. Ann Arbor, MI: University of Michigan Press, 1967.

Astaire, Fred, and Bob Thomas. *Astaire: The Man, The Dancer*. London: Weidenfeld and Nicholson, 1985.

Austin, Jane. *Pride and Prejudice*. London: T. Egerton, 1813.

Baker, Philip and Chris Corne. "Universals, Substrata and the Indian Ocean Creoles." In *Substrata Versus Universals in Creole Genesis: Papers from the Amsterdam Creole Workshop*, April 1986, edited by Pieter Muysken and Noval Smith. Amsterdam, 1986.

Bakhtin, Mikhail Mikhailovich. *Rabelais and His World*. Bloomington: Indiana University Press, 1984.

Barbot, John. *A Description of the Coasts of North and South Guinea; and of Ethiopia Interior, Vulgarly Angola; Being a New and Accurate Account of the Western Maritime Countries of Africa, Cited by Awnsham Churchill, A Collection of Voyages and Travels, Some Now First Printed from Original Manuscripts*. London, 1704.

Barnes, Sandra T. "The Many Faces of Ogun." In *Africa's Ogun*. Bloomington: Indiana University Press, 1989.

Basildon, David. *Africa in History*. New York: St. Martin's Press, 1991.

Baskerville, Charles Read. *The Elizabethan Jig and Related Drama*. Chicago: University of Chicago Press, 1929.

Baugh, John. *Black Street Speech*. Austin: University of Texas Press, 1983.

Bibliography

Bay, Mia. *The White Image in the Black Mind: African-American Ideas about White People, 1830–1925.* Oxford: Oxford University Press, 2000.

Beaumont, Cyril. *A Miscellany for Dancers.* London: Golden Cockerel Press, 1954.

Beckwith, Carol, and Angela Fisher. *African Ceremonies.* New York: Harry N. Abrams, 1999.

Beckwith, Martha Warren. *Black Roadways.* Chapel Hill: University of North Carolina Press, 1929.

Bell, J. Hesketh. *Obeah: Witchcraft in the West Indies.* Westport, CT: Negro Universities Press, 1970.

Benesh, Rudolf, and Joan Benesh. *An Introduction to Benesh Movement Notation.* London: A & C. Black, 1956.

Benesh, Rudolf, and Joan Benesh. *Reading Dance: The Birth of Choreology.* London: Souvenir Press, 1977.

Benitez-Rojo, Antonio. *The Repeating Island: The Caribbean and the Postmodern Perspective.* Durham, NC: Duke University Press, 1996.

Bennett Jr., Lerone. *Before the Mayflower.* Chicago: University of Chicago Press, 2003.

Berlin, Ira. *Many Thousands Gone: The First Two Centuries of Slavery in North America.* Cambridge, MA: Harvard University Press, 1998.

Berlyne, Daniel E. "Humor and Its Kin." In *The Psychology of Humor*, edited by Jeffrey Goldstein and Paul McGhee. New York: Academic, 1972.

Berry, Irmgard E. *Benesh Movement Notation Score Catalogue: An International Listing of Benesh Movement Notation Scores of Professional Dance Works Recorded 1955–1985.* London: Benesh Institute of Choreology Ltd, 1986.

Bhabha, Homi K. *The Location of Culture.* London: Routledge, 1994.

Bickell, R. *The West Indies as They Are, or a Real Picture of Slavery; but More Particular as it Exists in the Island of Jamaica.* London, Printed by R. Taylor, 1825.

Bickerton, Derek. *Roots of Language.* Ann Arbor, MI: Karoma Publishers, 1981.

_____. *Language & Species.* Chicago: University of Chicago Press, 1990.

Blasis, Carlo. *The Code of Terpsichore: The Art of Dancing, Comprising its Theory and Practice.* London: E. Bull, 1830.

_____. *An Elementary Treatise upon the Theory and Practice of the Art of Dancing.* New York, Dover Publications, 1968.

Blassingame, John W. *The Slave Community: Plantation Life in the Antebellum South.* Oxford: Oxford University Press, 1972.

Bolland, Nigel. *The Formation of a Colonial Society: Belize, from Conquest to Crown Colony.* Baltimore, MD: Johns Hopkins University Press, 1977.

Bosman, William. *A New and Accurate Description of the Coast of Guinea, Divided into the Gold, the Slave, and the Ivory Coast.* 2nd edition. Edited by James Knapton and Daniel Midwinter. London: Ballantyne Press, 1705.

_____. *A New and Accurate Description of the Coast of Guinea, Divided into the Gold, the Slave, and the Ivory Coast.* New edition with an introduction by John Ralph Willis, notes by J.D. Fage and R. E. Bradbury. London: Frank Cass, 1967.

Bowdich, Thomas Edward. *Mission from Cape Coast Castle to Ashantee, With a Statistical Account of that Kingdom, and Geographical Notices of Other Parts of the Interior of Africa.* Glasgow: Khull, Blackie, 1819.

Braffi, Emmanuel Kingsley. *The Esoteric Significance of the Asante Nation.* Kumasi: Educational Press and Manufactures, 1984.

Brathwaite, Edward. *The Development of Creole Society in Jamaica, 1770–1820* Oxford: Oxford University Press, 1971.

_____. *The Development of Early Modern British Colonies and the Formation of American Culture.* Chapel Hill: University of North Carolina Press, 1988.

Browning, Barbara. *Samba: Resistance in Motion.* Bloomington: Indiana University Press, 1995.

Burnard, Trevor and Kenneth Morgan. "The Dynamics of the Slave Market and Slave Purchasing Patterns in Jamaica, 1655–1788." *William and Mary Quarterly*, January, 2001.

Burt, Ramsay. *The Male Dancer: Bodies,*

Spectacle, Sexualities. London: Routledge, 1995.

Burton, Richard D. E. *Afro-Creole: Power, Opposition, and Play in the Caribbean.* Ithaca, NY: Cornell University Press, 1997.

Bygott, David. *Black and British.* Oxford: Oxford University Press, 1992.

Carey, Brycchan, Markman Ellis, and Sara Salih, eds. "The Hellish Means of Killing and Kidnapping': Ignatius Sancho and the Campaign against the 'Abominable Traffic for Slaves.'" In *Discourses of Slavery and Abolition: Britain and Its Colonies, 1760–1838.* Basingstoke: Palgrave Macmillan, 2004.

Carney, Judith. *Black Rice: The African Origins of Rice Cultivation in the Americas.* Cambridge, MA: Harvard University Press, 2001.

Carretta, Vincent. "Olaudah Equiano or Gustavus Vassa? New Light on an Eighteenth-century Question of identity." *Slavery and Abolition*, December 1999.

_____, ed. *The Interesting Narrative and Other Writings.* London: Penguin Classics, 2003.

Carty, Hilary S. *Folk Dances of Jamaica: An Insight* London: Dance Books, 1988.

Gadjigo, Samba, Ralph Faulkingham, Thomas Cassirer, and Reinhard Sander, eds. *Ousmane Sembène: Dialogues with Critics and Writers.* Amherst, MA: University of Massachusetts Press, 1993.

Cellarius, Henri. *The Drawing-Room Dances.* London: E. Churton, 1847.

Chernoff, John Miller. *African Rhythm and African Sensibility, Aesthetics and Social Action in African Musical Idioms.* Chicago: University of Chicago Press, 1979.

Chomsky, Noam. *Syntactic Structures.* The Hague: Mouton, 1957.

Chomsky, Noam. "A Minimalist Program for Linguistic Theory." In *MIT Occasional Papers in Linguistics, 1.* Cambridge: Cambridge University Press, 1992.

Cicero, Marcus Tullius. *De Oratore.* Translated by E. W. Sutton and H. Rickham. London: Heinemann, 1942.

Clarkson, Thomas. *The History of the Rise, Progress, and Accomplishment of the Abolition of the African Slave-Trade by the British Parliament.* London: L. Taylor, 1808.

Cole, Herbert M., and Doran H. Ross. *The Arts of Ghana.* Los Angeles: Museum of Cultural History, 1977.

Connah, Graham. *African Civilizations, Precolonial Cities and States in Tropical Africa: An Archaeological Perspective.* Cambridge: Cambridge University Press, 1994.

Cooper, Lane. *An Aristotelian Theory of Comedy, With an Adaptation of The Poetics and a Translation of The Tractatus Coislinanus.* Oxford: Clarendon Press, 1924.

Craine, Debra. "My dance is an offering." *The Times*, April 2, 2005.

Creech, William. *Edinburgh Fugitive Pieces.* Edinburgh: John Fairbairn, 1815.

Creel, Margaret Washington. *A Peculiar People: Slave Religion and Community Culture among the Gullahs.* New York: New York University Press, 1988.

Cumming, Tim. "From One African Legend to Another," *The Independent*, February 22, 2008.

Curtin, Philip D. *Atlantic Slave Trade: A Census.* Madison: University of Wisconsin Press, 1969.

Dance Black America, April 21–24, 1983. Brooklyn, NY: Brooklyn Academy of Music, 1983?

Daniels, Margaret. "Musette." In *International Encyclopedia of Dance.* New York: Oxford University Press, 1998.

Darwin, Bernard. *The Oxford Dictionary of Quotations.* Oxford: Oxford University Press, 1941.

Davis, David Brion. *From Homicide to Slavery: Studies in American Culture.* Oxford, Oxford University Press, 1986.

Davis, Lawrence M. *English Dialectology, an Introduction.* Tuscaloosa: University of Alabama Press, 1983.

Dean-Smith, Margaret. "Hornpipe." In *The New Grove Dictionary of Music and Musicians.* London: Macmillan, 1980.

_____. "Jig." In *The New Grove Dictionary of Music and Musicians*, London: Macmillan, 1980.

DeFrantz, Thomas F. *Dancing Many Drums: Excavation in African American Dance.*

Madison: University of Wisconsin Press, 2002.

Desmond, Jane. "Embodying Difference: Issues in Dance and Cultural Studies." In *Meaning in Motion: New Cultural Studies of Dance.* Durham, NC: Duke University Press, 1997.

Dixon-Gottschild, Brenda. "The Afrocentric Paradigm." *Design for Arts in Education,* January/February 1991.

Dover, Cedric. *Hell in the Sunshine.* London: Secker & Warburg, 1943.

Dow, George Francis. *Slave Ships and Slaving.* Salem, MA: Marine Research Society, 1927.

Drake, Richard. *Revelations of a Slave Smuggler: Being the Autobiography of Captain Rich'd Drake, An African Trader for Fifty Years, from 1807–1857; During Which Period He Was Concerned in the Transportation of Half a Million Blacks from African Coasts to America.* New York: Robert M. De Witt, 1860.

Dromgoole, Nicholas. *The Playwright as Rebel: Essays in Theatre History.* London : Oberon Books, 2001.

_____. *Performance Style and Gesture in Western Theatre.* London: Oberon Books, 2008.

DuBois, W. E. B. *The Suppression of the African Slave Trade to the United States of America 1638–1870.* Cambridge MA: Harvard University, 1896.

_____. *The Negro.* London: Williams & Norgate, 1915.

_____. *The Souls of Black Folk.* In *Three Negro Classics.* New York: Avon Books, 1965.

_____. *Darkwater: Voices from within the Veil.* New York: AMS Press, 1969.

Dunham, Katherine. *Katherine Dunham's Journey to Accompong.* New York: Henry Holt, 1946.

Dunham, Katherine. "The Dances of Haiti." *Acta Anthropologica* 2, no. 4 (November 1947).

Dutton, Richard, and Jean E. Howard, eds. *A Companion to Shakespeare's Works.* London: Blackwell, 2003.

Dyed, Brian. *A History of Antigua: The Unsuspected Isle.* New York: Interlink Publishing Group, 2000.

Eastwick, Samuel. *Considerations on the Negro Cause, Commonly So Called, Addressed to the Right Honourable Lord Mansfield, Lord Chief Justice of the Court of King's Bench.* London: J. Dodsley, 1773.

Ebron, Paulla A. *Performing Africa.* Princeton, NJ: Princeton University Press, 2002.

Edwards, Bryan. *The History, Civil and Commercial of the British Colonies in the West Indies,* Vol. II. London: G. and W. B. Whittaker, 1793.

_____. *An Historical Survey of the Island of Saint Domingo, Together With an Account of the Maroon Negroes in the Island of Jamaica; and a History of the War in the West Indies, in 1793 and 1794.* London, Printed for John Stockdale, 1801.

Elias, Norbert. *The Civilizing Process.* Translated by Edmund Jephcott. Oxford: Basil Blackwell, 1978.

Elkins, Stanley M. *Slavery: A Problem in American Institutional and Intellectual Life.* Chicago: University of Chicago Press, 1959.

Eltis, David. *The Rise of African Slavery in the Americas.* Cambridge: Cambridge University Press, 2000.

_____. "The Volume and Structure of the Transatlantic Slave Trade: A Reassessment." *William and Mary Quarterly,* 3rd Series, January 2001.

Emery, Lynne Fauley. *Black Dance in the United States from 1619–1970.* London: Dance Books, 1988.

Epstein, Dena J. *Sinful Tunes and Spirituals: Black Folk Music to the Civil War.* Chicago: University of Illinois Press, 1977.

Equiano, Olaudah or Gustavus Vassa. *The Interesting Narrative of the Life of Olaudah Equiano, or Gustavus Vassa, the African, Written by Himself.* Printed for the author by T. L. Wilkins, 1789.

Equiano, Olaudah. *The Interesting Narrative of the Life of Olaudah Equiano, or Gustavus Vassa, the African.* Abridged and edited by Paul Edwards. London: Heinemann Educational Books, 1967.

Ernst, Earle. *The Kabuki Theatre.* Oxford: Oxford University Press, 1956.

Eysenck, Hans Jurgen. *Dimensions of Per-*

sonality. London: Routledge & Kegan Paul, 1947.

Falconbridge, Alexander. *An Account of the Slave Trade on the Coast of Africa*. London: B. White, and J. Sewell, 1788.

Feldtenstein, C. J. *Erweiterung der Kunst nach der Chorographie zu Tanzen*. Translated by Lillian Moore. Frankfurt: C. J. von Braunschweig, 1772.

Feuillet, Raoul-Auger. *Recueil de Contredanses*. Paris: L'auteur, 1772.

Follett, Richard. *The Sugar Masters: Planters And Slaves in Louisiana's Cane World, 1820–1860*. Baton Rouge: Louisiana State University Press, 2005.

Francis, W. N. *Dialectology, an Introduction*. London: Longman, 1983.

Franks, A. H. *Social Dance: A Short History*. London: Routledge and Kegan Paul, 1963.

Frazier, Edward Franklin. *The Negro Family in the United States*. Chicago: University of Chicago Press, 1939, reprinted 1966.

_____. *The Negro Church in America*. New York: Alfred A. Knopf, 1964.

Freeman, Michael. *Francois Villon in His Works, the Villain's Tale, Faux Titre 195*. London: Rodopi, 2000.

Freud, Sigmund. *Jokes and their Relation to the Unconscious*. New York: Basic Books, 1960.

Fryer, Peter. *Staying Power: The History of Black People in Britain*. London: Pluto Press, 1984.

_____. *Black People in the British Empire*. London: Pluto Press, 1988.

_____. "The 'Discovery' and Appropriation of African Music and Dance." *Race and Class* 39 no.3 (January–March 1998).

Fryer, Peter. "William Cuffay." In *Oxford Dictionary of National Biography*. Edited by H. C. G. Mathew and Brian Harrison. Oxford: Oxford University Press, 2004.

Gallini, Giovanni-Andrea. *A Treatise on the Art of Dancing*. London: For the Author, 1772.

Gaspar, David Barry. "The Antigua Slave Conspiracy of 1736: A Case Study of the Origins of Collective Resistance." *William and Mary Quarterly*, April 1978.

_____. *Bondmen and Rebels: A Study of Master-Slave Relations in Antigua*. Baltimore and London, Johns Hopkins University Press, 1985.

Gates, Henry Louis, Jr. *The Signifying Monkey: A Theory of African American Literary Criticism*. New York: Oxford University Press, 1988.

_____. *Wonders of the African World*. New York: Alfred A. Knopf, 1999.

Genovese, Eugene D. *Roll, Jordan, Roll: The World the Slaves Made*. New York: Vintage, 1972.

Gerzina, Gretchen Holbrook. *Black London: Life before Emancipation*. New Brunswick, NJ: Rutgers University Press, 1995.

George, M. D. *London Life in the Eighteenth Century*. London: Penguin Books, 1925.

Ghana Statistical Service. "Analysis of Demographic Data." Accra, 1994.

_____. "Population and Housing Census Summary Report of Final Results." Accra, 2000–2002.

Gibson, A. E. M. "Slavery in Western Africa." *African Affairs*, 1903–4.

Gilroy, Paul. *The Black Atlantic: Modernity and Double Consciousness*. Cambridge, MA: Harvard University Press, 1993.

Girdlestone, Cuthbert. *Jean-Philippe Rameau, His Life and Work*. London: Cassell, 1959.

Glissant, Edouard. *Caribbean Discourse: Selected Essays*. Translated by J. Michael Dash. Charlottesville: University Press of Virginia, 1989.

Glissant, Edouard. *Poetique de la relation*. Paris: Gallimard, 1990.

Goings, Kenneth W. and Raymond A. Mohl, eds. *The New African American Urban History*. Thousand Oaks, CA: Sage, 1996.

Gombrich, Ernst H. *In Search of Cultural History*. Oxford: Clarendon Press, 1969.

Green, Jack P. *Pursuits of Happiness: The Social Development of Early Modern British Colonies and the American Culture*. Chapel Hill: University of North Carolina Press, 1988.

Green, Stanley and Burt Goldblatt, eds. *Starring Fred Astaire*. London: W. H. Allen, 1974.

Grétry, André Ernest Modest. *Zemire et Azore*. Paris: Duhan et Cie, 1771.

Grove, Lilly. *Dancing*. London: Longmans, Guen, 1895.
Gutman, Herbert George. *The Black Family in Slavery and Freedom, 1750–1925*. New York: Pantheon Books, 1976.
Hakluyt, Richard. *The Principal Navigations, Voyages and Discoveries of the English Nation 1598*. Glasgow, J. MacLehose and Sons, 1903–05.
Harlow, Vincent T. *Christopher Codrington, 1668–1710*. Oxford: Clarendon Press, 1928.
Harnan, Terry. *African Rhythm, American Dance: A Biography of Katherine Dunham*. New York: Alfred A. Knopf, 1974.
Harris. *Harris's List of Covent Garden Ladies, Or Man of Pleasure for the Year 1788*. London: H. Ranger, 1788.
Harris, Joel Chandler. *Uncle Remus and His Friends*. New York: Houghton Mifflin, 1892.
Harris, Randy Allen. *The Linguistics Wars*. Oxford: Oxford University Press, 1993.
Hecht, Jean J. *Continental and Colonial Servants in Eighteenth Century England*. Northampton, MA: Department of History, Smith College, 1954.
Herskovits, Melville J. *Life in a Haitian Valley*. New York: Alfred A. Knopf, 1937.
———. *The Myth of the Negro Past*. Boston: Beacon Press, 1958.
———. *The New World Negro*. New York: St. Martin's Press, 1966.
Herskovits, Melville J., and Frances S. Herskovits. *Trinidad Village*. New York: Alfred A. Knopf, 1947.
Hilton, Wendy. *Dance of Court & Theater: The French Noble Style 1690–1725*. Princeton, NJ: Princeton Book, 1981.
Hinton, Robert. "The Black Tradition in American Modern Dance." In *American Dance Festival*, edited by Gerald E. Myers. Durham, NC: American Dance Festival, Duke University, 1988–90.
Hoare, Prince. *Memoirs of Granville Sharp*. London: Henry Colburn, 1828.
Honour, Hugh. *The Image of the Black in Western Art*. Cambridge MA: Harvard University Press, 1989.
Horseford, John. *A Voice from the West Indies, Being a Review of the Character and Results of Missionary Efforts in the British and other Colonies in the Caribbean Sea With Some Remarks on the Usages, Prejudices, Etc of the Inhabitants*. London: Alexander and Heyhen, 1856.
Howell, Thomas. *A Complete Collection of State Trials and Proceedings for High Treason and other Crimes and Misdemeanours from the Earliest Period of the year 1783 with Notes and other Illustrations Compiled by T. Howell Esq. and Continues from the Year 1783 to Present Time*. London: T. C. Hansard, 1826.
Hudson, Richard. "Passacaglia." In *The New Grove Dictionary of Music and Musicians*, (London: Macmillan, 1980).
Inglehearn, Madeleine. *The Minuet in the Late Eighteenth Century*. London: M. Inglehearn, 1998.
Johns, Elizabeth. *Winslow Homer: The Nature of Observation*. Berkeley: University of California Press, 2002.
Johnson, Walter. *Soul by Soul: Life Inside the Antebellum Slave Market*. Cambridge, MA: Harvard University Press, 1999.
Jordan, Winthrop D. *White over Black: American Attitudes Toward the Negro 1550–1812*. Chapel Hill: University of North Carolina Press, 1968.
Joyner, Charles W. *Down by the Riverside: A South Carolina Slave Community*. Urbana: University of Illinois Press, 1984.
Kelly, Robin. *Race Rebels: Culture, Politics and the Black Working Class*. New York: Free Press, 1994.
Kenneys, J. G. *Free and Candid Reflections Occasioned by the late Additional Duties on Sugars and Rum*. London: Printed for the author and sold by T. Becket, 1783.
Koegler, Horst. *The Concise Oxford Dictionary of Ballet*. Oxford: Oxford University Press, 1982.
Lamb, Andrew. "Cotillion." In *The New Grove Dictionary of Music and Musicians*. London: Macmillan, 1980.
Lanaghan, Frances. *Antigua and the Antiguans: An Impartial View of Slavery and the Free Labour Systems*. London: Saunders & Otley, 1844.
Langer, Susanne K. *Feeling and Form: A Theory of Art*. London: Routledge and Kegan Paul, 1953.
Latimer, John. *Annals of Bristol in the Eigh-*

teenth Century. Forme: Printed for the Author, 1893.

Leach, Maria, ed. *Funk and Wagnalls Standard Dictionary of Folklore, Mythology, and Legend.* New York : Funk and Wagnalls, 1949.

Levine, Lawrence W. *Black Culture and Black Consciousness: Afro-American Folk Thought from Slavery to Freedom.* New York: Oxford University Press, 1977.

Lewis, John Lowell. *Ring of Liberation: Discourse in Brazilian Capoeira.* Chicago: University of Chicago Press, 1992.

Linebaugh Peter and Marcus Rediker. *The Many-Headed Hydra: Sailors, Slaves, Commoners, and the Hidden History of the Revolutionary Atlantic.* Boston: Beacon Press, 2000.

Little, Meredith Ellis. "Gavotte." In *The New Grove Dictionary of Music and Musicians.* London: Macmillan, 1980.

_____. "Gigue." In *The New Grove Dictionary of Music and Musicians.* London: Macmillan, 1980.

_____. "Bourrée." In *International Encyclopaedia of Dance.* London: Macmillan, 1998.

_____. "Rigaudon." In *International Encyclopaedia of Dance.* London: Macmillan, 1998.

Long, Richard A. "The Mission of Black Modern Dance." In *The Black Tradition in American Dance,* edited by Gerald E. Myers. Durham, NC: American Dance Festival, 1988.

_____. *The Black Tradition in American Dance.* New York: Da Capo Press, 1989.

Lovejoy, Paul E. and David V. Trotman, eds. *Trans-Atlantic Dimensions of Ethnicity in the African Diaspora.* London: Continuum, 2003.

Luffman, John. *A Brief Account of the Island of Antigua, Together with the Customs & Manners of Its Inhabitants.* London: J. Luffmam, Printed by T. Cadell, 1788.

Magri, Gennaro. *Theoretical and Practical Treatise on Dancing.* Naples: Orsino, 1779.

Manceron, Claude. *Men of Liberty: Europe on the Eve of the French Revolution, 1774–1778.* London: Eyre Methuen, 1977.

Mannix, Daniel P., and Cowley Malcolm. *Black Cargoes: A History of the Atlantic Slave Trade, 1518–1865.* London: Penguin Books, 1963.

Marsh, Carol G. "Passepied." In *International Encyclopaedia of Dance.* (London: Macmillan, 1998.

Martin, Samuel. *Essay upon Plantership, Humbly Inscribed to All the Planters of the British Sugar-Colonies in America, by an Old Planter.* London: T. Cadell, 1773.

Marx, Karl. *Das Kapital, Kritik der Politischen Oekonomie.* Hamburg: Meissner, 1857.

_____. *Capital, Volume1: A Critique of a Political Economy.* London: Penguin, 1976.

Mayers, Gerald E. *The Black Tradition in American Modern Dance.* New York: Prion, 1988.

McDonnell, Lawrence T. "Money Knows No Master: Market Relations and the American Slave Community." In *Developing Dixie: Modernization in a Traditional Society,* edited by W. B. Moore, et al. New York: Greenwood Press, 1988.

McDonnell, Lawrence T. *October Revolution: Communism's Last Stand.* London: Staplehurst, 1994.

McKinnen, Daniel. *A Tour through the British West Indies in the Years 1802 & 1803.* London: J. White; R. Taylor, 1804.

Mintz, Sidney W., and Richard. Price. "An Anthropological Approach to the Afro-American Past: A Caribbean Perspective." In *2 ISHI Occasional Papers in Social Change.* Philadelphia: Institute for the Study of Human Issues, 1976.

_____. *The Birth of African-American Culture: An Anthropological Perspective.* Boston: Beacon Press, 1976.

Monro, David Hector. *Argument of Laughter.* Notre Dame, IN: University of Notre Dame Press, 1963.

Moore, Lillian. "Moreau de St.-Mery and 'Danse.'" *Dance Index,* October 1946.

Morgan, Philip. *Slave Counterpoint: Black Culture in the Eighteenth-Century Chesapeake and Lowcountry.* Chapel Hill: University of North Carolina Press, 1998.

Morris, Christopher. *Becoming Southern: The Evolution of a Way of Life, Warren County and Vicksburg, Mississippi, 1770–*

1860. Oxford: Oxford University Press, 1995.

Moynihan, Daniel Patrick. "Social and Economic Conditions of Negroes in the United States." In *Bureau of Labor Statistics and Bureau of the Census BLS Rpt. No. 332 and Current Population Report* Series No. 24. Washington, DC, 1976.

Mueller, John. *Astaire Dancing: The Musical Films*. New York: Alfred A. Knopf, 1985.

Nash, Joe. "Talley Beaty." In *African American Genius in Modern Dance*, edited by Gerald E. Myers. American Dance Festival, 1993.

Nathan, Mathew. "Historical Chart of the Gold Coast, and Ashanti, Compiled from Various Sources." *African Affairs* 4 (1904).

Newton, John. *The Works of the Rev. John Newton Published by the Direction of his Executors*. (London: for the author's nephew, 1808.

Nketia, J. H. Kwabena. *Drumming in Akan Communities of Ghana*. London: Nelson, 1963.

———. "The Interrelations of African Music and Dance." *Studia Musicologica Academiae Scientiarum Hungaricae*, T. 7, Fasc. 1/4, 1965.

Opoku, K. A. "Choreography and the African Dance: Individual Research Report." *Institute of African Studies, Research Review*, New Series, 8, nos. 1&2 (1992).

———. "The Dance in Traditional African Society." *Institute of African Studies Research Review*, New Series, 8, nos. 1&2 (1992).

Owusu, Maxwell, "Rebellion, Revolution, and Tradition: Reinterpreting Coups in Ghana." *Comparative Studies in Society and History* 31, no. 2 (April 1989).

Park, Mungo. *Travels in the Interior Districts of Africa: Performed under the Direction and Patronage of the African Association in the Years 1795, 1796 and 1797*. London: John Murray, 1799.

Parker, Frank. *Linguistics for Non-Linguists*. Austin, TX: Pro-Ed, 1986.

Patterson, Orlando. *Slavery and Social Death: A Comparative Study*. Cambridge, MA: Harvard University Press, 1982.

Phillips, Thomas. "A Journal of a Voyage Made in the Hannibal of London, Ann. 1693, 1694, from England, to Cape Manseradoe, in Africa; and Thence Along the Coast of Guinez to the Island of St. Thomas, and so Forward to Barbados." In *A Collection of Voyages and Travels*. London, 1746.

Pinckard, George. *Notes on the West Indies*, Vol. I. London: Baldwin, 1816.

Piozzi, Hester Lynch. *Anecdotes of the Life of the Late Samuel Johnson, LL.D, during the Last Twenty Years of His Life*, edited by S. C. Roberts. Cambridge: Cambridge University Press, 1925.

Plumb, H. *England in the Eighteenth Century*. London: Penguin Books, 1950.

Pope-Hennessy, James. *Sins of the Fathers: The Atlantic Slave Traders, 1441–1807*. London: Capricorn Books, 1967.

Porter, Michael. *The Conspiracy to Destroy Black Women*. New York: African American Images, 2001.

Prince, Mary. *The History of Mary Prince, A West Indian Slave, Related by Herself, with a Supplement by the Editor; to Which is Added the Narrative of Asa-Asa, a Captured African*. London: F. Westley & A. H. Davis, 1831.

Quirey, Belinda. *May I Have The Pleasure: The Story of Popular Dancing*. London, BBC Books, 1976.

Raboteau, Albert J. *Slave Religion: The "Invisible Institution" in the Antebellum South*. Oxford: Oxford University Press, 1978.

Raffe, W. G., with M. E. Purdon. *Dictionary of the Dance*. London: Barnes, 1975.

Ralph, Richard. *The Life and Works of John Weaver*. London: Dance Horizons, 1985.

Rameau, Pierre. *Le Maitre a Danser*. Paris: Chez Jean Villette, Rue Saint Jacques, a la Croix d'Or, 1725.

Rath, Cullen Richard. "African Music in Seventeenth-Century Jamaica: Cultural Transit and Transition." *William and Mary Quarterly* 50, no.3 (1993).

———. "Drums and Power: Ways of Creolizing Music in Coastal South Carolina and Georgia, 1730–1790." In *Creolization in the Americas: Cultural Adapta-*

tions to the New World, edited by Steven G. Reinhardt and David Buisseret. College Station, TX: Texas A&M University Press, 2000.

Rattray, R. S. *Ashanti*. Oxford: Clarendon Press, 1923.

Richardson, Philip J. S. *The Social Dances of the Nineteenth Century in England*. London: Herbert Jenkins, 1960.

Roberts, John Stern. *Black Music of Two Worlds: African Caribbean, Latin and Afro-American Traditions*. New York: Praeger, 1972.

Rogers, Ellis. *The Quadrille: A Book on the History, Development and Practice of the Dance*. London, C & E Rogers, 2003.

Rule, John. *The Labouring Classes in Early Industrial England 1750–1850*. London: Longman, 1986.

Ryman, Cheryl. "The Jamaican Heritage in Dance: Developing a Traditional Typology," *Jamaica Journal* no. 44.

Said, Edward W. *Culture and Imperialism*. New York: Alfred A. Knopf, 1993.

St. Augustine. *Confessions (A.D 397)*. Translated by James J. O' Donnell. Oxford: Oxford University Press, 1992.

Saintsbury, G., ed. *Letters of the Late Ignatius Sancho, an African*. London: J. M. Dent, 1894.

Sancho, Ignatius. *The Letters of Ignatius Sancho, an African*, 5th ed. London: J. Nichols, 1803.

Savigliano, Martha E. *Tango and the Political Economy of Passion*. Boulder, CO: Westview Press, 1995.

Schama, Simon. *Rough Crossing: Britain, the Slaves and the American Revolution*. London: BBC Books, 2005.

Scholes, Helen, producer and director. *The Black Georgians*. Broadcast on BBC 4, June, 28, 2006.

Schwartz, Judith L. and Christena L. Schlundt. *French Court Dance and Dance Music: A Guide to Primary Source Writings 1643–1789*. New York: Pendragon Press, 1987.

Scott, James. *Weapons of the Weak: Everyday Forms of Peasant Resistance*. New Haven, CT: Yale University Press, 1985.

_____. *Domination and the Arts of Resistance: Hidden Transcripts*. New Haven, CT: Yale University Press, 1990.

Scott, Rebecca. *Slave Emancipation in Cuba: The Transition to Free Labour 1860 to 1899*. Princeton, NJ: Princeton University Press, 1995.

Scott, Rebecca, Frederick Cooper, and Thomas C. Holt. *Beyond Slavery: Explorations of Race, Labour, and Citizenship in Post-emancipation Societies*. Chapel Hill: University of North Carolina Press, 2000.

Shakespeare, William. *Shakespeare Complete Works: Macbeth*. Oxford, 1983.

Sheridan, Richard. "Samuel Martin, Innovating Sugar Planter of Antigua 1750–1776." *Agricultural History* 4 (1960).

_____. "The Rise of a Colonial Gentry: A Case Study of Antigua, 1730–1775." *Economic History Review*, 2nd Series, 13 (1960–1961).

Sherwood, Marika. "William Davidson." In *Oxford Dictionary of National Biography*. Oxford: Oxford University Press, 2004.

Shibles, Warren A. *Humor: A Critical Analysis*. Whitewater, WI: Language Press, 1978.

Shyllon, Folarin. *Black People in Britain 1555–1833*. Oxford: Oxford University Press, for the Institute of Race Relations, 1977.

Siegal, Jeff. *Language Contact in a Plantation Environment: A Sociolinguistic History of Fiji*. Cambridge: Cambridge University Press, 1987.

Slave Narratives: A Folk History of Slavery in the United States from Interviews with Former Slaves. Washington, D.C. 1936–38.

Sloane, Sir Hans. *A Voyage to the Islands Madeira, Barbados, Nieves, S. Christophers and Jamaica with the Natural History of the Herbs and Trees, Four-footed Beasts, Fishes, Birds, Insects, Reptiles, Etc. of the Last of Those Islands; to Which is Prefix'd an Introduction, Wherein is an Account of the Inhabitants, Air, Waters, Diseases, Trade, etc. of That Place, with Some Relations Concerning the Neighbouring Continent, and Islands of America*. London: Printed by B.M. for the Author, 1707–25.

Sloat, Susanna, ed. *Caribbean Dance, From Abakua To Zouk: How Movement Shapes*

Identity. Gainesville: University Press of Florida, 2002.

Stampp, Kenneth M. *The Peculiar Institution: Slavery in the Ante-bellum South*. New York: Alfred A. Knopf, 1956.

Stearns, Jean, and Marshall Stearns. *Jazz Dance: A Story of American Vernacular Dance: A History of Dancing to Jazz, from its African Origins to the Present*. New York: Macmillan, 1966.

Stedman, John Gabriel. *Narrative of a Five Years' Expedition against the Revolted Negroes of Surinam, in Guiana, on the Wild Coast of South America; from the Year 1772 to 1777: Eelucidating the History of That Country, and Describing Its Productions, Viz. Quadrupeds, Birds, Fishes, Reptiles, Trees, Shrubs, Fruits, & Roots; with an Account of the Indians of Guiana & Negroes of Guinea*, Vol. I. London: J. Johnson, 1796.

Steegman, John. *Victorian Taste: A Study of the Arts and Architecture from 1830–1870*. London: Thomas Nelson, 1970.

Steeh, Judith. *History of Ballet and Modern Dance*. Leicester: Manga Books, 1982.

Stern Roberts, John. *Black Music of Two Worlds: African, Caribbean, Latin and Afro-American Traditions*. New York: Praeger, 1972.

Steward, Austin. *Twenty-Two Years a Slave, Forty Years a Freeman: Embracing a Correspondence of Several Years while President of Wilberforce Colony, London, Canada West*. New York: W. Alling, 1857.

Stewart, James. *A View of the Past and Present State of the Island of Jamaica; with Remarks on the Moral and Physical Condition of the Slaves, and on the Abolition of Slavery in the Colonies*. Edinburgh, 1823.

Stolzoff, Norman C. *Wake the Town and Tell the People: Dancehall Culture in Jamaica*. Durham, NC: Duke University Press, 2000.

Stone, R. M. "Africa." In *The Garland Encyclopedia of World Music*. New York: Garland Publishing, 1998.

Strobel, Desmond F. "Quadrille." In *International Encyclopedia of Dance*. London: Macmillan, 1998.

Stuckey, Sterling. *Slave Culture: Nationalist Theory and the Foundations of Black America*. New Haven, CT: Yale University Press, 1985.

Sweet, James H. *Recreating Africa: Culture, Kinship and Religion in the African-Portuguese World, 1441–1770*. Chapel Hill: University of North Carolina Press, 2003.

Thackeray, William Makepeace. *The Paris Sketch Book*. London: Bradbury, Evans, 1870.

Thomas, Helen. *The Body: Dance and Cultural Theory*. Houndmills: Palgrave Macmillan, 2003.

Thompson, E. P. *The Making of the English Working Class*. London: Victor Gollancz, 1963.

Tierou, Alphonse. *Doople: The Eternal Law of African Dance*. Paris: Harwood Academic Publishers, 1989.

Tomalin, Clare. *Samuel Pepys: The Unequalled Self*. New York: Alfred A. Knopf, 2002.

Tomlinson, Kellom. *The Art of Dancing Explained by Reading and Figures*. London: Published by the author, 1735.

Thompson, Robert Ferris. "Dance and Culture, an Aesthetic of the Cool." *African Forum* 2, (Fall 1966).

Thompson, Robert Ferris. *African Art in Motion*. Berkeley: University of California Press, 1974.

Thornton, John Kelly. *Africa and Africans in the Making of the Atlantic World, 1400–1800*. Cambridge: Cambridge University Press, 1992.

Walvin, James. *Slaves and Slavery: The British Colonial Experience*. Manchester: Manchester University Press, 1992.

Way, Peter. "Labor's Love Lost: Observation on the Historiography of Class and Ethnicity in the Nineteenth Century." *Journal of American Studies* 28 (1994).

———. "Soldiers and Misfortune: New England Regulars and the Fall of Oswego, 1755–1756." *Massachusetts Historical Review* 1 (2001).

White, Graham, and Shane White. *Stylin': African American Expressive Culture from Its Beginnings to the Zoot Suit*. Ithaca, NY: Cornell University Press, 1998.

Wilberforce, Samuel D. D. *Life of William*

Wilberforce. London: Macmillan, Hurst, 1868.
Wilks, Janet. *Benesh Movement Notation Beginners' Manual*. London: Burke Publishing, 1955.
Williams, Eric. *Capitalism and Slavery*. London: Andre Deutsch, 1964.
Williams, Raymond. *Culture*. London: Fontana, 1981.
Wilson, G. B. L. *A Dictionary of Ballet*. London: Theatre Arts Books, 1976.
Wilson, Peter. *Crab Antics: The Social Anthropology of English Speaking Negro Societies of the Caribbean*. New Haven, CT: Yale University Press, 1973.
Wilson, Thomas. *The Quadrille and the Cotillion Panorama*. London: R & E Williamson, 1818.
Wood, Christopher. *The Dictionary of Victorian Painters*. London: Jupiter, 1978.
Wood, Marcus. *Blind Memory: Visual Representations of Slavery in England and America 1780–1885*. Manchester: Manchester University Press, 2000.
Wood, Peter. *Economic Beginnings in Colonial South Carolina, 1670–1730*. Columbia: University of South Carolina Press, 1971.
_____. *Black Majority: Negroes in Colonial South Carolina from 1670 through the Stono Rebellion*. New York: Knopf, 1974.
_____. "Gimme de Kneebone Bent: African Body Language and the Evolution of American Dance Forms." In *The Black Tradition in American Dance*, edited by Gerald E. Myers. Durham, NC: American Dance Festival, 1988.
Wyndham, H. A. *The Atlantic and Slavery,*. London: Oxford University Press, 1935.
Young, William. *A Tour through the Several Islands of Barbados, St Vincent, Antigua, Tobago, and Grenada in the Years 1791 & 1792*. London: Printed for John Stockdale, 1801.
Yorke, Philip C. *The Diary of John Baker: Barrister of the Middle Temple Solicitor-General of the Leeward Islands*. London: Hutchinson, 1931.
Yupp, Nick. *The French Millennium*. Koln: Konemann, 2001.

Index

Page numbers in **_bold italics_** indicate pages with illustrations.

abolitionist movement 19, 88, 115, 124; Parliamentary Committee for the Abolition of Slavery, hearings 84, 87
abolition of slavery 108, 115, 155
The Abolition of the Slave Trade (Cruikshank) 83, ***84***, 87, 88–89
Adair, Christy 23
Adinku, W. Ofotsu 40
African culture: broadness of, over many regions 8, 37, 49, 101; in the Carolinas, evidence of 28; characteristics of dance 151; contributor to American culture 9; Creoles' understanding of 94–95; dance prohibited on plantations 127–128, 158; dances, survival of, in New World 11, 16, 53, 74–75, 92–93, 95, 97–98, 146–147; dancing style, carried to New World 11, 80, 134; drumming, in New World 101; Europeans' incomprehension of 38; musical instruments, in New World 98; regional differences 82; religious traditions 8, 10–11, 18, 75, 95; *see also* dance, pervasiveness in African life
Africanisms 8, 10, 22–23, 134; in white dance 14
Afro-Creole (Burton) 120
Ailey, Alvin 14–15
Akan people 37, 53, 91; chief, role of tribal 47; clothing 48–49; dance traditions 36, 47, 53; drumming 50; *see also* Court/Klass revolt
Albert, Charles d' 147
Alford, Violet 62
Anderson, Benedict 30
Anecdotes of the life of the late Samuel Johnson (Piozzi) 154
Annales school 18
anti-abolitionists 117, 141, 142
Antigua: Court/Klass revolt (1736) 91–95, 146–147; life expectancy of slaves 91; planters' power 95; sugar industry 90–91, 98

Antigua and the Antiguans (Lanaghan) 97
Argentina 16–17
Aristotle 78
Arnold, James 84–85
The Art of Dancing Explained by Reading and Figures (Tomlinson) 56–57, 61
asafo dance 36, 93, 99, 146–147
Ashanti people 38, 46, 93
Asiento of 1713 107, 108
assembly room dances 63, 64, 147–148
assimilation into British society: difficulties in 111, 123–125; evidence of 104, 154–155
The Atlantic and Slavery (Wyndham) 109
Atlantic triangle 106–107, ***107***–108
audience perceptions: in understanding dance 13–14, 14–15, 17, 39, 42, 51, 93–94, 95; in understanding humor 148, 150, 151–152
Austen, Jane 98
authenticity 12–15

Baker, John 96–97
Bakhtin, Mikhail Mikhailovich 120
ballet 54, 55, 70–71
Barbados 26, 107
Barber, Francis 154, 155
Beckwith, Carol 48
Beckwith, Martha Warren 106
Beef, Jack 96–97, 114
Beghin-Say sugar company 108
Bell, Hesketh J. 143–145, 146
Benesh, Rudolf 41
Benesh dance notation 9, 41
Benitez-Rojo, Antonio 25–26, 27–28
Berlin, Ira 4, 28
Berlyne, Daniel E. 76
Bernard, John 19
Bhabha, Homi K. 123
A Bivouac Fire on the Potomac (Homer) 20, ***22***, 73
black balls: admission prices 143; bonding of the community 113, 114, 126, 145, 158;

191

in the Caribbean 144–145; Creolization of dances 5; descriptions of 113, 158; satire and humor 121, 142–143, 145, 148; Somerset case, celebration at decision in 115; values, display of 121–122

black community in 18th and 19th-century London: aspirations upward in society 142, 155; Caribbean origins of majority 82; creole culture of 4–5; dual identity, sense of 111; historical evidence for 5; identity and solidarity 103–104, 113, 114–115, 116, 118, 123, 141; population estimates 104–105; prosperity of 143; separateness from working class whites 103, 104, 110, 112, 123–125, 148; slaves brought directly from Africa 108; *see also* assimilation into British society; black balls

black dance: defined 33; European descriptions of 6, 11, 19, 24, 44, 45, 86, 98, 99; failings of term 23–24; integration with European dances 70, 146; in present-day London 157; as protest 86, 89, 101, 119; purposes of 126, 141, 148; rhythm, importance of 24, 45, 48–49, 50, 51–52, 126–127, 145; strangeness of, to European eyes 6, 24, 45, 86, 138, 145; *see also* black balls

Black Dance in the United States from 1619–1970 (Emery) 21

Black People in Britain 1555–1833 (Shyllon) 104

black populations in early Britain 105–106, 108–109

Blacking, John 41
Blasis, Carlo 69, 74, 139
Blassingame, John 11
Blind Memory (Wood) 88–89
Bloa Nam dance school 40
Bolland, O. Nigel 116
Bosman, William 38
bourrée 63–64, 66
Bowdich, T. Edward 45
Braffi, Emmanuel Kingsley 46
Brazil 15–16, 100, 101
The Breaking Up (Summers) 148, **149**, 151
Browning, Barbara 15, 16
Burnard, Trevor 36
Burton, Richard D.E. 120
Bush, George W. 156
Butler, Thomas 100
Bygott, David 105, 106

candomblé 15, 16
capoeira 15, 16, 100
Carey, Brycchan 111
Caribbean islands' differences 27
Caribbean's mixed cultural origins 8, 26–27, 27, 36
Carney, Judith 28
carnival 99, 120, 122, 147

Carty, Hilary S. 148
Cato Street conspiracy 118–119
chaconne 60–61, 66
chegancas 73–74
Chelsea Pensioners Reading the News of the Battle of Waterloo (Wilkie) 109
Chernoff, John Miller 24, 51, 51–52
Chesterfield, Lord 53–54
chica 74–75
chief, role of tribal 47–48, 94
Christianity, integrated into African traditions 10–11, 21, 28
Cicero 77
Clarkson, Thomas 83
Clay, Edward Williams 142, 148
clothing 24, 48–49, 62, 65
Code of Terpsichore (Blasis) 74
Codrington, Christopher 90, 91
Cole, Herbert M. *see* Cole and Ross
Cole and Ross 37, 45, 46, 48–49
colonial gaze 17, 138
color, vibrancy of, in textiles 24
Confessions (St. Augustine) 39
Connah, Graham 38
Contredanses 58, 66, 67, 69
Coromantees 91–95
cotillion 60, 67–68, 70
Court/Klass revolt 91–95
Crab Antics (Wilson) 121–122
Creech, William 60
Creel, Margaret Washington 28
creole culture 3, 4–5, 29, 80–81, 116, 122
creolization 3–4, 4–5, 20–21, 27–32, 76, 99, 100–101; *see also* dance, creolization of
Creoles 4, 30, 36, 93, 94–95
Crowell, Nathaniel Hamilton, Jr. 101
Cruikshank, Isaac 83, **84**, 87, 88–89
Cuba 26, 27
Cuffay, William 123, 124–125
Curtin, Philip 36

"The Damnation of Women" (DuBois) 89
dance: adoption upwards in society 55; communication 25, 48, 55–56, 92–93, 100, 101, 114; creolization of 4, 48, 79–80, 99–101, 127, 138, 139; cultural uniqueness of 39, 41–42; difficulties in writing about 33–34; emotional outlet 20, 56, 85, 116; pervasiveness in African life 9, 25, 40–41, 42, 43, 45–47, 157, 158; posture and bearing 50–51, 56, 57, 60, 79, 134–135, 145–146
The Dance in Traditional African Society (Opoku, A.M.) 40, 47–48
dance positions 135, **136–137**
Dancing (Grove) 45
dancing masters 55, 57, 63, 100, 135
"dancing the slaves" 83–85, 88
Danse (Saint-Mery) 58, 73, 74–75

Dash, Michael 25
Davidson, William 118–119
Davis, Angela Y. 89–90
Davis, David Brion 116
De Oratore (Cicero) 77
Dean-Smith, Margaret 63
DeFrantz, Thomas 22–23
Degler, Carl 15
derision 17, 22, 79; *see also* satire and humor
Desmond, Jane 12, 14
Diabaté, Toumani 48
divisions, social: class 14, 110, 116–117, 118, 128; race 103–104, 110–112, 117, 118–119, 123, 124
Dixon-Gottschild, Brenda 23
Dominican Quadrille Group 176
double identity 19, 94, 123, 124, 125
Dover, Cedric 106
Drake, Richard 85
Dromgoole, Nicholas 54
drumming 48, 49–50, 100, 101, 138, 145
DuBois, W.E.B. 19, 89, 123
Dunham, Katherine 6, 20–21
Dyde, Brian 98

Ebron, Paulla A. 51
education of high-status Africans in Britain 109
Edwards, Bryan 90
Edwards, Paul 43, 111
An Elementary Treatise Upon the Theory and Practice of the Art of Dancing (Blasis) 69, **139**
Elias, Norbert 54, 57
Elkins, Stanley 9–10
Ellis, J.D. 132
Eltis, David 36, 109
Emery, Lynne Fauley 21
Epstein, Dena J. 19
Equiano, Olaudah 42–43, 86–87, 97
Essay Upon Plantership (Martin) 95
Estwick, Samuel 104
European dance: African influence on 71–74, 138; in Caribbean 58–59, 97, 99, 127; changes during industrial revolution 54, 65–67; male displays 53–54; melody, importance of 50, 51, 145; types of dance 54–69
exoticism 17, 20
Eysenck, Hans Jurgen 77

Falconbridge, Alexander 83–84, 85
Feuillet, Raoul-Auger 59, 60, 63, 67
Fisher, Angela 48
folk life studies movement 18
Follet, Richard 116
Frail, Noel de 59
France 68, 107–108; *see also* European dance, types of dances

Frazier, Edward Franklin 7, 9–10, 102
Frazier-Herskovits debate 7–11
Freud, Sigmund 77–78, 78–79
Freyre, Gilberto 15
Fryer, Peter 104, 112
Fugitive Pieces (Creech) 60

Gainsborough, Thomas 155, 177
Gallini, Giovanni-Andrea 57, 73–74
Gaspar, David Barry 91, 93
Gates, Henry Louis 151
Gates, Henry Louis, Jr. 28
gavotte 61, 66
gender, differing values 121–122
Genovese, Eugene D. 115–116, 117
George, Dorothy 110
Gerzina, Gretchen Holbrook 104, 105, 108
Ghana 37, 38, 44, 50; dance 40, 41, 46, 93, 95, 146–147
gigue *see* jig
Gillray, James 148
Gilroy, Paul 25, 27
Girdlestone, Cuthbert 60
Glissant, Edouard 25, 28, 30–31, 32
Goines, Leonard 51
Gombrich, Ernst H. 64–65
Gordon Riots 110, 111–112, 117
Granny Sarah 96
Greene, Jack P. 30
Grove, Lilly 45
Gutman, Herbert George 11

Haiti 74–75; slave revolt of 1793 24, 113–114
Hakluyt, Richard 106–107
Harlem Renaissance 18
Harris's List of Covent Garden Ladies (Derrick) 143
Hawkins, John 106–107
Hermit Songs (Ailey) *ii*
Herskovits, Frances 134
Herskovits, Melville J. 2, 7–9, 80, 134, 157
Hibiscus Quadrille Troupe 176
hierarchy among slaves 94, 127–128
Hilton, Wendy 63–64
Hinton, Robert 40, 113–114
History of Antigua, the Unsuspected Isle (Dyde) 98
Homer, Winslow 20, **22**, 73
Honour, Hugh 142, 143
hornpipe 59, 63, 66, 72–73, 76
The Horrors of Slavery (Wedderburn) 124
Horsford, John 95–96
humor and satire *see* satire and humor

The Image of the Black in Western Art (Honour) 142
Indian dance 39
industrial revolution 54, 58, 64–65, 66–67, 70, 121

Index

"intentional fallacy" 12
The Interesting Narrative of the Life of Olaudah Equiano (Equiano) 43, 87, 97

Jamaica 6, 27, 36, 122, 135, 138, 156
James, Rebecca (author's great-grandmother) 127, 175
Jazz Dance (Stearn & Stearn) 21, 142–143, 151
jig 20, 59–60, 66, 71–72, **72**, 99–100
Johnson, Samuel 135, 154
Johnson, Walter 119
Jokes and Their Relation of the Unconscious (Freud) 77–78
Joyner, Charles 28

Kelly, Robin 119
Kemps' Jig **72**
Kenneys, John Gardner 133–134
Khan, Akram 39
Kimber, Captain John, case of 87–89
King, Robert 86
King-Dorset, Eileen 156, 175, 176
King-Dorset, Eric 175
King-Dorset, Rodreguez 4, 6
Kivy, Peter 13
Klass, King (Court) 91–95

Labouring Classes in Early Industrial England, 1750–1850 (Rule) 121
Lamb, Andrew 60
Lanaghan, Frances 97
Langer, Susanne K. 33
language, link to culture 28–30, 30–31, 44
Latrobe, Benjamin 24
Letters of the Late Ignatius Sancho, an African (Sancho) 110, 111, 155
Levine, Lawrence W. 6, 12–13, 18, 78–79, 79–80
Life in Philadelphia (Clay) 142, 148
Linebaugh, Peter 112
Locke, John 53
London, Caribbean slaves visits to 96–97
Long, Edward 114
Long, Richard A. 18
Louisiana 113–114
Louther, William ii, 6
Lucianite Dancers 176, 177
Luffman, John 98–99

Le Maitre a Danser (Rameau) 135, **136–137**, 138
The Making of the English Working Class (Thompson) 121
Malemort (Glissant) 30–31, 32
Mansfield, Lord (William Murray, first Earl Mansfield) 110
Mansfield Park (Austen) 98
Martin, Samuel 91, 95

Martinique 30–31, 32
Marx, Karl 116–117
Marxist analyses 117, 118, 119
McDonnell, Lawrence T. 118
melody, importance of, in European dance 50, 51, 145
middle-class: attitude towards dance 68, 70; rise of 65, 68
middle passage *see* ships, slave
Mintz-Price interpretation 11–12, 28, 28–29, 30
Mintz, Sidney W. *see* Mintz-Price interpretation
minuet 5, 56–59, 61, 66
minuet congo 73, 75–76, 97–98
monkeys 133
Monro, David Hector 76, 77
Moore, Lillian 73
Moreton, J.B. 6
Morgan, Kenneth 36
Morgan, Philip 116
Morris, Christopher 116
Moynihan, Daniel Patrick 9–10
mudras hand movements 39
musette 61, 66
musical instruments 19, 44, 45, 48, 97, 98, 99, 100
Myth of the Negro Past (Herkovits) 7, 8, 8–9

Narrative of a Five Years' Expedition Against the Revolted Negroes of Surinam, in Guiana, on the Wild Coast of South America, from the Year 1772 to 1777 (Stedman) 44, 45, 155
Nash, Joe 10
The Negro Family in the United States (Frazier) 9
A New and Accurate Description of the Coast of Guinea, Divided into the Gold, the Slave and the Ivory Coast (Bosman) 38
New West-India Dance, to the Tune of 20 Millions (HB) **140**, 141–142
Newton, John 91
Nketia, J.H. Kwabena 46, 50
Northup, Solomon 24–25
notation systems for dance 9, 33, 41–42, 63

October Revolution (McDonnell) 118
The Old Plantation 20
Opoku, A.M. 40, 47–48
Opoku, K.A. 45, 46, 47
Oswego, fall of 117, 118

Park, Mungo 45
Parke, Daniel 96
passacaglia 60–61, 66
passepied 59, 66
Patterson, Orlando 30, 31–32
Peninsular War 132

Pepys, Samuel 108–109
Performance Style and Gesture in Western Theatre (Dromgoole) 54
Phillips, Thomas 83
Phoenix Dance Company 23
pidginization 29
Pinckard, George 86
Piozzi, Hester Lynch 154
The Playwright as Rebel (Dromgoole) 54
Poetics (Aristotle) 78
political activism 110, 111–112, 123–124, 124–125
polka 65–66, 68, 69, 70
Pope, Alexander 71
Portugal 37–38, 73–74, 106, 107
prejudice, racial *see* divisions, social: race
Price, Richard *see* Mintz-Price interpretation
Prince, Mary 97
Providencia 121–122
"pushing and dancing" 100

quadrille 66, *132*, 147, 152–154, *153*; in Caribbean, present-day 122, 138–139, 156; creolization of 5, 99, 128, 153, 154; improvisation in 134–135, 146; in London, present-day 155–156; origins of 66, 67–70; satirical use of 120, 120–121, 127, 135–136, 148; *see also* black balls
Quadrille and Cotillion Panorama (Wilson) 67–68
Quirey, Belinda 39, 50, 66

Rabelais and His World (Bakhtin) 120
Raboteau, Albert J. 139
Rameau, Pierre 135, *136*
Ramsay, Burt 14–15
rape 15, 86–87, 88, 89–90
Rath, Richard Cullen 28, 29, 44, 99–100, 101
Ravenal, Henry W. 100
Recueil de Contredanses (Feuillet) 67
Recueil de Danses (Feuillet) 60
Rediker, Marcus 112
"respectability and reputation" 121–122
"RFW watercolor sketch and verse" 128, *129*, 130, 132–133
"RFW watercolor sketches" *131*, *132*, 133, 134–135, 138
rhythm, importance of, in African dance 24, 45, 48–49, 50, 51–52, 126–127, 145
rice cultivation 28
Rickman, John 104–105
rigaudon 62, 66
ring shout 10, 11, 80, 141
Rogers, Ellis 134–135
Roll Jordan, Roll (Genovese) 115–116, 117
Ross, Doran H. *see* Cole and Ross
The Route (Summers) 148, *149*, 151

Royal African Company 107
Rule, John 121

St. Augustine 39
St. Lucia 138
Saint-Mery, M.L.E. Moreau de 58, 73, 74–75
Sales, Roger 120
Sancho, Ignatius 110, 110–111, 117, 155, 177
sarabande 54–55, 56, 60, 66
satire and humor 76–80; blacks making fun of whites 79–80, 127, 138, 142, 143, 144, 146, 148, 150, 152; whites incomprehension of blacks' humor 149–150, 152; whites making fun of blacks 141, 142, 148
Savigliano, Martha E. 16–17
Say, Louis 108
Scott, James 119
Scott, Rebecca 117
secretiveness of slaves' activities 10, 18–19, 32, 92–93, 94, 100
sex, interracial 15
sexual interpretations of dance 15–16, 17
Sharp, Granville 115
Sheridan, Richard 96
Shibles, Warren A. 77
ships, slave: African dance 83, 86; "dancing the slaves" 83–85, 88; disease 85; loading 83; rape 86–87, 88
shout 10, 11, 80, 141
Shyllon, Folarin 104
The Signifying Monkey (Gates) 151
slavery: abolition, in British Empire 115, 155; abolition, in France 108; British trade in, beginnings of 106–107, 108; brutality 31–32, 83–85, 88, 112, 166–167; European trade in, beginnings of 37–38, 106; Frazier's theory on its effect on cultural retention 10; geographic origins of slaves 36, 75, 90–91; struggle of slaves against 112–113, 113–114, 115–116; *see also* rape
Sloane, Hans 44–45
Smith, William 6
"social death" 30–31, 31–32
social unrest in London 110, 111–112, 116–117, 118–119, 124–125, 147–148
society, European, changes in 54, 58, 64–65, 66–67, 70, 121
soldiers, black 105, 105–106, 132
Soldiers of Misfortune (Way) 117–118
Some Thoughts on Education (Locke) 53
Somerset, James, case of 110, 115
South Carolina revolt (1733) 99–101
Spain 26–27, 60, 106, 107
Stampp, Kenneth 9–10
Staying Power (Fryer) 112–113
Stearn, Marshall and Jean 21, 142, 151
Stedman, John Gabriel 44, 45, 155
stereotypes 15, 38

Sterne, Laurence 111
Stevens, Marshall 51, 52
Steward, Austin 127–128
Stolzoff, Norman C. 127
Stone, R.M. 40–41
Stuckey, Sterling 10, 18
Stylin' (White & White) 4, 11, 98, 99, 138
sugar industry 26, 27, 90–91, 98, 107, 108, 116
The Sugar Masters (Follet) 116
Summers, W. 139, 142, 143, 148–150, **149**
Sweet, James H. 75
syncretism 25–26, 28–29

Taglioni, Marie 70–71
tango 16–17
Taruskin, Richard 12, 13
Terpsichore in the Flat Creek Quarters, Pea Ridge 152–154, **153**
theater dance 62, 70–71
Thicknesse, Phillip 114, 143
Third Catalogue (Khan) 39
Thomas, Helen 12
Thompson, E.P. 121
Thompson, Robert Farris 16, 22, 134
Tierou, Aphonse 40
Tomalin, Clare 108–109
Tomboy 93, 94
Tomlinson, Gary 12–13
Tomlinson, Kellom 56–57, 61
Towne, Laura 11
The Tractatus Coislinanus (Aristotle) 78
Treatise on the Art of Dancing (Gallini) 73–74

Treaty of Utrecht 107
Tregear, Gabriel Shire 139, 142, 143, 148–150
Tregear's Black Jokes (Tregear) 139, 142, 143, 148–150, **149**
Trinidad 36, 134
Tristram Shandy (Sterne) 111
Trotter, Dr. Thomas 83

Uncle Remus tales 79

Vestris, Gaetano 71
The Visual Representation, Role and Origin of Black Soldiers (Ellis) 132

Walker, Darren 176
waltz 65–66, 68, 69, 70, 146
war dances 46, 92–93, 94, 95, 99, 146–147
Warner, Edward 90
Watson, Robert F. 128, **129**, **131**, **132**, 132–133, 134–135, 138
Way, Peter 117, 118
Wedderburn, Robert 123–124
White, Shane and Graham 6, 11, 23–24, 138
Wilberforce, William 87, 88, 141
Wilkie, David 109
Wilson, Peter J. 121–122
Wilson, Thomas 67–68, 68
Wood, Marcus 88–89
Wood, Peter H. 20, 28
Wyndham, H.A. 109

Yorke, Philip C. 114
Young, Sir William 86, 99